PERSPECTIVES

ON CHILDREN'S SPIRITUAL FORMATION

PERSPECTIVES

ON CHILDREN'S SPIRITUAL FORMATION

GREG CARLSON · TIM ELLIS

TRISHA GRAVES · SCOTTIE MAY

EDITED BY MICHAEL J. ANTHONY

4 VIEWS

NASHVILLE, TENNESSEE

ISBN: 978-0-8054-4186-4

Published by B&H Publishing Group
Nashville, Tennessee

Dewey Decimal Classification: 259.22
Subject Heading: CHURCH WORK WITH CHILDREN \ MINISTRY

7 8 9 10 11 12 • 22 21 20 19 18
VP

This book is affectionately dedicated to

Eileen C. Anthony

One can never underestimate the importance of a godly
Christian mother during the formative years of life.

Thanks, Mom, for all of your sacrifices and for bringing
me to church so faithfully as a young child.
2 Timothy 1:5

Contents

Contributors

Introduction

Michael J. Anthony
Professor of Christian Education at Talbot School of Theology/
Biola University

Michael Anthony has authored numerous books in the field of Christian education including *The Evangelical Dictionary of Christian Education* and *Management Essentials for Christian Ministries.*

Chapter One

Scottie May
Associate Professor of Educational Ministries, Wheaton College

Scottie May is coauthor of *Children Matter* and contributor to *Children's Spirituality: Christian Perspectives, Research, and Application.* She has been influential in shaping the field of children's spiritual formation across North America.

Chapter Two

Gregory C. Carlson
Global Training Director and Director of Rorheim Institute
Awana Clubs International

Greg Carlson is the author of *Understanding Teaching, Effective Biblical Teaching for the 21st Century*. In addition, he serves as the director of Rorheim Institute, which is the adult leadership development network for Awana Clubs International.

John K. Crupper
Director of Rorheim Institute Development,
Awana Clubs International

John Crupper is responsible for partnerships as well as creative development and strategy development for Rorheim Institute. He has served as a senior pastor and has also spent a number of years in the business world in operations management

Chapter Three

Trisha Graves
Pastor of Children's Ministry, Mariners Church, Irvine, California

Trisha Graves has been on staff at Mariners Church, one of Southern California's largest megachurches, for the past thirteen years. She was instrumental in the design and development of their new children's ministry building called Port Mariners Kid Zone. She is a frequent conference speaker on developing effective children's ministries.

Chapter Four

Tim Ellis
KIDMO, Franklin, Tennessee

Tim Ellis graduated from Azusa Pacific University with a B.A. in music and an M.A. in conducting. He is executive producer for all KIDMO & Lil' K productions.

Bill Baumgart
Orbit Church, Franklin, Tennessee

Former director of A&R for Sparrow Records, Bill Baumgart is president of Orbit Church and also serves as executive producer for its media and music productions.

Greg Carper
Children's Pastor, Carmel Presbyterian Church, Carmel, California

In addition to working as children's pastor of Carmel Presbyterian Church, Greg Carper also serves as a speaker, lecturer, and writer for KIDMO Access and is completing his third year of law school at Monterey College of Law.

Acknowledgments

This has been a fun project to work on over the past couple of years. It has allowed me to collaborate with some good friends and to meet new ones as well. Dr. Scottie May and I have been active members of the North American Professors of Christian Education (NAPCE) association for over twenty years. In that capacity we have had the opportunity to sit at meals together, attend workshops, and interact on educational and ministry theories for some time. She has stimulated my thinking in profound ways, and it's always fun to come to this annual gathering to see how God has been active in her life.

Scottie's husband passed away a couple of weeks before I asked her to take on this project. At first I didn't want to ask her because I knew she had enough on her plate to deal with at home and at Wheaton College where she teaches. However, the fact remained that no one could articulate the biblical basis and philosophical rationale for the Contemplative-Reflective Model as well as she could. So I held my breath, took a risk, and asked her one day. I'm so grateful for her kindness in accepting my invitation. What a sacrifice of love she has given us in her work!

Scottie would like to acknowledge the contributions that were made on her chapter and critiques by several individuals.

She would like to acknowledge the support of her research assistants: David Westergaard for culling the outline and structure by going through her notes and lectures; and Joann Olson for the editorial skills she brought to the task.

I met Dr. Greg Carlson at NAPCE as well. In fact, we've been roommates at some of these conferences. He has had an active career teaching both undergraduate and graduate students at several institutions of higher education. Only recently has he transitioned over to being director of the Rorheim Institute. A more qualified individual to lead this important organization couldn't be found. Greg's mixture of biblical scholarship together with his administrative savvy blend to form the ideal candidate for his responsibilities. Only a few months after accepting his new role, and the various demands that come with learning a new role, I invited him to join our team of authors. He would have had every reason to turn me down, but who better to represent the Instructional-Analytical Model than Dr. AWANA himself? Thanks, Greg, for accepting this invitation and for finding a way to write your thoughts during so many months of international travel.

Greg would like to express his sincere appreciation to those who assisted him in this project. Among those are Donna, Geoff, Vince, and Sean: you're a great family and gifts from the Lord Jesus. To the Rorheim Institute team, John C., Bob, Diane, Larry, Mike, and John B. Thank you!

I first met Trisha Graves when she and her fiancé came to my office at Mariners Church in 1990 to ask if I would officiate at their wedding. It was a joy to share in that special moment. I also had the privilege of baptizing her when they later joined the young couples fellowship group I pastored at the church. Since that time she has become an active mother of four (including triplets) as well as the children's pastor at one of North America's largest churches. Only a fellow pastor can understand and appreciate the amount of pride and respect I have for the way she has grown and matured over the years. Not only is she an incredibly gifted ministry leader; she is also a dedicated mother and wife. She is one of those rare ministry leaders that maintains a balance between the demands of a growing church and the needs of her family at home. As you can imagine, it was not easy for her to take on another project of this magnitude, but I appreciate her willingness to make an investment in the kingdom by doing the necessary research and writing for this book.

I first became acquainted with the KIDMO Team through my wife's ministry. As a children's pastor at a megachurch in Southern California, she was familiar with this unique ministry paradigm. She had recommended it to several churches where she had been hired as a consultant to help organize children's ministries. Kai Vilhelmsen, who is the familiar face and emcee of their Lil' K preschool curriculum, was once an undergraduate student of mine at Biola University.

The KIDMO team consisted of several highly talented and extremely busy individuals. For that reason I am extremely grateful for their willingness to take on this assignment in the midst of their many projects and obligations. Johnny Rogers is the on-screen personality of KIDMO and serves as their creative genius. Bill Baumgart is president of Orbit Church. Tim Ellis is executive producer for all KIDMO & Lil' K productions, and Greg Carper is the copastor/codirector of children's ministry at Carmel Presbyterian Church and a speaker, lecturer, and writer for KIDMO Access. In addition to this team, the critiques at the end of each chapter were written by several other gifted players from the KIDMO organization. They include Dr. Keith H. Reeves, Randy Isola, and Greg Carper. In addition to this writing team, the following individuals made valuable contributions: Dave Bunker, George Barna, Randy King, and Jeannie Wherley.

I also want to acknowledge my appreciation to Dr. Richard Leyda, department chair of Christian Education at Talbot School of Theology/Biola University for providing me with a teaching schedule that freed me up on Tuesdays so I could write. This book just wouldn't have happened without his support. In addition, Dr. Kevin Lawson, the director of our PhD and EdD programs at Talbot School of Theology, has been a helpful sounding board. He knows far more about children's spirituality than I and was willing to share his books with me and offer constructive critique when I needed it.

Also I want to acknowledge the unseen force behind this book. My wife, Michelle, has been the voice that has guided my thinking and reflection along this journey. It's one thing to write on the subject of children's ministry; it's quite another to practice it! For nearly fifteen years she has led several churches in the role of children's pastor or director of family ministries. In this capacity she has not only thought deeply about this area, but she has also been diligent in applying theory to practice. Admittedly, few are masterful at both, but she certainly is. Thanks for helping me gather my random thoughts and for giving me needed clarity.

Finally, I want to express my indebtedness to Len Goss at Broadman & Holman who was willing to take a gamble on this proposal when I first presented it to him. As an experienced editor he has been a significant source of support and encouragement to me throughout the entire process. I look forward to partnering with him on future projects as well.

Putting Children's Spirituality in Perspective

MICHAEL J. ANTHONY

More and more churches are realizing that a major factor in church growth is a well-staffed and trained children's ministry team. The most effective ministry models have professionals leading the team due to the heavy demands of programmatic designs. Many Bible colleges and seminaries are experiencing a resurgence in demands for training and preparation in this career specialization.

One of the tensions between theologians who explore children's spirituality issues and pastors who do the work of children's ministry is reconciling theory and practice. There really aren't any pure theories that can be condensed into a neatly packaged, descriptive paradigm. The most effective means of exploring the theology, philosophy, and theoretical development of children's spiritual formation is to examine the major children's ministry programs with a critical eye toward their rationale. Examining each of the four major programs of children's spiritual formation will be the focus of this book.

Connecting theory to practice has been a challenge for ministry leaders for generations. This is particularly true for those in the age level specializations of children, youth, and singles. Although programs exist in each of these avenues, it's often difficult to get successful ministry practitioners to articulate just *why* their programs are successful. Without this descriptive analysis it's difficult to determine whether their success is based on clearly thought-out theological or philosophical reasoning or just plain good luck. In some cases the success may be based on the "fad of the day" approach to ministry experience.

As both a theoretician and a practitioner, I want to help connect theory to practice by providing a forum for the leaders of four major models of children's spiritual formation to articulate their theological foundations of children's ministry, their philosophical presuppositions, and also a detailed analysis of their programmatic design. Many previous works have detailed the theological or philosophical presuppositions of children's spiritual formation; but few, if any, go the extra step of connecting both to the practice of children's ministry programming. Some espouse their particular belief in order to secure the reader's "buy in," but this text is unique in that its purpose is to present the various views and allow readers the opportunity to choose or reject elements of each and develop their own from this range of perspectives. However, before such an endeavor can proceed, we need to come to an understanding about some essential discussion points.

First, matters of theology, personal philosophy, and programmatic design are held deeply by all of us. Challenging the theological presuppositions of persons will generally put you on the outside of their world looking in. Such a perspective labels you as an outsider, and entry into their world of personal beliefs and values is viewed as a "by invitation only" proposition. Try pushing back on the theological view of a colleague at lunch one day, and you'll quickly see what I mean. We hold our personal beliefs as sacred and don't open them up to critical analysis without some degree of apprehension or perhaps even defensiveness. Throughout history wars have been fought and lives have been sacrificed over issues of theology. Denominations were birthed over spirited differences in philosophy of ministry, so it should come as no surprise that we continue to hold these matters close to the chest.

Before any meaningful dialogue can take place between those who hold differing views on matters of the heart, it needs to be said that we'll enter and exit this debate with a spirit of mutual respect. We'll agree to disagree with one another and to do it agreeably. Jesus would expect nothing less of us. We can (and will) disagree with the viewpoints of a particular author, but we'll do so in a manner that does not challenge the integrity of that person's personal character or commitment to God's kingdom. Even though we may firmly disagree, we remain committed to the task of presenting every person complete in Christ.

This opening introduction is intended to provide two benefits for the reader. The first half of the introduction provides the reader with an overview of the literature associated with the concept of spirituality. Gaining the "big picture" perspective will help you understand how it's been used (and abused) over many years of exploration. If you're already well read in the field of spirituality, you may want to skip ahead a few pages. However, for those practitioners who may not be aware of the greater scope of the literature, you are advised to take the time to read this important section. It will provide you with the various terms and constructs necessary for conducting a meaningful dialogue on the subject. The second half of this introduction will provide the reader with a theology of children's spirituality and suggest a model for describing and applying spirituality to the field of children's ministry.

Putting Spirituality into Perspective

Misconceptions about Spirituality

It's been said that everyone knows what spirituality is until they're forced to define it. At that point they stare blankly into space, muttering phrases that don't make a great deal of sense. Perhaps a better way to start is to state up front what spirituality is not. Taking that approach may help us develop a sharper picture about what it actually is. I've comprised a list of the top ten commonly held misconceptions about spirituality. As you review this list, some may seem strangely familiar to you.[1]

1. *Spirituality requires you to join the Roman Catholic or Eastern Orthodox Church and adhere to their theological practices by doing things like praying to Mary, attending Mass, celebrating the Eucharist, or saying the rosary.* Many of those who have advocated the concept of religious spirituality came from the Catholic or Eastern Orthodox faith, but that doesn't mean you have to become a member of one of these traditions in order to foster your own personal spirituality. Growing spiritually is not related to any one particular faith tradition.

2. *Spirituality means you will attend long retreats in the mountains or desert and stare blindly into space for hours at a time while quoting mind-numbing mantras.* To be sure, some of the more ardent adherents of religious spirituality spent time attending personal retreats. Meditation is a spiritual discipline, like many others cited in Scripture, which Christians are encouraged to practice. One does not have to travel great distances to practice it as we're encouraged to meditate on the Scriptures as we go about our daily travels.

3. *Developing one's spirituality is reserved for the elite of the faith and isn't for the average Christian.* Although growing in one's spirituality is related to spiritual maturity, it certainly isn't reserved for those with seminary degrees or years of occupational experience. Growing spiritually should be the goal of every Christian.

4. *Spirituality is a passing fad and won't last long. It's the religious "trend of the month" kind of experience.* Developing one's spiritual relationship with God has been going on since man was first created. There is nothing trendy about it. Those who desire a closer relationship with their Creator take the necessary time to invest in nurturing such a relationship.

5. *Spirituality is acquired by reading classic books on prayer, meditation, and fasting. Those who read such books often quote Latin phrases to impress their friends.* It's unfortunate that some people draw attention to themselves by trying to act religious.

---

1. The following list is extracted and significantly edited from Peter Toon, *What Is Spirituality and Is It for Me?* (London: Daybreak, 1989), 15.

Jesus condemned the Pharisees for their outward show of religious egotism. However, sometimes the insights of others (e.g. authors, pastors, etc.) are helpful in guiding us in our journey toward discovering new ways of experiencing God. Books written by these individuals help us do just that.

6. *Spirituality begins when you're "baptized in the Holy Spirit" and is viewed as a "second blessing" available to a few select believers.* It's true that a closer relationship with God will display itself in desiring to use your spiritual gifts. That's evidence of spiritual maturity. Each individual's gifts are his or her own, and we should all look for ways to use the unique area of giftedness that God has blessed us with in life.

7. *Spirituality requires people to get really involved and busy doing things for God.* Being busy isn't evidence of spirituality. In fact, sometimes being too busy doing religious activities is a sign of spiritual immaturity. The issue is not how much time you spend doing religious things but the motives of the heart for doing them in the first place. God is more concerned about the condition of your heart than activities you manifest.

8. *Spirituality involves denying yourself the things you like to do and living the life of a monk.* Twenty-first-century spirituality is not a return to the asceticism that was practiced by cavedwelling priests in the ancient church. God calls us to community and involvement in the lives of those around us, both in our neighborhoods and in our churches. Remember, a light shines brightest when it's in a dark environment. Spirituality gives your light the energy it needs to shine brightly.

9. *Spirituality requires a lot of reading, particularly the latest top ten best-sellers from the local Christian bookstore.* Growing in your spiritual life is not a passing trend. It involves reading the Bible and perhaps some additional devotional materials selected according to your individual needs. Not everyone has the same spiritual needs, so what is "top ten" to one person may have no meaning to another. Let God help you find the materials that will help you nurture your relationship with him, not someone else's contrived list designed to market and sell religious products.

10. *Acquiring spirituality is like going to camp and having a mountaintop experience. It's fun for the moment but doesn't last long.* Growing in your relationship with God is a lifelong process. There are seasons of growth and seasons where growth is not as evident. That doesn't mean it isn't happening, just that you don't have the proper perspective to see it. For some people, getting away from the distractions of a fast-paced existence allows them to focus on their relationship with God. That's how they're wired. Returning to that fast-paced lifestyle makes it hard to maintain that clarity which was experienced away from home. However, that doesn't make a relationship with God any less real or possible. God's relationship with us isn't limited by geographic location.

Coming to Terms

An old adage says, "He who defines the terms controls the argument." That axiom is based on the belief that no meaningful dialogue or debate can take place until all the participants have first agreed on the definitions of the terms involved in the discussion. Without such agreement it's difficult to conduct any reasonable dialogue. However, in the nearly two thousand years since the church's inception, we honestly have to admit that the church has never agreed on a definition for the term *spirituality*. Spiritual formation, that process of developing one's personal and/or corporate spirituality, has been hotly contested and debated for centuries; and it's doubtful that the argument will be resolved anytime soon. However, with that in mind, it's not unreasonable for us to come to some agreement regarding the general nature of spirituality as applied to the unique audience of children. Though others may disagree with our parameters, they are nevertheless essential for us to articulate so as to be sure that we are all on the same page. This is much easier said than done; but since each of the authors of this text approach their discussion from the parameters of a Protestant Christian worldview, it's much more reasonable to ascertain. This would not be the case if each were coming from a secular or postmodern perspective.

Some key terms need to be explored and defined. Terms such as *spirituality, spiritual formation, spiritual maturity,* and *spiritual development* may appear to some to be synonyms for the same concept. However, to others, each term represents differing perspectives, angles, and positions. For example, Hindus, Muslims, Christians, and Jews hold to differing views on the nature of spirituality. One may see it as a mystical experience played out in solitude whereas another may view it as an applied conviction of personal faith evidenced in one's relationship to those around them. "Spirituality is all about the human search for identity, meaning, purpose, God, self-transcendence, mystical experience, integration and inner harmony. Thus there are spiritualities related to all religions and to many human pursuits which arise in the human spirit."[2] Seen in this way, perhaps each faith tradition has something to add to our understanding and is worthy of consideration.

Another somewhat controversial aspect of this topic is trying to determine if spiritual formation is a means or an end in itself. For many, spiritual formation, if it's to be meaningful at all, must be viewed as a means to an end—the end being a Christlike existence played out in the streets of humanity across geographic and cultural borders. Where there is no authentic Christian lifestyle, there can be no genuine spiritual formation. That's not the case for everyone though. To many, spiritual formation is viewed as a spiritual discipline that is practiced in private and reserved for the exclusive use of the individual. Like the eremite who sits in the solitude of his cave, this spiritual leader acclaims a level of spirituality that's divorced from daily living and finds its ultimate purpose in personal spiritual enrichment. Perhaps like Plato's allegory of the cave, spiritual formation is illusive and in the eye of the beholder.

Each reader will need to take a moment and shed preconceived notions about what constitutes genuine spirituality until after a full exploration of the topic has been presented. Denominational trappings are not easily shed, and personal blinders prevent many ministry leaders from acknowledging their existence.

---

2. Ibid., 15.

For those who are willing to enter into such an exploration, the fruits of discovery are well worth the investment of time and energy.

A Rose by Any Other Name

William Shakespeare said, "That which we call a rose by any other name would smell as sweet." And while that may be true in matters of horticulture, it's certainly not applicable to the manner in which spirituality is defined in the literature. Not all definitions of spirituality are the same. In fact, some can be shocking to those who are not acquainted with the full spectrum of literature in the field.

For many who read books on this subject, it's assumed that a discussion regarding the spiritual formation of a child, or anyone else for that matter, is predicated upon a belief that God is part of the equation. Indeed, to them, leaving religion out of the picture negates the argument for or against spirituality altogether. They would say, "Why bother?" However, for many who are embedded in the study of this topic, the subject of religion has little, if anything, to do with the study of spirituality. The natural side of this debate uses many of the same terms and concepts but looks different to those who can't imagine a discussion of spirituality apart from its connection to the Creator himself.

Considering the volume of work on spirituality that has been put forward in the past ten years alone, one would think that by now we would have come to some agreement on defining a few common terms. Shouldn't we at least be able to agree on a definition for the term *spirituality*? Such is sadly not the case. Commenting on the plethora of discussion yet the lack of a common definition, Downey laments, "In view of this tidal wave, this spiritual sprawl, what is needed is a clear definition of spirituality, one which would allow enough room for all that's authentic in the quest for the sacred, while at the same time providing some criteria for discernment in the face of the many instances of human self-expression now huddling under that umbrella-like term 'spirituality.'"[3]

---

3. Michael Downey, *Understanding Christian Spirituality* (New York: Paulist Press, 1997), 13–14.

Spirituality then, much like beauty, may be more in the eye of the beholder. Three descriptions will be presented here from the literature with the hope that readers might be able to identify elements of various definitions that resonate with them. Definition 1: "The Christian path [spirituality] consists of the awakening of the personal center of the human being, by God's personal grace and Christ's compassionate, redemptive personal love, within the Christian community, in a journey that leads to personal union with the tri-personal God."[4]

Definition 2: "In its Christian sense, 'spirituality' is about the process of renewal and rebirth that comes about through the action of the Holy Spirit, which makes us more like Christ. It's about spiritual growth and development, and includes the development of just about every aspect of our life of Christian faith."[5]

Definition 3: "Developing the spiritual . . . is synonymous with developing mature human beings, who possess such attributes as self-acceptance, a sense of responsibility, concern for others, a sense of wonder and awe, and sensitivity to reality beyond the physical senses of the material."[6]

Since there are no agreed-upon definitions for many of the terms we use in this arena, even for the term *spirituality* for that matter, it's incumbent on us to take some necessary time to provide a few foundational definitions. Metaphorically speaking, the literature on spirituality is like a major body of water. Flowing out of this body are two large rivers. Each of these rivers further divides into smaller streams. Each stream has its own list of associated theorists, theories, terms, schools, and professional associations. Some refer to these two rivers as *internally focused* or *externally focused*.[7] Others label them simply *secular* or *sacred*.

---

4. Ewert Cousins, "What Is Spirituality?" in *Modern Christian Spirituality: Methodological and Historical Essays,* ed. Bradley Hanson, (Atlanta, Ga.: Scholars Press, 1990), 44.
5. Alister McGrath, "Beyond the Quiet Time," in Barry Callen, *Authentic Spirituality: Moving Beyond Mere Religion* (Grand Rapids, Mich.: Baker Books, 2001), 218.
6. Christopher Meehan, "Resolving the Confusion in the Spiritual Development Debate," *International Journal of Children's Spirituality* 7, no. 3 (2002): 292.
7. M. C. Kitschoff, "The Role of Religious Education in Building a Nation in Multi-ethnic South Africa," *Religious Education* 89, no. 3 (1994): 313–37.

One research psychologist refers to secular spirituality as *natural* spirituality and offers the following definition:

Spirituality is the response to a deep and mysterious human yearning for self-transcendence and surrender. This yearning results from having been created in such a fashion that we are incomplete when we are self-encapsulated. As important as relationships with others are, we need something more than involvement with others; something within us yearns for surrender to the service of some person or cause bigger than ourselves. When we experience this self-transcendent surrender, we suddenly realize that we have found our place. However, when we find it we immediately know that this is where we belong. Again, spirituality is our response to these longings.[8]

Traveling down these secular/sacred rivers is exploring hostile territory for many evangelical Christians. Trying to develop an understanding of spirituality without including God in the equation is futile. They would boldly claim, "You can't get there from here." However, many have explored this river and have provided valuable insights to those who have eyes to see and ears to hear. Branching off these main tributaries are streams of literature with labels such as *existential, humanistic, postmodern, developmental,* and *psychological* spirituality. Time doesn't allow a detailed description of each, but a brief snapshot may be of help to the reader for putting our subject in perspective.

Secular Views of Spirituality

Existential Spirituality. European philosophers Kierkegaard, Nietzsche, and Heidegger espoused an existential spirituality where personal existence and meaning making were most significant and required significant subjectivity. This philosophical approach "presumes that human individuals are universally characterized by having a concern about the meaning of their being and spirituality is understood to be an engagement with the meaning of one's life. The meanings that have central im-

---

8. David Benner, *Psychotherapy and the Spiritual Quest* (Grand Rapids, Mich.: Baker Books, 1988), 104.

portance for this existential framework of spirituality are those that relate specifically to one's being and fundamental purposes of life."[9]

Existential spirituality concerns itself with answering deep and personal questions about life's meaning. Questions such as these represent the essence of existential spirituality: How can I live a more effective life in a complex world? How can I find deeper meaning in a world filled with absurdity? How can I remain peaceful in the midst of the tensions of life? and How can I avoid being a superficial person?[10]

Humanistic Spirituality. Humanistic spirituality is concerned primarily with deepening, enhancing, or enriching life from a holistic point of view. The Enlightenment brought about a shift of focus from the divine to the human. Increasing one's spirituality was seen as a process of growing in depth, range, harmony, and intensity in relation to some facet of great value, often drawn from sources that may have had no connection to religion whatsoever. Hence, this humanistic emphasis of spirituality sought to find meaning and purpose in universal *human* experience rather than *religious* experience.[11]

Postmodern Spirituality. Postmodern spirituality is likewise devoid of overt theological absolutes though it does flirt with religion in the broad sense. Commenting on this delicate dance, researchers Ratcliff and May state:

> While the idea of a parallel reality, coexisting with and regularly intersecting with the material world, fell into disfavor during the Enlightenment era and its intellectual offspring, modernism, the possibility of a spiritual realm is more resonant with some aspects of postmodern thought. Since postmodernity has demonstrated that ample portions of reality surpass the measurements by objective scientific methods, perhaps more individuals are open to the idea that the material world is not the sum total of all of life, even

---

9. R. Scott Webster, "An Existential Framework of Spirituality," *International Journal of Children's Spirituality* 9, no. 1 (April 2004): 7–19.

10. James Bacik, *Catholic Spirituality, It's History and Challenge* (New York: Paulist Press, 2002), 4.

11. Meehan, "Resolving the Confusion in the Spiritual Development Debate," 292.

though most individuals are more acutely aware of this tangible world than the spiritual realm.[12]

The modernist philosopher John Locke (1632–1704) argued that once Christianity was freed from unnecessary dogmatic baggage it would become the most reasonable form of religion. Christian theology was the examination of biblical theology and its subsequent cataloging of divine facts hidden away in the Bible. Faith became a science as religious knowledge morphed into rational presuppositions which had logical consequences. Viewed this way, the Bible itself became modernized. Modernist theology had a high regard for mental reasoning and cognitive thought processing but was profoundly lacking in affective engagement. Thus, entering the twenty-first century, reality appeared far more complex and convoluted than unyielding categories of human rationality. Progress and peace had not become the obvious outcomes of rational thought. Emerging from the rubble of modernist theology came a postmodern spirituality that sought to engage both the mind of the individual and the soul.[13]

Theologian Millard Erickson offers seven motifs of this emerging postmodern spirituality. They serve as a foundation for understanding how postmodern spirituality is theologically informed.

1. The objectivity of knowledge is denied. Knowledge is not a neutral means of discovery. The knower is conditioned by the particularities of his or her situation.

2. Knowledge is uncertain. The idea that knowledge can be erected on some bedrock of indubitable first principles ("Foundationalism") must be abandoned.

3. All-inclusive systems of knowledge are impossible. Systems that seek to interpret reality for all people for all times are impossible and should be abandoned.

---

12. Donald Ratcliff with Scottie May, "Identifying Children's Spirituality, Walter Wangerin's Perspectives, and an Overview of This Book," in *Children's Spirituality: Christian Perspectives, Research and Applications,* ed. Donald Ratcliffe (Eugene, Oreg.: Cascade Books, 2004), 9–10.

13. Callen, *Authentic Spirituality,* 231.

4. The inherent goodness of knowledge is not a given. Modern people have not saved the world with the immensity of contemporary knowledge but have often turned it to destructive ends.

5. Progress is not inevitable. Increased knowledge and cultural change can lead backward. Newer is different but not necessarily better.

6. Truth is a community reality. We must abandon the model of the isolated knower as the ideal and move to community-based knowledge. All truth is defined by and for the community.

7. Truth is to be known through multiple means (not simply or even primarily through reason and the scientific method). Intuition, for instance, is a legitimate means of knowing.[14]

Religion has a limited role to play in postmodern spirituality as long as it doesn't restrict the personal freedoms and expressions of the individual. Truth, faith, and spirituality are relative to the individual and highly subjective.

Even though it is fashionable today, nonetheless it is foolish to call for religion without theology. If there could be such a thing as spirituality without a theological spine, it surely would degenerate into little more than pious sentimentalism. The current postmodern inclination is toward a religion that rests on the thin base of cynicism and personal preference. It is widely assumed that the only wrong idea is any universal truth, and the only recognized sin is to actually believe in sin. In this setting, the self becomes god, truth is relative and objectivity is an illusion. Ideas, doctrines, and religious forms are accepted or rejected on the basis of whether or not persons like them and whether or not they are found useful and personally fulfilling.[15]

---

14. Millard Erickson, *Postmodernizing the Faith* (Grand Rapids, Mich.: Baker Books, 1998), as cited in Callen, *Authentic Spirituality*, 231.
15. Callen, *Authentic Spirituality*, 34.

In light of this religious plurality and theological relativity, postmodern spirituality is difficult to define and articulate because it's highly personal and individualistic. What is a spiritual experience for one may not be for another and, hence, subject to interpretation or dismissal as authentic. Much like beauty, postmodern spirituality is in the eye of the beholder.

Development Spirituality. Developmental forms of spirituality draw their origins from detailed examinations into the structure of human existence. A number of theorists describe human development as passing through a series of stages or seasons. Each stage is dissected to include further characteristics of those who have successfully mastered that level. Healthy progress is seen as the natural progression through the various stages at the appropriate chronological time. A sampling of these would include Freud's psychosexual stages, Erickson's psychosocial model, Piaget's stages of cognitive development, Fowler's faith development, or Kohlberg's moral development. Some spirituality theorists view its development as a set of progressive stages neatly labeled as clearly defined steps along life's journey.

Psychological Spirituality. Psychological spirituality is closely aligned with developmental spirituality since both draw their terms and understanding of theoretical constructs from the realm of developmental psychology.

> From the psychological perspective we may point to what may be described as the deep mysterious longing/yearning for self-transcendence and surrender in human souls. This can be interpreted as an unconscious searching for our "roots" as human creatures. . . . This search for self-discovery can easily become or be turned into a quest for self-satisfaction and self-fulfillment. And much of what in these days is called spirituality is in fact a kind of psychological spirituality which supplies a temporary form of inner harmony and fulfillment.[16]

Some organizations articulated an integrated program based on both a psychological spirituality and a religious spirituality.

---

16. Toon, *What Is Spirituality and Is It for Me?* 27.

An example of this is Alcoholics Anonymous, which encourages its members to draw on the resources of a "Higher Power" for guidance, strength, and self-control. It doesn't really matter what this Being/Power is called so long as the individual has fostered a relationship with him/her/it.

In summary, there is a body of literature which draws its understanding of spirituality from nonreligious antecedents. Viewed from this perspective, "the concepts 'spirit' and 'spiritual' point to qualities of human existence which transcend the physical and animal aspects of being, and which can be found in the thinking, feeling, and willing of human beings. In other words, human beings are capable of *transcendence,* that's the ability to stand above the flow of time and contemplate the reality of which one is part."[17]

As a helpful summary the chart on the following page illustrates the various natural and quasi-religious views of spirituality that have been covered thus far. It will also serve as an advanced organizer for the next section of this chapter which will be to review the major religious theoretic constructs of spirituality that are prominent in the literature today. This will provide the reader with a broad base for understanding how a model of children's spiritual formation flows out of a particular theological paradigm.

One of the difficulties of presenting a diagram to illustrate an abstract concept is the tendency for that diagram to come across as too simplistic. Complex thoughts can rarely be limited to a diagram. Something inevitably gets lost in translation. Such is the case when we try to illustrate evangelical spirituality. What kind of diagram is appropriate? Would a metaphor be any better at communicating multifaceted details? Either way, something will inevitably get left out in translation.

When Scottie May (author of chapter 1) and I recently sat down to review this chapter, she offered some constructive critique. "My view of evangelical spirituality isn't as delineated as what this chart portrays," she said. "The diagram you use (p. 16) doesn't show how other forms of spirituality, including some of

---

17. Meechan, "Resolving the Confusion in the Spiritual Development Debate," 294.

Theological Perspectives on Spirituality

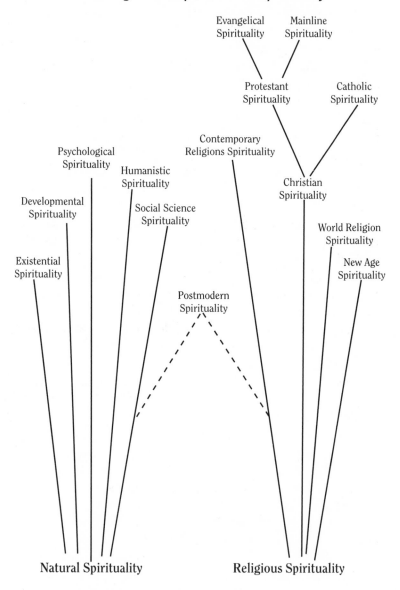

the naturalistic ones, inform my view of evangelical spirituality."
"You're absolutely right," I said. "That's one of the limitations of
using a diagram."
Perhaps a better illustration would be a double helix DNA
strand. Comprised of two strands or core material, the strands
are joined together by multiple rungs comprised of thousands of
microscopic genes. This combination of dominant and recessive
genes is what makes each person a unique individual. Perhaps
in the same way, one's spirituality starts with a common core, in
this case the *imago dei*. From that common starting point one's
family of origin, cultural upbringing, education, life experiences,
and thousands of other elements come together to form each
person's unique spiritual DNA. Maybe that's why it's so difficult
to understand spirituality. The components that contribute to
one's spirituality are unique to each individual.

Bridging the Divide

In concluding this section on definitions of secular spirituality, it's worth noting that some have attempted to bridge the
divide between the secular and the sacred rivers of spirituality
literature and have formulated a more integrative model. One example of this is seen in a model of children's spirituality brought
forward by John Bradford. He maintains that the concept of spirituality is best viewed as tripartite: human, devotional, and practical. Human spirituality is concerned with the need individuals
have to be loved, affirmed, feel secure, and respond in wonder to
their environment. It's primarily related to one's personal and
social development. Devotional spirituality is advanced as one
appropriates and practices the teachings of a particular religious
body or faith tradition. Becoming an adherent to a particular
religious group characterizes this form of spirituality. Practical
spirituality is defined as the integration of human and devotional
spirituality. It's the point at which one lives out personal convictions in the day-to-day practice of life. It's reflected in the capacity that individuals have for affection, personal friendships, resil-
ience during adversity, endeavor, enquiry, reverence, reflection,

and a sense of interpersonal and social responsibility.[18] Though not overtly religious, Bradford's model seeks to demonstrate that religion can, and often does, play an integral role in the formation of one's spirituality.

Rebecca Nye used extensive qualitative research on children in the United Kingdom to espouse a construct which she refers to as "relational consciousness." Based on extensive interviews of children, she describes children's spirituality "as an unusual level of consciousness or perceptiveness relative to other passages of that child."[19] It is characterized by the perceptions of the child in relationship to other people, God, or themselves. This relational consciousness is built upon three categories of spiritual sensitivity. Each category comes with three examples from their research.

First is awareness-sensing, including the "here-and-now" experience such as meditation sometimes practiced by Buddhists; "tuning" which is an awareness that emerges during aesthetic experience; the intense and undivided concentration that is labeled "flow"; and "focusing" which involves a holistic awareness of the body. The second category is mystery-sensing and includes the experience of wonder and awe associated with the ultimate mystery of life, or the use of active imagination that transcends everyday experience. The third category of spiritual sensitivity is value-sensing, as expressed in delight or despair; related to ideas of worth or value; a sense of ultimate goodness and trust in life; and the quest for ultimate meaning and identity related to that meaning.[20]

Exploring Christian Spiritual Formation

Catholic Spirituality. The Catholic form of spirituality involves a journey of faith in the context of community and his-

---

18. John Bradford, *Caring for the Whole Child: A Holistic Approach to Spirituality* (London: The Children's Society, 1995), as cited in Meechan, "Resolving the Confusion in the Spiritual Development Debate," 299.

19. Rebecca Nye, "Psychological Perspectives on Children's Spirituality" (Doctoral Dissertation, University of Nottingham, U.K., 1998), 237.

20. Donald Ratcliff, "Rituals in a School Hallway: Evidence of a Latent Spirituality of Children," *Journal of Christian Education* 5, no. 2 (Fall 2001): 9–26.

toric traditions. In this form of spirituality, the gospel is mediated through specific sacramental instruments administered by a hierarchy of priestly representatives. God is essentially present; and God's revelation of himself is confined to specific contexts, priesthood, cultic practices, and holy places. Ritual is not viewed as getting in the way of relationship but as a means to facilitate it. Historically speaking, this form of spirituality values and emphasizes the unity found in community, images and icons, mysticism, and an openness to natural theology.[21]

Catholic spirituality, as found in the United States during the nineteenth and early twentieth centuries, was marked by strict adherence to prescribed church teaching. Personal Bible study was discouraged while attendance at Mass each week was mandated. There was an emphasis on prayer and devotional reflection using materials provided by the priest. This form of spirituality provided for a sense of security in an unsettled world filled with war and strife. It fostered an institutional identity and loyalty. Spirituality was something that was practiced in daily living by attending Mass, eating fish on Fridays, adherence to church laws, and obedience to church leaders. Since the Mass was conducted in Latin with the priest's back to the congregation, it did not foster a personal spiritual vitality. There was little emphasis on the role of the Holy Spirit in the Christian life. Eventually, Catholic spirituality degenerated to a list of do's and don'ts, which resulted in shallow and apathetic involvement on the part of the participant.[22]

After the Second Vatican Council called by Pope John Paul XXIII (1962–1965), there was a revitalization of Catholic spirituality. The German Jesuit Karl Rahner (1904–1984) offered a solid foundation for an incarnational spirituality that provided practical insights for many Catholics who were genuinely trying to practice their faith in daily living. Hans Urs von Balthasar, viewed by some as the greatest Catholic theologian of the twentieth century (1905–1988), had a profound impact on contemporary Catholic spirituality. He taught that through private prayer,

21. Philip Sheldrake, *Spirituality and History* (Maryknoll, N.Y.: Orbis Books, 1995), 209.
22. Bacik, *Catholic Spirituality*, 31–32.

which properly began by listening intently to the Scriptures, believers could develop a contemplative spirit so as to allow them to worship God in the liturgy and participate wholeheartedly in the church's mission to redeem the world.[23]

The Second Vatican Council itself promoted a reawakening among Catholic believers to genuine spirituality.

By emphasizing biblical images of the church, such as the people of God and the Body of Christ, the council prompted Catholics to assume greater responsibility for the church and their own spiritual development. . . . Vatican II nudged Catholics toward a spirituality more clearly rooted in Scripture. Finally, the council has greatly affected contemporary spirituality by reminding laypersons of their importance and dignity, their call to holiness, their essential role in the church and their task of humanizing the world.[24]

In a more contemporary setting, Catholic believers still struggle with finding ways to reconcile their faith in God with life in an ever increasingly pluralistic and relativistic society. They wrestle with the disconnect between dogma and daily living, between ancient church teachings in an electronic and technological age of rapid change. Tradition is viewed with suspicion as they entertain the integration of new forms of "truth" into what they have been taught in the past. Catholic spirituality, like the spirituality of their Protestant cousins, is searching for meaning and relevance.

Protestant Spirituality. Protestant spirituality, drawn in sharp contrast from the forms of spirituality seen in the Catholic church for nearly two thousand years, draws mankind into a relationship with God using means which are viewed as more specific and respecting of individual distinctives. Rather than having to come to God through the doors of the church per se, God is viewed as the Great Shepherd who goes out searching for his lost sheep. God does the searching and conditions the heart of man to repent. Spiritual transformation often takes place via a dramatic moment of awareness of personal sin which usually

23. Ibid., 38–40.
24. Ibid., 40–41.

results in a decision to live a different life, one which is now focused more on spiritual resources. The Scriptures talk of this as a regeneration (Titus 3:5–6) or spiritual rebirth experience (John 3:3). For Protestants, the process of growing spirituality starts at this point of conversion and continues throughout the rest of life by means of a variety of venues (e.g., church services, camping retreats, home Bible studies, para-church organizations, religious books, television, movies, etc.). Regardless of the methods used, the end result of growing spiritually mature is the desired outcome.

The hallmark battle cries of the Protestant reformation were Christ alone, grace alone, faith alone, and Scripture alone. So it should come as no surprise to see that Protestant spirituality emphasizes dependency solely on God, hearing the voice of God through his Word, personal accountability for sin with subsequent repentance, and an adherence to a belief in a future eschatological kingdom. Protestant spirituality depicts God as distant, transcendent, and as a figure of authority deserving of awe, fear, and respect. God is heard but remains invisible. He is free to intervene in human affairs as he wills, is critical, and constantly calls mankind to personal commitment.

While traditional Catholic and Protestant spirituality both agree that salvation is by grace and through Christ, the foundations are substantially different. For the Reformers, God forgives sin once and for all and salvation is assured solely by a gracious God in a completely free act. Traditional Catholic spirituality, by contrast, suggested that by grace God makes human actions worthy in his sight. The sacraments communicate grace that really sanctifies our incomplete works. Thus room is left for the human action in the salvation process, even if essentially aided and even initiated by grace.[25]

To some degree it comes down to perspective. In Protestant spirituality, the soul of man yearns after God and ascends to a higher spiritual plane, allowing the sinner to enter into a

---

25. Sheldrake, *Spirituality and History*, 211.

personal relationship with God. The invitation is extended, and it's up to the individual to receive and accept the invitation. From the Catholic spirituality perspective, God alone seeks, strives, and descends to us, thereby making an encounter possible.[26] Both result in an ongoing relationship, but each starts with a different theological presupposition.

Both traditions seek to unite people to God and to a form of communal experience. "Within the Christian community, spiritual development builds on an understanding of a transcendent and immanent God as well as a community of faithful companions on the journey, all of which bring meaning, purpose and significance."[27] Although the end result of both the Catholic and Protestant forms of spirituality may look similar, e.g., a closer, more robust personal relationship with God through Christ, the means of accomplishing that end may look different. The point I want to make here is simply that viewing children's spirituality, much like any discussion of spirituality, is going to take an open mind and a willingness to entertain differing views without becoming defensive. It's possible that one or more of the models represented in this book will challenge your personal theology. It may require you to think outside the box and challenge set patterns of practice.

Concluding Remarks about Definitions

Given the broad scope of literature, from a biblical perspective as well as from the social sciences, and the wide range of views and opinions about spirituality research, it would be presumptuous at this point to espouse a particular definition that would satisfy everyone. It's hard to grasp the multidimensional nature of this subject and condense it into a "one size fits all" description. As Nye writes, "Attempts to define [spirituality] closely, and derive an adequate 'operational definition' can be sure of one thing: misrepresenting spirituality's complexity, depth, and fluidity. Spirituality is like the wind—though it might be ex-

26. Gene Veith, "Sinne and Love," in *Reformation Spirituality: The Religion of George Herbert* (Lewisburg, Penn.: Bucknell University Press, 1985), 19, 24–28.
27. Eugene Roehlkepartain, "Exploring Scientific and Theological Perspectives on Children's Spirituality," in *Children's Spirituality: Christian Perspectives, Research and Applications,* 122.

perienced, observed and described, it cannot be 'captured'—we delude ourselves to think otherwise, either in the design of research or in analytic conclusions."[28]

One researcher aptly summarizes the decades of confusion regarding the lack of consensus on a definition of spirituality when he states:

> What appeared to have happened this century (and to have been accelerated in the last two or three decades) is that the basic understanding of the spirit/Spirit is no longer controlled by the general doctrines of the Christian religion. Any activity of the human spirit is eligible for being described as spirituality. And the fact that we live in a pluralistic and secularist society gives a certain validity to this comprehensive and vague definition. This situation certainly means that if anyone is to use the word today then he/she must be clear what particular meaning is being offered or developed.[29]

So, given that admonition, it would be wise to state here and now that in the context of this examination of spirituality, we are addressing it from the unique and somewhat limited perspective of the evangelical stream. Authors who are presenting their particular perspectives for consideration (and critique) are doing so from the Christian, Protestant, and evangelical point of view. We have chosen an approach which is not so broad as to be of little value in exploration (i.e., trying to look at Catholic, Protestant, Orthodox, and other world religions), yet not so specific that it can't be compared and contrasted (i.e., four views of Baptist spirituality).

When we speak of children's spirituality, we are addressing the point at which a young child initiates an awareness of a spiritual dimension in life and desires to explore this feeling. This journey may begin through a dramatic moment of evangelistic

---

28. Rebecca Nye, "Relational Consciousness and the Spiritual Lives of Children: Convergence with Children's Spiritual and Religious Development," in K. H. Reich, F. K. Oser, and W. G. Scarlett, eds., *The Case of Religion, Vol. 2: Psychological Studies on Spiritual and Religious Development* (Lengrerich, Germany: Pabst, 1999), 57–82.

29. Toon, *What Is Spirituality and Is It for Me?* 15.

decision (i.e., Child Evangelism Fellowship's preference) or evolve slowly over time while living in the context of a family (i.e., Bushnell's preference). At any rate, spirituality should be viewed as a journey and not a destination. Children's spirituality is not limited to religious conversion. Likewise, it should not be confused with points along the way. Attending a retreat or church function (e.g., Vacation Bible School) may provide a means for assisting in one's spiritual development but is not the end in and of itself. Children's spirituality is multidimensional and convoluted. At best it defies simplistic attempts to define and describe; however, it's knowable and worthy of investigation.

Forming an Evangelical Theology of Children's Spirutality

Countless questions form the basis of developing a theology of children's spirituality. Questions such as: What is the status of a child prior to the age of accountability? Having been created in the image of God, what influences mar that image and prevent a child from maintaining and reflecting that image across a life span? How do one's family of origin, cultural upbringing, education, and life experiences contribute to forming a child's spirituality? Will the child that is nurtured in a godly home arrive at an age of discretion before one that is not? What is the nature of inherited sin in the life of a child? Can a child be saved prior to achieving an age of accountability? How can infant baptism be spiritually beneficial to the child if he/she cannot understand its meaning? What spiritual decisions need to be made during the development from childlike spirituality to adultlike spirituality? These questions, and hundreds more, are pondered by those who seek to develop a theology of children's spiritual formation.

Sometimes looking at spirituality's component parts allows you to get a better understanding as to how all of the parts function together. Though the parts are many and varied, we will limit ourselves to a relative few in this book. In this case the component parts of forming a theology of children's spirituality are fourfold: determining when a child is old enough to become aware of personal sin (i.e., age of accountability), the means by which spiritual regeneration should be initiated (i.e., child evangelism), when a child should be baptized, and finally, how a child grows spiritually while taking into consideration the cognitive, emotional, relational, and psychological realities of maturation.

Age of Accountability. Traditionally there has been a difference of opinion on a childhood sin nature. Most theologians throughout history have taught that children are infected with a sin nature, but they disagree on the extent to which they are responsible for it. The church father Augustine (354–430), bishop of Hippo, held to a strict interpretation of the passages which spoke of human depravity. He taught that an infant who had died without experiencing the church sacrament of baptism was destined to an eternity of hell. Children, much like adults, were viewed as lost and in need of God's redeeming grace. This resulted in an urgency on the part of the child's parents to ensure that their child received the sacrament of infant baptism as soon after birth as possible.

Another view holds that infants are in a state of "noninnocence," in that they are affected by original sin but not held accountable since they are physically incapable of sinning at such an early age. As they grow, they gain the capacity to speak and develop reasoning abilities. At some point during their maturation, they move from this state of noninnocence to a position of personal accountability for personal sin. The difficulty arises in trying to ascertain at what age this occurs.

A third view of childhood salvation, which is affirmed by the Wesleyan tradition, is seen more as a lifelong maturing relationship with God rather than as a defining conversion event. Along this spiritual journey one encounters God through a variety of experiences, each designed to draw the individual closer in relationship with God. Wesley believed that God did not hold people accountable for inherited sin or sins of ignorance but faced condemnation only for those sins which they knowingly committed. Since infants were not capable of becoming aware of their sin, they were not held accountable. However, parents were expected to provide their children with an environment which provided strong religious instruction. This included receiving the sacrament of infant baptism, attendance at Sunday services, daily Bible reading, small group attendance, and living a consistent faith in the context of the home.

Child Evangelism. Those who hold to the view that a child does not need a dramatic conversion experience point to the passages of Scripture where children who came to faith in Christ always did so in the context of their family. Christian parents are seen as the condition which is necessary for children to become Christians themselves. Nowhere in Scripture do we read of evangelistic efforts being directed toward children apart from the context of their parents. However, such a position begs the question, Does this reflect theological preferences of cultural limitations? The answer is not inconsequential!

A different view regarding childhood evangelism came along during the revivalism period soon after the end of the Civil War. Leaders such as Charles Finney, Dwight L. Moody, and Ira Sankey increased efforts at childhood evangelism due to the revivalist belief that children must grow up in their sin in order to become the object of a conversion experience once they had achieved a level of mental reasoning. During this period a child evangelist by the name of Edward Payson Hammond spent thirty years of his life directing his efforts at the conversion of children. His two books on the subject, *The Conversion of Children* and *Little Ones in the Fold,* taught that children could understand the basic elements of the Christian faith enough to undergo a conversion experience.[30] He wrote:

> Every child that is old enough to sin, is old enough to be conscious of sin; and the consciousness of sin always prepares the way for the Saviour. And when a Saviour is presented, the child seizes hold of the idea, just as the man does. A drowning child will struggle for life, will catch at straws even, just as the man will. It would be a strange thing if, when so large a proportion of children die in infancy or childhood, the plan of salvation were so beyond their apprehension that they could not lay hold of it.[31]

---

30. Gideon Yoder, *The Nurture and Evangelism of Children* (Scottdale, Penn.: Herald Press, 1959), 21.

31. Edward Hammond, *The Conversion of Children* (New York: Fleming H. Revell, [1887]), 6.

This approach to child evangelism is often referred to as "crisis" evangelism due to its emphasis on pointing to a particular crisis in the life of children that precipitated a decision to give their life to Christ. This dramatic moment serves as the turning point from their life of waywardness to one of regenerated renewal.

A Congregational minister by the name of Horace Bushnell reacted strongly against the efforts of childhood evangelism during this revivalist era. Rather than seeing the child as the focus of evangelistic efforts, he advocated a form of children's spiritual formation whereupon the child grew up in a Christian home never knowing himself/herself to be anything otherwise. The key to this form of spiritual formation was a godly Christian home that consistently demonstrated the teachings of Christ that a child would also assimilate such values and ethics and "transition" into the Christian faith with such ease that they would find it difficult to see themselves as ever being anything but a Christian themselves. This view is often referred to as "educational" evangelism because of its emphasis on lifelong training and nurturing of the individual.

Children's Baptism. Based on the theological position of Augustine and the early church fathers, children were required to receive the church sacrament of baptism or spend an eternity in hell. It mattered not whether the child had reached an "age of discretion" since it was the sacrament that brought about true conversion, not the reasoning ability of the child. This view, known as "baptismal regeneration," is the preferred method of initiating childhood spirituality in many mainline denominations today. Seeing the faith of the child's sponsor, generally the child's parents, the priest administers the sacrament under the assumption the child will one day grow to a point of personal spiritual decision making. Until then the child is safely within the fold.

At some point along their development, it is assumed that these children will enroll in confirmation classes. The purpose of confirmation is to strengthen the spiritual commitment that began during the early days of the child's life. During the preadolescent years children attend a series of classes taught by the local vicar. The content of these classes includes instruction in the doctrines of the church, memorizing several of the creeds (e.g., apostles' Creed, Nicene Creed), learning the Ten Commandments, and instructions on how to take their first Communion. They are subsequently presented to the bishop who anoints their foreheads with oil in the shape of the cross.

Most evangelical churches do not practice infant baptism today because they believe that individuals must first become aware of their sin nature by observing their sin practices. Once they're convinced of their need to repent from their sinful lifestyles, they're in need of a conversion experience. Obviously this is not possible for an infant. Instead of infant baptism, many evangelical churches prefer to practice infant dedication. This service is held to set apart the parents as dedicated Christians and to formalize their commitment to raise their child in the context of a Christian home whereupon children will come to understand their sin nature and be guided toward making a decision to accept Christ at an early age. Baptism takes place only after the child has made a decision to accept and follow Christ as an act of spiritual dedication. In this way baptism is seen as the outward evidence of an inward decision that has been previously made by the child. Unfortunately, since there is such variance regarding the practice of childhood baptism, the topic is often avoided in children's curriculum. The result is that some children never receive instruction on the importance of baptism and reach adulthood without ever being confronted with its necessity.

Developmental Considerations. One of the difficulties many children's ministries have is in trying to determine at what age certain theological topics are appropriate for children at various ages. For example, is it appropriate to teach three year olds about the Holy Ghost when their only concept of a ghost is negative? Should preschool children be taught about the rapture of the church, and to what degree is it reassuring to them to know that they might be snatched away from their loved ones without notice? Does a five-year-old really understand how to invite Jesus, a grown man, into her heart? How does a grown man fit into a four-inch organ in the center of her chest, and what is he going to do there anyway? A young child can only understand so much, and anything taught beyond that will either be missed or confusing. Admittedly, some things need to wait until the child is old enough to understand, but who makes that decision and on what basis?

A Swiss researcher by the name of Jean Piaget studied children at the French school of a friend, Alfred Binet. There, while observing the interaction of children with their peers, he espoused a series of stages depicting what a child could understand and at what age. These stages of cognitive development have become the standard by which most curriculum companies write their materials. He categorized childhood cognitive development into four stages: preoperational, operational, concrete operational, and abstract reasoning. Each stage is qualitatively different, and each has to be navigated in sequence. No stage could be skipped or eliminated. The following description will provide the reader with an overview of the contents of each stage:[32]

Piagets Stages of Cognitive Development	
Stage	**General Characteristics**
Sensorimotor (age 0–2)	Reality is determined based on the child's senses (e.g., taste, touch, see, smell, hear). Objects of thought are limited to these senses alone.
Preoperational	Incomplete thinking.
Preconceptual (age 2–4)	The child's ability to understand is incomplete since the child cannot differentiate identical items from the same class.
Intuitive (age 4–7)	Thinking is more logical, although governed more by perception than logic.
Concrete Operational (age 7–11)	Logical thought can now be applied to specific (concrete) situations that involve real objects.
Formal Operational (age 12–15)	Logical thought can be applied using abstract concepts and examples with symbols substituting for real objects.

32. Dennis Dirks, "Foundations of Human Development," in *Foundations of Ministry: An Introduction to Christian Education for a New Generation,* ed. Michael Anthony, (Grand Rapids, Mich.: Baker Books, 1992), 77.

The obvious application of these insights helps ministry leaders working with children and adolescents know how much a child can reasonably understand and at what stage of maturation. When ministry leaders present material which is beyond the capability of a child's understanding, they may be doing more harm than good.

A Paradigm of Children's Spiritual Formation

One thing I've learned after more than twenty years of teaching in a college or seminary classroom is that a diagram can go a long way in helping students understand vague concepts. I can talk for hours trying to help children understand a difficult abstract concept, but the moment I illustrate it with a diagram, the cognitive lights come on, and I hear the "Oh, that's what you mean" response. But as I've mentioned earlier in this chapter, the downside of depicting complex theories with a diagram is that not all constructs can be reduced to a simple illustration. Something gets lost in translation, and eventually someone asks a question that reveals the difficulty of trying to illustrate a theory with a picture.

With that obvious limitation I'd like to illustrate a paradigm of children's spirituality that may be of help in our discussion. It's an integrative model based on two helpful typologies. The first is Urban Holmes's helpful illustration depicting human spirituality and his phenomenology of prayer taken from his book *A History of Spirituality*. He takes the premise that prayer is an essential means of facilitating spiritual formation and as both a devotional activity and also a daily life. He offers a diagram which depicts a helpful typology for the spiritual life.[33]

The horizontal axis represents the apophatic/kataphatic scale. This depicts the degree to which the ascetical method advocates an emptying (apophatic) technique of meditation as opposed to an imaginal (kataphatic) technique of meditation. The vertical axis of the diagram represents the speculative/affective scale. This depicts the degree to which one's methods of fostering spiritual formation emphasizes the illumination of the

---

33. Urban Holmes, *A History of Spirituality* (New York: Seabury Press, 1980).

mind (speculative) or the heart or emotions (affective). By comparing these two axes, it is possible to define spiritual practice and its immediate objectives with some degree of clarity. "We can also use this description of the apophatic/kataphatic and speculative/affective scales to distinguish certain dangers of exaggeration."[34] These dangers are depicted on the diagram using italics. The resulting typology contains four schools of thought on spiritual formation: speculative-kataphatic, affective-kataphatic, affective-apophatic, and speculative-apophatic.[35]

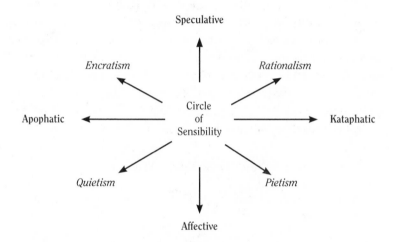

The second matrix that is insightful to our understanding of spiritual formation is David Kolb's Learning Cycle.[36] It allows teachers and learners alike to account for individual differences found in the process of learning. Learning, much like developing spiritual maturity, is highly personal; and no one description fits all individuals. Kolb's model helps account for these individual differences found within students. This model also employs a

34. Ibid., 4.
35. Ibid., 4–6. See also John Westerhoff, *Spiritual Life: The Foundation for Preaching and Teaching* (Louisville, Ky.: John Knox Press, 1994), 53.
36. David Kolb, *Learning: Experience as the Source of Learning and Development* (Englewood Cliffs, N.J.: Prentice Hall, 1984). Other helpful resources include David Kolb, "Learning styles and disciplinary differences," in Arthur Chickering, ed., *The Modern American College* (San Francisco: Jossey-Bass, 1985) and also David Kolb and Roger Fry, "Toward an Applied Theory of Experiential Learning," in C. Cooper, ed., *Theories of Group Process* (London: John Wiley, 1975).

double axis typology which describes how individuals come to experience and process new information in their world. Since spiritual formation is a learned process and requires considerable time developing across the life span, it stands to reason that a comprehensive look at how one develops spiritually should include some consideration of the learning cycle.

Kolb's vertical axis describes how the student comes to perceive new information. One end of the axis depicts concrete experience (feeling), and at the other end is abstract conceptualization (thinking). (This is similar to the view of Holmes.) According to Kolb's learning cycle, students *perceive* new information on the basis of intuitive feeling or cognitive reasoning. The horizontal axis depicts the manner in which students *process* new information. At one end is reflective observation (watching), and at the other end is active experimentation (doing). In essence, students process new information by either watching others interact with it or by getting personally involved through hands-on interaction.

Kolb's Learning Cycle

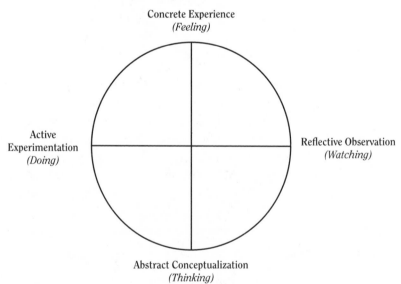

Concrete Experience
(Feeling)

Active Experimentation
(Doing)

Reflective Observation
(Watching)

Abstract Conceptualization
(Thinking)

One typology provides useful insights as to how one develops spiritually while the other provides beneficial understanding regarding how one learns cognitively. What I am proposing is not a new theory per se but more of an integration of these models to describe this complex process of developing spiritual formation, particularly in the life of a child, although it might apply in similar manner to adults as well.

Based on our earlier discussions, it's obvious that people come to experience God and learn about him in unique and personal ways. In summary, spiritual formation is seen as an interactive relationship between these two variables: *experiencing* and *knowing*. We *experience* God in profound and personal ways when we sense him drawing us into a relationship with him. It can occur at the oddest of times. Perhaps while staring out into the vastness of an ocean or gazing into the simplistic beauty of a handpicked backyard flower. At some point we realize that there is something to life that's much bigger than ourselves, and we sense that God is real. It's hard to define, but we know that voice within us is real and alive. Something or someone is beckoning us to explore a new way of thinking about what life is all about. Slowly we are drawn into a relationship with an eternal God. We experience his gentle voice and recognize his influence. It isn't the same for everyone. Why would a creative God limit himself to formulaic actions? It's uniquely personal but experienced nonetheless.

We know God as we build a relationship with him. He has beckoned us to come, and we have accepted his invitation. Along the way we interact, dialogue, and commune. Some days are filled with excitement and discovery while others are quiet and contemplative. Our relationship is anything but predictive. We pass through a season of remarkable growth as we study a book or a Scripture which seems to open our soul and speak to our heart's need. Then we pass through a season where our growth accelerates because of the depth of personal relationships we enjoy with others who are on a similar journey. As we "do life together," we feel alive and encouraged. Soon a new season will issue in, and we come to know the ways of God through times of reflective journaling and self-analysis. Throughout life the means may be many and varied, but each one is every bit as real as the other. Again, knowing God in this way may be difficult to define and dissect, but that doesn't negate its reality.

The two elements of experiencing and knowing God can be displayed as a matrix. We come to *experience* God (vertical axis), and we come to *know* God (horizontal axis) in dynamic interface.

Regarding the vertical axis, there have always been two outcomes of the spiritual life. The first focuses on an affective spirituality that focuses on the engagement of one's affective expression (i.e., feelings, emotions, inner impressions, etc.). The second is a less speculative spirituality that is housed in cognitive reasoning (i.e., thinking, reasoning, rational thought, etc.). Viewed this way, we experience God on a continuum somewhere between how we feel about God (a function of our affect, or feeling) and what we believe to be true about God (a function of our mind, or thinking).

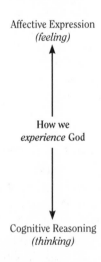

Affective Expression
(feeling)

How we
experience God

Cognitive Reasoning
(thinking)

The horizontal axis describes how people come to learn about God. At one end of the axis are those who prefer to learn about God by reflective observation. They watch closely the faith of their parents, Sunday school teacher, camp counselor, pastor, etc. Their faith is developed through less kinesthetic means such as study, group prayer, and small-group interaction.

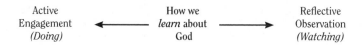

| Active
Engagement
(Doing) | How we
learn about
God | Reflective
Observation
(Watching) |

At the other end of the axis are those who prefer to learn about God through hands-on activities. They are busy testing the biblical principles to see if they are valid. They like action-oriented activities with real-life application. Bible study to these individuals is dry and lifeless. They would much rather volunteer for a day assisting at a homeless shelter than sitting for an hour listening to someone preach about helping those in need. They might not be able to quote chapter and verse for why they do what they do, but they know it's what Jesus would do if he were in their shoes today, and that is all the information they need before taking action. In essence, they prefer doing over watching.

Overlapping these two axes creates a typology that combines the personal manner in which people come to experience a relationship with God with how they develop an ongoing relationship with him. Both are needed for spiritual formation. To experience God without sustaining that relationship with a knowledge base is dangerous and does little more than make one susceptible to cults. Likewise, knowledge also needs some personal expression, or it becomes simply an academic exercise.

The four quadrants revealed by overlapping these two axes form a basis for helping us understand how children come to faith in Christ and grow in their relationship to him. In the midst of so many mind-numbing individual differences, the diagram Models of Children's Spiritual Formation allows us to view spiritual formation from a larger perspective so we can understand what's taking place inside the heart and mind of the believer. Let's take a few moments to explain the process of spiritual formation from the perspective of those living in each of the four quadrants.

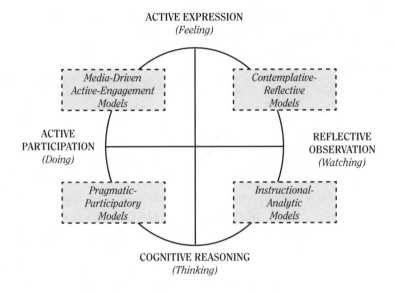

ACTIVE EXPRESSION
(Feeling)

Media-Driven
Active-Engagement
Models

Contemplative-
Reflective
Models

ACTIVE
PARTICIPATION
(Doing)

REFLECTIVE
OBSERVATION
(Watching)

Pragmatic-
Participatory
Models

Instructional-
Analytic
Models

COGNITIVE REASONING
(Thinking)

Models of Children's Spiritual Formation

Quadrant 1: Contemplative-Reflective. This quadrant is characterized by periods of quiet reflection, introspective prayer, and storytelling. Its goal is twofold: first to empty the mind of self-absorbed thoughts and to come before God as a clean vessel. Confession and honest self-assessment are essential to this process. The second goal is to find a place of solitude for quiet meditation. One can meditate on a passage of Scripture, reflect on a quiet song playing in the background, or gaze at a piece of artistic expression of spirituality (e.g., sculpture, painting, etc.). Prayer is the primary outcome of this expression of spirituality. These individuals feel deeply about spiritual events in their life. Their walk with God is punctuated with times when God was "real" to them during turmoil, doubt, or transition. They value stories of the faith and often ponder the great insights brought about by the early church fathers in their historic writings. They are verbal people when it comes to describing their own relationship with God and are often engaged in dialogue with others about matters of spirituality.

"This school is dominated by contemplative prayer. Centering prayers are typical. Their purpose is to occupy and free the mind so that one can dwell with God. The rattling off of prayers known by heart can achieve the same purpose. The oldest prayers in the church are centering prayers such as 'Lord Jesus Christ, Son of God, have mercy on me a sinner.'"[37] Thomas Merton, a Trappist monk with the religious name of Father Louis, has become one of the most prominent names associated with spirituality in the twentieth century. Speaking on the issue of contemplative prayer he writes:

> Contemplation is the highest expression of man's intellectual and spiritual life. It is that life itself, fully awake, fully active, fully aware that it is alive. It is a spiritual wonder. It is spontaneous awe at the sacredness of life, of being. It is gratitude for life, for awareness and for being. It is a vivid realization of the fact that life and being in us proceed from an invisible, transcendent and infinitely abundant Source. . . . Hence it is more than a consideration of abstract truths about God, more even than affective meditation on things we believe. It is awakening, enlightenment and the amazing intuitive grasp by which love gains certitude of God's creative and dynamic intervention on our daily life.[38]

Those in this quadrant believe that Christian spirituality must go beyond the simple transmission of biblical information. "Christians must move through the words of revelation into vital and personal contact with the risen Christ who desires to live now as the eternal God in our souls. Beyond mere religion, even beyond being saved, there should be the active pursuit of intimate relationship with God."[39]

From a programmatic point of view, it is heralded by Jerome Berryman, founder of the Center for the Theology of Childhood and author of the popular book *Godly Play: A Way of Religious*

37. John Westerhoff, *Spiritual Life: The Foundation for Preaching and Teaching* (Louisville, Ky.: John Knox Press, 1994), 57.

38. Thomas Merton, *New Seeds of Contemplation* (Trappist, Ky.: Abbey of Gethsemani, Inc.: 1972), 1–6, as cited in John Tyson, ed., *An Invitation to Christian Spirituality: An Ecumenical Anthology* (New York: Oxford University Press, 1999), 421–22.

39. Callen, *Authentic Spirituality*, 94.

Education.[40] Three other advocates of this position are Ivy Beck-with,[41] Scottie May,[42] and Catherine Stonehouse.[43] The latter two have published an excellent book on their use of contemplation, godly play, and guided imagery in programming children's ministry.

The author of chapter 1, Dr. Scottie May, is a professor of Christian education at Wheaton College. She advocates an application of this quadrant for children's ministry. She has clearly thought through the theological implications and masterfully integrated her theological convictions into ministry application. Her chapter is a compilation of course lectures, seminar presentations, published articles, and a recent book that she co-authored. Her adaptation of Berryman's research applied to the context of an evangelical perspective provides an excellent opportunity for us to see how this emphasis can be applied into the children's ministry program at a local church.

Quadrant 2: Instructional-Analytic. This quadrant has a high regard for cognitive thought processing. These individuals grow and nurture their spiritual formation through a consistent and systematic study of God's Word. They take the time to explore the Scriptures in detail looking for authoritative answers. They often punctuate their conversations with "Dr. So and So says . . ." or "My pastor claims . . ." as they use this authoritative individual to defend their point. As children they loved Bible memorization activities like quizzes and sword drills. They gravitate to memorization programs like AWANA because they receive positive reinforcement for their efforts. They rarely forget their Bibles when going to church and might even have an extra for someone who forgot his. It's characterized by a systematic presentation of

---

40. Jerome Berryman, *Godly Play: A Way of Religious Education* (San Francisco, Calif.: Harper Collins, 1991). Also, *Teaching Godly Play: The Sunday Morning Handbook* (Nashville: Abingdon Press, 1995).

41. Ivy Beckwith, *Postmodern Children's Ministry: Ministry to Children in the 21st Century Church* (Grand Rapids, Mich.: Zondervan, 2004).

42. See Scottie May, Beth Posterski, Catherine Stonehouse, and Linda Cannell, *Children Matter: Celebrating Their Place in the Church, Family, and Community* (Grand Rapids, Mich.: Eerdmans, 2005).

43. See Catherine Stonehouse, *Patterns of Moral Development* (Waco, Tex.: Word Publishers, 1980); *Joining Children on the Spiritual Journey: Nurturing a Life of Faith* (Grand Rapids, Mich.: Baker, 1998); and also "Knowing God in Childhood: A Study of Godly Play and the Spirituality of Children," in *Christian Education Journal* 5, no. 2 (1985): 27–45.

biblical teaching, emphasis on Scripture memory with elaborate reward systems and hierarchical design structures. Ministry models such as AWANA, Boys Brigade, and Pioneer Girls are indicative of this paradigm. AWANA was founded by Pastor Lance "Doc" Latham and Art Rorheim of the North Side Gospel Centre in Chicago, Illinois in the 1940s. It became organized as a ministry in 1950 and quickly caught on with other churches. Children loved the positive reinforcements of stickers, badges, and patches which motivated young children to compete with others for these prizes. The acronym stands for Approved Workmen Are Not Ashamed based on 2 Timothy 2:15. Today more than 10,400 churches in the United States run AWANA. There are clubs in all fifty states. AWANA can be found in thirty-two hundred churches in 109 countries on six continents. Although many programs could fit into this particular quadrant, AWANA seems best to personify its characteristics for our purposes here. The two writers of chapter 2 of this text are intimately aware of the details of AWANA and believe strongly in its mission and purpose.

Dr. Greg Carlson is the executive director of the Rorheim Institute, which is the adult leadership development network for AWANA Clubs International. He taught Christian education for twenty years at Grace Seminary and has authored several books. In addition, he is assisted by Dr. John Crupper, who serves as the director of Strategic Partnerships for AWANA.

Quadrant 3: Pragmatic-Participatory. Ministry models that fit within this rubric would include those with a propensity toward choreographed singing, dramatic presentations of Bible stories, numerous activities in a teaching hour, and a mild integration of instructional technology. "Learning in a context of activity and fun" might be the mantra that's advanced by those in this quadrant. These kids are active learners and rarely enjoy sitting still for long. These students want to get involved. They are active learners and need assistance staying on task. They look for practical application to Bible stories and enjoy opportunities for "getting their feet wet" in the fundamentals of the faith. They ask a lot of perceptive questions during Bible studies because they need to know that Bible stories have relevance for today. They need to test their faith to see if it's real. Sometimes this questioning is viewed by ministry leaders as threatening or argumentative rather than as an important way for these students to learn. As children they like to make crafts and explore. To them, long hours of sitting while listening to stories is dry, dull, and boring. They would rather go and feed the homeless at a shelter on Saturday night than listen to a Bible story about helping those in need on Sunday morning. In essence, they are the doers of our world.

From a ministry program perspective, the ninety minutes that may encompass a learning session on Sunday morning will be divided into five or more segments. Each segment has a purpose, and transitions between segments are carefully thought through so as to facilitate a seamless progression. A typical morning program would include elements such as singing, skits, drama, Bible story, puppets, games, and narratives. Technology is a critical component of the program; and various elements are presented via technology such as CD music, PowerPoint, video segments, and the use of television or movie clips. At some point during the presentation, time is given for the students to break into smaller groupings so an adult can participate in the interaction. These small groups provide personal contact with the students who might otherwise remain anonymous.

Children's ministries across North America that characterize this approach include Willow Creek's (South Barrington, Illinois) popular Promiseland curriculum, Saddleback Community Church's (Mission Viejo, California) Empowering Kids curriculum, or North Point Church's (Alpharetta, Georgia) KidStuf curriculum. Group Publishing is also a strong proponent of this paradigm through their action-oriented children's curriculum products (e.g., Active Learning).

This chapter is represented by Trisha Graves, the children's pastor at Port Mariners Kid Zone, the children's ministry of Mariners Church in Irvine, California. Mariners Church is listed as one of the largest churches in North America, which includes about fifteen hundred children each weekend. The children's ministry at Mariners recently completed a major capital campaign. Their recently dedicated sixty-five-thousand-square-feet children's ministry center (decorated by Disney consultants) stands as a testimony to the priority that the church places on children's ministry.

Quadrant 4: Media-Driven Active-Engagement. This ministry model is characterized by high-energy, heavily vested in instructional technology, with children always in motion. These children love creative expression, guided imagery, music, drama, and activities. These students are always in motion and love the process of learning as much as the end result. For them the joy of discovery may be more enjoyable than achieving the instructional objective of the lesson. For those who may not be familiar with guided imagery, it's a much more passionate form of storytelling. Whereas storytelling is a preferred way of learning for those in quadrant 1, those in this quadrant need more. Guided imagery provides that. In this form of expression, the storyteller moves from describing the events of the passage to getting the students to enter into the story itself. By describing the details of the event, acting out the story, changing voices to match the dialogue, using props to display actions, and perhaps even wearing costumes which depict various roles, this form of storytelling allows the student to engage the heart and feeling nature of the learner. It's an extreme version of storytelling that goes beyond the cognitive transfer of information to engage the heart of the learner.

These learners also enjoy using creative expression in order to facilitate learning. Rather than telling a story about a parable, they would much prefer dressing the parts and participating in a role play to act out the story. They might even prefer changing the story to make it a contemporary adaptation so students can discover how to apply the lesson in today's context. Remember, these students have the capacity to feel deeply about the issues of life and desire to participate actively in solving problems that are discovered. They're generally optimistic about life and look for what could become as opposed to what has already happened. They view authority with suspicion and enjoy working with students like themselves. They generally don't prefer to read or sit for long without some creative expression or activity. From a programmatic perspective, engaging these students requires using dramatic arts, video, and impacting music. No program component should last for more than ten minutes as this reflects their value for constant motion and activity. Although there are a number of excellent examples of this model around today, KIDMO is the poster child of this paradigm and is an extremely popular children's ministry program across North America. It is currently in two thousand churches and is growing by approximately forty churches per month. It's based on a philosophy of ministry that believes reaching children should involve fun, active games, technology, and interactive music. Few churches can operate at the level of quality that's required for learners in this quadrant, so KIDMO has developed a media-enhanced program for childhood and preschool children that's self-contained on multiple DVDs. The church starts the program by playing the DVD and stops at appropriate places along the way for interpersonal interaction with the students. Small groups are essential and a vital link for long-term learning.

This chapter is written by a team of KIDMO specialists. They include Johnny Rogers, the up-front personality and creative genius behind KIDMO. Assisting him is Bill Baumgart, president of Orbit Church. Tim Ellis is the executive producer for all KIDMO and Lil' K productions, and Greg Carper is the copastor/codirector of children's ministry at Carmel Presbyterian Church. In addition to these roles, he is also a conference speaker, lecturer, and writer for KIDMO Access.

Though there are no agreed-upon definitions for spirituality, spiritual formation, or spiritual maturity, that shouldn't preclude one from investigating it. For summary purposes *Christian spirituality* may be defined as "the interaction between one's theology and the living out of that theology in daily practice." "A central feature is that spirituality derives its identity from the Christian belief that as human beings we are capable of entering into a relationship with God who is both transcendent and, at the same time, indwelling in the heart of all created things."[44] Christian spirituality is intended to be lived out in the context of community with other believers and also in the midst of the lost. The Holy Spirit enables the spiritually minded believer to be drawn into fellowship with God and empowers him/her in the Christian commitment.

Programs that are designed to help facilitate this spiritual maturing process, which are created with children in mind, must take into consideration the maturation process. Accommodating the various stages of cognitive, psychosocial, and emotional development are essential for successful assimilation of new material. The Scriptures must be taught in a way that does not violate how God created us to learn since how one person perceives and processes spiritual insights may be different from another. The teacher-learner process is a valid basis for achieving spiritual development. This book intends to provide the reader with multiple models for achieving children's spiritual formation so that from this broad spectrum the ministry leader will be better equipped to make wise choices regarding the use of curriculum, volunteer leadership, facilities, and training requirements necessary for effective children's ministry.

44. Sheldrake, *Spirituality and History*, 60.

CHAPTER 1

The Contemplative-Reflective Model

SCOTTIE MAY

To watch a group of children gathered in hushed reverence because they sense the presence of the holy is an experience not soon forgotten. In a contemplative environment the careful observer is able to watch the children transition from ordinary time and space to a special time and space that reveals deep contentedness on their faces and in their posture. This transition does not happen quickly but rather subtly. It seems as if the spirit of the child is communing with the Spirit of God. The Contemplative-Reflective Model of children's ministry seeks to facilitate experiences such as these.

The aim of the Contemplative-Reflective Model of children's ministry is this: to help children encounter God in ways that result in a sense of awe and wonder, to help them consider things of God with continued attention. The model seeks to assist them in finding the quiet place within themselves—a place that all children have—where they can sense the presence of God and hear his voice.[1] What is a Contemplative-Reflective Model? What would it look like? Is it possible for children to contemplate, or is it even desirable? A helpful starting place for exploring these questions is to define the word *contemplation*. According to *Oxford English Dictionary*, to *contemplate* means "to give long and attentive consideration, especially of spiritual matters." In a similar vein, to *meditate* means "to focus one's thoughts or to ponder, to engage in contemplation." As the dictionary defines these words, in ordinary usage, the two words are essentially interchangeable.

Scripture does not directly contain the word *contemplate* but makes references through equivalent words.[2] *Meditate* and *meditation* are used numerous times.[3] Genesis 24:63 states that Isaac went into the field at night to meditate, but it does not describe the process he undertook. The book of Psalms contains more than 75 percent of the "meditate" references in the Bible. It is obvious that meditation was a significant part of David's spiritual life. Psalm 119 is especially rich in those references. Yet none of the references involves children.

Therefore, one might conclude that the words *children* and *contemplation* do not belong in the same sentence. The past experiences of many may deem a Contemplative-Reflective Model as incongruous with each other because children are assumed to have short attention spans, to be unable to reflect, and to be uninterested in spiritual matters. But perhaps those people have acted on assumptions based on what children say they want rather than carefully observing what the children actually long for—yearnings for which most children do not have words. In fact, children indeed are spiritual beings and are able to engage in deep reflection even as young as preschool age.

---

1. Noted educator Elliot Eisner says that "what we choose to 'spend' time on says something about what we value." Decisions about what and how we teach "influence what children perceive to be of value in the school [and church] and in the culture at large." "The Impoverished Mind," *Educational Leadership* 35, no. 8 (May 1978): 616.

2. First Corinthians 3:18 states that believers in Christ *reflect* God's glory. That word also may be translated *contemplate* (see the TNIV translation of that verse).

3. Ironically, the Bible contains the word *study* fewer than five times. (The exact number varies with different translations.)

Why should awe and wonder, as was mentioned earlier, be goals for children in our ministries? North American children frequently use the word *awesome* to describe the newest ride at a theme park or the latest electronic game. But when awe and wonder are found in Scripture, they almost always refer to God's laws, his actions, or his character.[4] Advocates of the Contemplative-Reflective Model desire this type of response from children because these advocates have experienced what God is like; they have seen the wonder of his great love (Ps. 17:7).

Additionally, Adrian Van Kaam, in his two-volume work *Formative Spirituality,* states that "awe has a primordial place in the hierarchy of dispositions of the heart."[5] Awe, he states, is transcendent to sensory perception and has mystery formation as its object. "The disposition of awe may give rise to an experience so profound, fascinating, and overwhelming that it seems to inundate our full field of consciousness."[6] The reader may be asking how Van Kaam's views relate to children's ministry. Hopefully, the relevance will soon become evident.

This chapter introduces and examines a model that is unfamiliar to many. The contemplative approach intentionally creates an environment that enables children to move at a slow pace, in relative quiet, so that they can reflect on a story from Scripture that helps them know who God is. The acceptance and application of the model may be affected by factors such as the tradition of the church, the value a congregation gives to contemplation or meditation, the views of the place of children, and the willingness of church leaders to examine the theological and philosophical foundations of the model.

We begin by considering children's spirituality and some of the references to children in the Bible. We will then review the history of the development of the model, the foundational framework and its unique character; present the implications

---

4. Consider the many passages that contain *awe* and *wonder*. God's people stand in awe of him and describe his work as *awesome* throughout the Old Testament. Doctor Luke's books have the phrase *filled with awe* to describe responses to Jesus' ministry. *Awesome* occurs frequently in the Psalms. The same is true for *wonder* and *wonderful.*

5. Adrian Van Kaam, "Human Formation," *Formative Spirituality,* vol. 2 (New York: Crossroad, 1985), 177.

6. Ibid., 183.

and outcomes of the model; and describe ways the model has been implemented.

Children and Spirituality

The spiritual nature of the child is one of the prime considerations of this model. Spirituality is complex and multifaceted.[7] In some traditions the concept of the age of accountability lends itself to the erroneous idea that children, before they reach a certain age (an age which differs widely between groups that hold this view), are not spiritual in the sense that they do not have a relationship with God. But spirituality also connotes a broader meaning, in a sense, a universal spirituality, though not all spirituality is Christian. This model validates that all children are spiritual and have the potential for Christian spirituality as do all people.

The word *spirituality* is hard to grasp with a simple definition since contemporary society uses and misuses it in various ways. Spirituality is described by some as awareness beyond the self, personal or impersonal, and may be named God, a power, or a presence.[8] The spiritual is the nonphysical aspect of self, yet it is related to self in that we are physical beings.[9]

Rebecca Nye, a British researcher of children's spirituality, uses the phrase "relational consciousness" to describe this quality in children. This consciousness possesses an existential awareness, a sensing of mystery, as well as aspects of the value of the meaning of life.[10]

"'Spiritual' is not just something we *ought* to be. It is something we *are* and cannot escape, regardless of how we may think or feel about it. It is our nature and our destiny."[11] It is part of our

---

7. Because the subject of this chapter is a Contemplative-Reflective Model of children's ministry, a thorough exploration of the topic of spirituality is not possible.

8. Iris Cully and Kendig Cully, eds., *Encyclopedia of Religious Education* (San Francisco: Harper and Row, 1990), 607.

9. Dallas Willard, *The Divine Conspiracy: Rediscovering Our Hidden Life in God* (San Francisco: HarperCollins, 1998), 79.

10. Rebecca Nye, "Christian Perspectives on Children's Spirituality: Social Science Contributions" in *Children's Spirituality: Christian Perspectives, Spirituality and Applications*, ed. Donald Ratcliffe (Brockton, Mass.: Cascade, 2004), 90–107.

11. Ibid., 79.

human nature because we are all created by God in his image. The spiritual life may be described as the "sum total of responses which one makes to what is perceived as the inner call of God."[12] Whether Christian or not, "the individual is increasingly aware of a spiritual craving within. He or she is drawn by one of the aspects of being . . . which leads to a profound personal conviction that one possesses a spark of the Divine."[13]

In the New Testament the most common Greek word for *spiritual* is *pneumatikos,* meaning "noncarnal or nonphysical," although the context may lead the reader to deduce accurately that the meaning may indicate godliness, Christlikeness, or the influence of the Holy Spirit. According to Benedict Groeschel, the Franciscan director of an office of Christian Development located in New York, "The center of Christian spirituality is the Incarnate Word of God" in the person of Jesus Christ.[14]

Catherine Stonehouse supports the work of other Christian scholars who regard children as spiritual beings. She writes: "With ease [children] grasp the reality of the transcendent and are even more open to God than many adults. . . . Children are born with the potential for spiritual experience, and God is the one who stimulates the activation of that potential."[15]

The landmark research of Robert Coles on the spiritual life of children involved intensive interviews of many children spanning several years. He writes the following about the subjects of his study:

> To be sure, we talked with a lot of children whose specific religious customs and beliefs came under discussion; but we also talked with children whose interest in God, in the supernatural, in the ultimate meaning of life, in the sacred side of things, was not by any means mediated by visits to churches, mosques, or synagogues. Some were the sons and daughters of professed agnostics or atheists; others belonged

---

12. Benedict Groeschel, *Spiritual Passages: The Psychology of Spiritual Development* (New York: Crossroad, 1992), 4.
13. Ibid., 13.
14. Ibid., 17.
15. Catherine Stonehouse, *Joining Children on the Spiritual Journey: Nurturing a Life of Faith* (Grand Rapids: Baker, 1998), 181.

to "religious" families but asked spiritual questions that were not at all in keeping with the tenets of their religion. Such children . . . have expressed visionary thoughts, thoughts sharply critical of organized religion.[16]

Many of these children summarized the effect of their perception of spirituality this way: "It's up to God, not us."

The Christian spirituality of children is nurtured through openness to the Holy Spirit as mediated by life within the faith community. It is strengthened by corporate uses of Scripture, forms of prayer, hymns, ritual and sacraments, retreats, and the cycles of the liturgical year, which include feasts and celebrations. This nurture cannot happen in isolation.[17]

If the context for the child is not Christian, the child still has the quality of spirituality with accompanying questions about life, self, and meaning. The environment then strongly influences the direction that spirituality takes—whether a child finds her or his life in Jesus Christ or not.

Spirituality is an aspect of all children in that they consider and ponder aspects of themselves that are less physical—nonphysical concepts that are "other" than themselves. Therefore, a Contemplative-Reflective Model enables the spiritual aspects of the child to be nurtured. When the adults caring for the children are Christian and actively involved in the spiritual life of their community of faith, the children more readily realize the power and vitality of the spiritual. The child is then freer to receive the work of the Holy Spirit.

Children in Scripture: "Jesus put a child among them"

People often assume that the Bible is a book for adults about adults. This is true, but there are also many references to children in both Old and New Testaments. In fact, Scripture has a

---

16. Robert Coles, *The Spiritual Life of Children: The Inner Lives of Children* (Boston: Houghton Mifflin, 1990), xvii.
17. Cully and Cully, *Encyclopedia of Religious Education,* 611.

surprising number of things to say about children once the reader begins to look for them.[18] The attitudes of the Lord Jesus toward children are especially significant for this discussion. What he taught the disciples regarding children is relevant to ministry today.[19] All three Synoptic Gospels relate a familiar incident involving a child. As the story begins, the disciples are bickering among themselves about status (Matt. 18:1–6).

At that time the disciples came to Jesus and asked, "Who is the greatest in the kingdom of heaven?" He called a little child and had him stand among them. And he said: "I tell you the truth, unless you change and become like little children, you will never enter the kingdom of heaven. Therefore, whoever humbles himself like this child is the greatest in the kingdom of heaven. And whoever welcomes a little child like this in my name welcomes me. But if anyone causes one of these little ones who believe in me to sin, it would be better for him to have a large millstone hung around his neck and to be drowned in the depths of the sea."

This scene is also described in Mark 9:33–37 and Luke 9:46–48. Jesus put a child *among them*. Some translations say he put the child "in the midst of them." His action was a direct response to their initial question. When the disciples asked, "Who is the greatest in the kingdom?" Jesus immediately gave them a visible illustration by placing a child among them. Clearly he recognized the issue couched in their initial question: their power plays appear to have come from selfishness and pride. Ironically, Jesus uses a child to reveal their spiritual immaturity.

Through his actions and words, Jesus reveals the value he holds for the child as a significant part of the faith community. So precious to God is the child that he uses this little one to teach the disciples by simply placing this child before them.

18. For a more complete discussion of this subject, see chapter 2, "Children in the Bible" in *Children Matter*, the book Catherine Stonehouse, Beth Posterski, Linda Cannell, and I coauthored (Grand Rapids: Eerdmans, 2005).

19. An excellent treatment of Jesus' view of children has been written by Judith M. Gundry-Volf, "The least and the greatest," in *The Child in Christian Thought*, ed. Marcia Bunge (Grand Rapids: Eerdmans, 2001), 29–60.

Jesus elevates the lowly status of a child in the culture of his day, and he reveals the value he places on humility over status. Jesus' actions must have stunned the disciples. He has the audacity to tell the disciples to change and become like little children or they would never enter the kingdom of heaven. Not only will they not be the greatest; they will not even be part of the kingdom. Christ explicitly states that whoever humbles himself like that child is the greatest in the kingdom of heaven.

Jesus continues: "Whoever welcomes a little child . . . in my name, welcomes me." In so doing, he reveals his heart toward these little ones. It is as if he is saying that the disciples should treat children as they would treat him. How one treats the weakest, most impressionable part of society matters to Jesus. Also, in contrast, if someone neglects or harms one of the children, there will be a just, serious punishment. At another time, while he was praying, Jesus declared praise to his Father because he had hidden certain things from the wise yet revealed them to little children (Matt. 11:25; Luke 10:21).[20] Their attitude was that of childlike trust, enabling him to reveal himself to them easily.

Given Jesus' words and actions, how should we respond to children? We are to include and embrace them just as he did. We are to avoid anything that might cause one of them to sin. We are to welcome children in such a way that they are able to sense the presence of God.

A contemplative approach to ministry with children will facilitate that process, helping to keep the child from a spirituality based solely on "self and parental images," leading them to a spiritual life "derived from an actual encounter with the living God."[21] Since to *contemplate* means "to look with continued attention and to observe thoughtfully," the environment for this model enables that to happen because the focus is on God himself, often initially through the parable of the good shepherd. The model intentionally guides the child to linger *in* the story, to gaze upon the good shepherd, to *wonder* about him.

---

20. Note: The Greek word used here for "little children" could refer to either youngsters or to new believers.
21. James Loder, *The Logic of the Spirit* (San Francisco: Jossey-Bass, 1998), 169.

After beginning with a look at an incident involving Jesus and a child, further insights about children and their spirituality can be gained from other passages of Scripture that refer directly to children. Scripture clearly states that children are sinful (Gen. 8:21), yet there are distinctive qualities about children. They must be carefully taught (Deut. 11:19–21), and they are to gather and learn with adults (31:12). They are also to be present with adults for many aspects of congregational life (1 Chron. 20:13; Ezra 10:1; Neh. 12:43). Several proverbs state that they need discipline and training (Prov. 13:24; 22:6; 23:13), yet even young children can praise God (Ps. 8:2; Matt. 21:15–16).[22]

Although it would be inappropriate to assume that the following examples should be construed as normative, aspects of some of these biblical children's spirituality need recognition. The boy Samuel "grew up in the presence of the LORD" (1 Sam. 2:21b), having been given to the Lord after he was weaned (1:24). In Psalm 22:9, David acknowledges God from birth and declares that he trusted God even as an infant.[23] The prophet Jeremiah realizes that he was appointed by God prior to his birth (Jer. 1:4). John the Baptist, while still in his mother's womb, was filled with the Holy Spirit (Luke 1:15) and responded actively when Mary, who was pregnant with Jesus, greeted Elizabeth, John's mother (1:41). Even Paul was set apart from birth and called by God's grace (Gal. 1:15). And Timothy knew the Scriptures from infancy (from preschool age) that made him wise for salvation (2 Tim. 3:15). The children in the above examples all had encounters with the holy as young children or as yet unborn children.

As demonstrated, Scripture relates the spiritual encounters of several children in biblical times. It also articulates the significant position the Lord Jesus gives children, and there are many references to meditation, awe, and wonder. Biblical support for

---

22. These references by no means exhaust the texts regarding children; they are simply representative of passages referring to children.

23. This passage appears to be in sharp contrast to the oft-quoted Psalm 51:5 in which David declares his sinfulness from birth, even from conception. The genre of Scripture and the intent of the psalmist in these two passages demand careful attention. There is a tendency by children's workers to dismiss one or the other of the passages without recognizing that they may need to be held in tension.

the Contemplative-Reflective Model may be drawn from this evidence.

The Historical Development of the Contemplative-Reflective Model

The development of an intentionally Contemplative-Reflective Model has taken place over the last century and a half. It begins with the rich, innovative work of Maria Montessori, Italy's first female physician. Born in 1870, she found that the gender bias of the day made it difficult for her to practice medicine in a traditional way.[24] She chose instead to focus on children, specifically mentally retarded children. She established *Casa Bambini* where she amazed government officials by teaching literacy skills as well as life skills to these children who previously had been "warehoused" in institutions. Her high view of children, including those devalued by the culture, enabled her to envision an educational setting that prepared any child for life and learning. She equipped the learning environment with child-sized furnishings. She developed materials that, after an initial instruction, children could manipulate at their own pace, helping them understand concepts that would otherwise have seemed appropriate for much older children.

A devout Catholic, Montessori also believed that every child is a spiritual being, whole and complete—a belief that was in opposition to the popular position of that day. Her personal faith, her view of children, and the learning principles she was exploring led naturally into religious education. Though not known as a religious educator, she wrote *The Child in the Church* and *Spontaneous Activity and Education,* works that lay groundwork for a contemplative approach to ministry with children. Part of her approach was to help children prepare "their first communion by harvesting the wheat, baking the bread, and marking the hosts for communion with appropriate symbols. She wrote, 'The

---

24. Much has been and continues to be written about this remarkable woman and her revolutionary approach to education. For a significant biography written some time ago by E. M. Standing, see *Maria Montessori: Her Life and Work* (New York: New American Library, 1962).

Montessori Method was furnished with a long-sought opportunity of penetrating deeper into the life of the child's soul, and of thus fulfilling its true educational mission.'"[25]

Sofia Cavalletti formalized Montessori's approach to religious education though she never met Montessori. The connection happened through Gianna Gobbi, a student of Montessori and a competent Montessori educator in her own right. In the 1950s shortly after Montessori's death, Gobbi was drawn to her friend Cavalletti's ability as a noted Hebrew scholar, skilled in the translation of the biblical text. Cavalletti was not skilled in working with children, nor did she have any interest until Gobbi asked for her help as a Bible scholar. Soon, with Gobbi guiding her in the Montessori approach, Cavalletti began a journey of more than fifty years to help children attain what Cavalletti views as the "real goal of the Christian life: to live a life hidden with God in Christ."[26]

In time she developed *Catechesis of the Good Shepherd,* a Montessori-based, contemplative approach that helps young children meet and fall in love with the good shepherd. The experience happens in an atrium (not a classroom), led by a catechist (not a teacher). The different terminology is intentional because the design and use of space and the role of the adult leader are not typical.

Cavalletti developed three three-year levels: three to six years, six to nine years, and nine to twelve years. Each level has a different focus based on her research as to what most draws the child into the biblical story. For the first level, it is the parable of the good shepherd; for the middle level it is the concept of the vine and the branches; the third level focuses on redemption history.[27] This results in a carefully developed, nine-year curriculum with clear emphases. Though based in Italy, catechesis has been offered in the United States as well as other countries since

---

25. Jerome Berryman, *Teaching Godly Play: The Sunday Morning Handbook* (Nashville: Abingdon, 1995), 19.

26. Sofia Cavalletti, *The Religious Potential of the Child* (Oak Park, Ill.: Catechesis of the Good Shepherd, 1992), 3.

27. Sofia Cavalletti, *Discovering the Real Spiritual Life of Children* (video; Archdiocese of Chicago: Liturgy Training Publications, 2000).

the late 1970s, primarily in Catholic, Episcopal, and Lutheran churches.[28]

Next in the development of a contemplative-reflective approach comes an American-based adaptation of the Montessori-Cavalletti work. Kansas-born Jerome Berryman traveled to Italy in 1971 for advanced Montessori studies. Before this he had been working in Arkansas, and his preschool-age children attended a Montessori school. The approach fascinated him; he wanted to learn more, so he took his young family to Italy to study in the place where the Montessori approach was birthed. That year he met Sofia Cavalletti and began a long-term relationship with her as his mentor/tutor. The result is what he calls *Godly Play*.[29]

In the late 1980s, Berryman collaborated with Sonya Stewart, producing the helpful book *Young Children and Worship* that explains their application of the Contemplative-Reflective Model. This useful book contains more than thirty presentations and explains how to implement their approach. Since then, Berryman and Stewart have worked independently. Berryman established the Center for the Theology of Childhood in Houston, Texas. Stewart taught at Western Theological Seminary in Holland, Michigan. Both have continued writing materials for their similar approaches: Stewart with *Young Children and Worship;* Berryman with *Godly Play.*

This latter contemplative approach is gaining in popularity in the United States. It requires a less elaborate, more flexible environment than does catechesis. Also, it may be self-taught more readily through the writings of Berryman and Stewart. Catechesis requires extensive training for each level but results in highly qualified, committed catechists.

The principles identified through the thorough work of Montessori, Cavalletti, Berryman, and Stewart enable children's

---

28. For more information about Catechesis of the Good Shepherd, see Cavalletti's writings, primarily *The Religious Potential of the Child* (Oak Park, Ill.: Catechesis of the Good Shepherd, 1992) and *The Religious Potential of the Child 6 to 12 Years Old* (Oak Park, Ill.: Catechesis of the Good Shepherd, 2002). You may also want to visit the Web site of the National Association of Catechesis of the Good Shepherd: www.cgsusa.org.

29. Jerome Berryman, *Godly Play: An Imaginative Approach to Religious Education* (Minneapolis: Augsburg, 1991), 23–27.

ministers to draw on their insights and shape a contemplative-reflective approach appropriate for their setting.

Values Behind a Contemplative-Reflective Model

If the Lord Jesus' instructions to the faith community are to learn from children, to change and become humble as they are, and to welcome children into the congregation, it is critical to examine any ministry approach to make sure it aligns with the mission Christ has given. Many activities, attitudes, and ways of thinking may facilitate what God wants to accomplish, yet there are those which may be counterproductive to what God desires to achieve in children and ultimately in the faith community. There is no perfect model of ministry with children, but our gracious God is at work in lives and in ministries in spite of flawed approaches and human shortcomings.

In the introduction of *The Child in Christian Thought,*[30] editor Marcia Bunge identifies themes regarding children drawn from Scripture and Christian history. Bunge deduces that children are whole, complete human beings made in the image of God who need instruction and guidance as they are developing; that children are gifts of God to us and are also sinful creatures and moral agents; that children are models of faith for adults; and that they are also orphans, neighbors, and strangers who need justice and mercy.

If Bunge's themes rightly characterize the nature of these little ones, what implications do these themes hold for children's ministry? What tasks lie ahead? What personal work did Jesus model for us in the lives of little ones? What tools must be used in our ministry efforts? The contemplative-reflective approach begins to address some of those questions. As we explore this approach, four issues emerge: (1) We must know the child. (2) We must know the story, and that story must be the center of all that is taught. (3) We must know the culture and the context. (4) We each must know our God. Our approach to these issues

---

30. Marcia Bunge, *The Child in Christian Thought* (Grand Rapids: William B. Eerdmans, 2000), 1–28.

determines the manner in which we go about God's work with children.

Knowing the Child

Because children are different from adults in many ways, they act and react differently from adults in similar settings. Their imaginations are engaged in ways that adults often do not understand. In many church settings, children become restless, exhibiting short attention spans. But sometimes, from my own observations, in settings that are slow and gentle, filled with rich symbols and visual objects, children settle calmly, even reflectively. For the young child, "imagination may be the vehicle of powerful religious experiences."[31]

Language. In the biblical references to specific children mentioned earlier, many of the encounters of the child's spirit with the Spirit of God took place when the child was prelanguage, before articulation of the event was possible. Language is not therefore a precursor to spiritual experience. The emotional component of those experiences must be distinguished from the ability to speak about the experience. Too often spirituality has been associated with correct language. Words and deeds don't always match in religious life. In the same way feelings and experiences are often disconnected from words, especially for children.

In *Godly Play*, Jerome Berryman writes about the significance of language and experience for the young child. His carefully prepared, contemplative environment seeks to create space to allow children to begin to formulate and ask existential questions at church or at home—questions such as, "What happens when someone dies?" "Mommy, what if you don't come back?" or, "What should I be when I grow up?"[32]

The environment must create opportunity for interplay between experience and language that the child lacks at first. If experiences of God are provided, language to describe those experiences may develop. Language shapes experience, and experience shapes language.[33] But helpful language must be used. The

---

31. Loder, *Logic of the Spirit*, 154.
32. Berryman, *Godly Play: An Imaginative Approach to Religious Education*, 59.
33. Ibid., 153.

language of religion, of spiritual formation, is the language of mystery and of relationship. As the child enters into symbols, parables, and narratives, the child may experience the presence of God.[34] But language may also be spiritually deforming, introducing fear or mistrust of God or even irrelevance. Language can keep children from drawing closer to God if God is defined with detail and precision; if self is described in conditional terms, such as "if you can be good, then . . ." or "God doesn't love you when you're naughty"; or if the sense of awe and wonder is not part of worship.

Ways of Knowing. The separation of language from spiritual experience highlights an important distinction between *connatural knowing* and *speculative knowing.* Connatural knowing is an *encounter* with what is to be known. In a way it is the desire to know because of interest, longing, even love of the object. Initially infants learn language and sounds in this manner. Speculative knowing is *detached,* rational, theoretical, propositional—the more traditional "schooling" approach.[35] It seeks knowledge for the sake of knowledge.[36]

A study showed that children disengage from the learning process if speculative knowing is used extensively in teaching them things of faith. The study suggests purposefully altering traditional religious education by introducing connatural knowing to young children so that they may *encounter* God rather than initially being taught about him. Consistent early experiences *with* God may allow the desire to know *about* God to grow. This proposed sequence of knowing seems to parallel a child's knowing about her parents: connatural knowing comes first, with the desire for speculative knowing gradually coming later. Thus, a relationship with God, certainly the chief goal of children's ministry, might be established with positive emotional grounding.

---

34. Ibid., 148.

35. Christopher Renz, "Christian Education and the Confirmation Debate: Towards a Theology of Catechesis," *Journal of Christian Education* 41, no. 1 (1998): 53–65.

36. It is not hard to see the parallel between speculative and connatural knowing with the thinking of Martin Buber in his book, *I and Thou* (New York: Scribner's Sons, 1958). Buber's use of I/Thou equates with connatural knowing, while his I/It with speculative knowing.

Other scholars concur with this study, noting that the child's relational experience precedes the development of spiritual narrative.[37] In other words, if a child has a relationship with God first, she or he will in time be able to articulate a faith story. The nonverbal "inner speech" may become the foundation for spirituality. As speech is linked with an internal experience of God, the child is slowly then able to personalize spirituality. The child uses symbols from narratives or a concrete experience as the basis for relational consciousness with Other (God) not unlike the concept of bonding.[38] As the child integrates the meaning of the symbols with circumstances in life, identification with God as Other and with self may take place in relational terms.

The emphasis in recent generations on "speculative" knowing, driven by the assumed importance of cognition for children, demands careful study by practitioners and curriculum developers in children's ministry. David Hay, Rebecca Nye, and Roger Murphy write: "Over the past thirty years the dominance of cognitive developmental theory in the field of religious education has led to a severe neglect of the study of the spirituality of the child and to a distortion of what goes on in the religious education classroom."[39] This undoubtedly is caused in part by the challenge of finding appropriate methodology but also in part by the narrowness of developmental stage theories that come "near to dissolving religion into reason and therefore childhood religion into a form of immaturity or inadequacy."[40]

If cognitive development and facility are viewed as necessary for the spiritual development of children, they also force a question about the faith of mentally retarded children. The logical human conclusion—that mentally challenged children are not able to learn enough about God to really know him—would be most unfortunate and also undoubtedly wrong. For effective for-

---

37. Kevin Reimer and James Furrow, "A Qualitative Exploration of Relational Consciousness in Christian Children," *International Journal of Children's Spirituality* 6, no. 1 (2001): 10.
38. Ibid., 20.
39. David Hay, Rebecca Nye, and Roger Murphy, "Thinking about Childhood Spirituality: Review of Research and Current Directions," in *Research in Religious Education*, ed. Leslie Francis, William Kay, and William Campbell (Macon, Ga.: Smyth & Helwys, 1996), 47.
40. Ibid., 56.

mational education to take place in children's ministry, the child must have both connatural and speculative experiences, but, if the research is correct,[41] connatural knowing should happen first regardless of the age of the child or the child's cognitive ability.

Recent ongoing scholarship examines some of the work of noted cognitive theorist Jean Piaget.[42] Piaget argues that a child's early concepts of God are shaped by perceptions of her or his parents, a position that is not fully supported by the current research. Current research suggests that young children have conceptual abilities to reason about God that they do not use regarding humans. The study of Barrett and Richert suggests that children have a "preparedness" or "sensitive" period[43] for learning about God. If their hypotheses are valid, "contrary to common, Piagetian-derived assumptions, it should be possible to teach children about many seemingly sophisticated aspects of theology at a very early age. Particularly, preschoolers seem capable of reasoning about God as an immortal, infallible, super-powerful being. . . . Teaching children about divine attributes at a young age could have more robust consequences with less investment than at a later stage in development."[44]

Children's Brains. God's design of the human being is amazing. From the newborn infant to the geriatric person, the workings of the body fill one with awe at the work of our Creator. The brain is among the more remarkable organs of the body, and it is the object of increasingly intense study, given the exploratory abilities of recent technology. The two large cerebral hemispheres (neocortex or cerebrum) are familiar to many. Some people reductionistically think that the left hemisphere regulates thinking while the right one influences creativity. Not many are as familiar with the midbrain or limbic system. These three major

---

41. See footnote 14.

42. Justin Barrett and Rebekah Richert, "Anthropomorphism or Preparedness? Exploring Children's God Concepts," *Review of Religious Research* 44, no. 3 (2003): 300–12.

43. A "sensitive" period is also a common phrase use by Montessori for times when children indicate significant readiness to learn certain concepts.

44. Justin Barrett and Rebekah Richert, "Anthropomorphism or Preparedness? Exploring Children's God Concepts," 310–11.

parts of the brain (sometimes called the triune brain) are interacting with one another all the time.

An interview in *Discover*, a journal of science, presented the findings of researcher Antonio Damasio, head of neurology at the University of Iowa.[45] Much of his work focuses on the role of the brain and emotions. Damasio, among others, discusses the *amygdala*, an important part of the limbic system.[46] It plays a crucial role in emotional response and is, in that way, significantly tied to rational decision making. Historically, particularly since the Enlightenment, rationalism has been a dominant aspect of Western society, so much so that emotions are often considered suspect. Emotions do not make the decisions, but they do influence how persons make decisions and how persons feel about the decisions that have been made. According to Damasio, the emotional processing that takes place regarding decisions a person makes is connected to the resulting conviction and also the morals and values used while making that judgment. In addition, and very importantly, this processing cannot be hurried.

Damasio suggests that all parts of the brain do not work at the same speed. The neural pathways associated with cognition have a myelin coating that allows for faster and faster processing through training and experience. Damasio reports that the fibers of the amygdala and other parts of the midbrain are unmyelinated so that the conduction of those impulses is constant and slow. He states, "The risk of emotional neutrality becomes greater and greater as the speed of cognition increases."[47] The implication is that as we develop, we may rely more and more on cognition, and then we risk losing our emotional and moral connections regarding decisions we make. Electronic technol-

45. Steven Johnson, "Antonio Damasio's Theory of Thinking Faster and Faster," *Discover* 25, no. 5 (2004): 45–49.

46. Some of the others who are researching the connection of the midbrain to spirituality are: Rene Joseph, "The Limbic System and the Soul: Evolution and the Neuroanatomy of Religious Experience," *Zygon* 36, no. 1 (2001): 105–35; Chauncey Leake, "Human Purpose, the Limbic System, and the Sense of Satisfaction," *Zygon* 10, no. 1 (1975): 86–94; Joseph LeDoux, *The Emotional Brain: The Mysterious Underpinnings of Emotional Life* (New York: Simon and Schuster, 1996); Andrew Newberg, Eugene d'Aquill, and Vince Rause, *Why God Won't Go Away* (New York: Ballantine, 2002); and Jerome Berryman, *Godly Play: An Imaginative Approach to Religious Education* (Minneapolis: Augsburg, 1991).

47. Johnson, "Antonio Damasio's Theory of Thinking Faster and Faster," 49.

ogy and media enable children to multitask with greater speed and with what appears to be increased efficiency; but if Damasio is correct, that speed comes with the price of short-circuiting emotional connections. It will be beneficial to look at ways to help children connect emotionally and relationally with God, with other children, and with the significant adults in their lives. These neurological findings shed insight on the role of the midbrain in emotional processing and the need to allow adequate time and space for children to process spiritual things in an unhurried manner even more so than for a cognitive response. Berryman says that an awareness must be developed that recognizes nonverbal limbic responses in children as well as verbal, neocortex (more cognitive) responses because falling in love [with the Lord Jesus] through grace happens through the limbic system, whereas it is spoken about through the left hemisphere of the neocortex.[48]

For generations language has been the focus in ministry with children, relying on the cognitive left hemisphere of the neocortex. In recent decades the creative right hemisphere of the neocortex has received increasing attention. Given Damasio's position about the limbic system presented here, it seems crucial to take seriously the possibility that children's experiences or encounters with God can be facilitated by preparing environments that allow connatural knowing and relational consciousness to emerge. Nye's concept of relational consciousness is powerfully relevant for ministry praxis in the spiritual formation of children.[49] The Contemplative-Reflective Model attempts to have the child's spirituality influence the form ministry takes rather than letting the stage of a developmental construct or a cultural trend shape the ministry.

Repetition and Routine. Another key to understanding children is their fascination and contentment with repetition. Because of this, ritual and symbols can help provide formational stability and familiarity. Have you noticed how little ones love

48. Jerome Berryman, "Children and Mature Spirituality," in *Children's Spirituality: Christian Perspectives, Research and Application,* ed. Donald Ratcliff (Eugene, Or.: Wipf & Stock Pub., 2004, 33.

49. Rebecca Nye, "Christian Perspectives on Children's Spirituality: Social Science Contributions," 90–107.

songs, rhymes, and ditties? Children are often not content unless the tunes are repeated ad nauseum. This love for routine can be seen in bedtime rituals, daily routines, and in liturgical worship. Rituals from my own elementary school days gave security, telling me, "It's a new day, and all is well with my world." Repetition and routine support children's need to know that they can trust those responsible for caring for them. Without these consistent patterns, children may perceive their own world as chaotic and their well-being at risk.

Often as adults we may assume something is boring for them or that they need "fresh" creativity. In fact, repetition may well be one thing for which children yearn. G. K. Chesterton expounds on this point beautifully. He writes:

> Because children have abounding vitality, because they are in spirit fierce and free, therefore they want things repeated and unchanged. They always say, "Do it again"; and the grown-up does it again until he is nearly dead. But perhaps God is strong enough to exult in monotony. It is possible that God says every morning, "Do it again" to the sun; and every evening, "Do it again" to the moon. It may not be automatic necessity that makes all daisies alike; it may be that God makes every daisy separately, but has never got tired of making them. It may be that He has the eternal appetite for infancy; for we have sinned and grown, and our Father is younger than we.[50]

It is interesting to note that all liturgy, the work of the people, has a rhythm to it. Through liturgy, ritual, and repetition, when experienced among adults who participate with conviction, children learn the language of faith. "Forever and ever" leads to "Amen," and "Alleluia" leads to the gospel.[51]

Knowing the Story

Children's ministers recognize that children are capable of knowing God at any age in ways appropriate for that age. That means children must come to know and experience God's re-

---

50. G. K. Chesterton, *Orthodoxy* (Garden City, N.Y.: Image Books, 1959), 59.
51. Gabe Huck, "Understanding Liturgy," *Liturgy* 19, no. 1 (2004): 3.

demptive story intimately to provide the language for their faith and relationship with God. It must be the focal point of all that is done. This *knowing* should be first connatural then speculative. Children need particularly to know that they are *in* that story.

A value of the Contemplative-Reflective Model is to be able to enter into the story so that it is real and comes alive for them rather than only knowing about it in an informational way. This means that Scripture must be central: the whole redemption story taught without letting it become a "kiddie gospel."[52]

The story has the potential of drawing children into it, depending on how it is presented. (Two examples of children's teaching models that maintain the story as the center are Berryman's *Godly Play* and Cavalletti's *Catechesis of the Good Shepherd,* which will be described later in this chapter.) The story is at the center while the child is respectfully, wholly among those gathered. The child is not the center; the biblical story is. Instead of the story being an *object* to be studied as in speculative knowing, it becomes the *subject* to be entered and with which to be engaged.[53] Using the terms of Jewish theologian Martin Buber, the story is no longer *It* but *Thou.*[54] When the story is center and when the leaders or presenters have experienced it personally, they can tell it in such a way that the children are able to enter into it and experience it.

Knowing the Purpose of Worship

Not only is knowing and keeping the story essential, but another core value of the Contemplative-Reflective Model is to enable children to participate in authentic worship. In order for that to happen, the culture and context of the children must be considered. This model, in most every way, seems in opposition to contemporary North American culture. It is, in fact, and that is one of its intended strengths. On the surface this may seem

---

52. "Kiddie gospel" is the phrase used by Gretchen Pritchard in *Offering the Gospel to Children* (Cambridge, Mass.: Cowley, 1992), 39, to describe the tendency of some to "dumb down" God's story and to omit the "hard" parts of the story for children.

53. This view of the subject is reminiscent of the approaches of Paulo Freire, *Pedagogy of the Oppressed* (London: Continuum, 2000) and *Education for Critical Consciousness* (New York: Crossroad, 1974), and Parker Palmer, *To Know as We Are Known* (San Francisco: Harper San Francisco, 1993).

54. Martin Buber, *I and Thou* (New York: Scribner's Sons, 1958).

contradictory, but the model attempts critically to retrieve what has been lost in recent generations regarding the thoughtful nurture of children and their ability to worship.

It is a challenge to try to distinguish children's needs and yearnings from their wants. Marketing through various media creates wants that are obvious, resulting for many children in a form of impoverishment—a poverty of affluence—since many parents desire to meet children's wants. Yet children also have yearnings and needs for belonging, feeling welcome, being secure, having quietness, understanding, meaning, and connecting with God. The Contemplative-Reflective Model is intended to meet some of those needs.

One place many of the yearnings of little ones are met is in the charity and security of a reasonably healthy family. It can be a safe haven from the thundering assaults on children that exploit their lack of strong defenses. Thus, the significance of the family must be recognized and supported within the faith community. But for children from families that are less than healthy, the support of the faith community is even more important. The Contemplative-Reflective Model provides a setting where the Lord Jesus becomes deeply significant and comforting for such children.

Ritual separated from the story may become empty, lifeless, boring, and meaningless. However, thoughtful, intentional, worshipful settings can provide rich opportunities to help children encounter God. Frederick Buechner describes worship in practical, concrete terms that can be appropriate and meaningful for children. He writes: "To worship God means to serve him. Basically, there are two ways to do it. One way is to do things for him that he needs to have done—run errands for him, carry messages for him, fight on his side, feed his lambs, and so on. The other way is to do things for him that you need to do—sing songs for him, create beautiful things for him, give things up for him, tell him what's on your mind and in your heart, in general, rejoice in him and make a fool of yourself for him the way lovers have always made fools of themselves for the one they love."[55]

55. Frederich Buechner, *Listening to Your Life* (San Francisco: HarperCollins, 1992), 182.

To use the word *worship* as a noun describes an encounter with God. In light of Buechner's comments, much worship in the Bible is also described in terms of verbs that children do. The following excerpts from 1 Chronicles 16 present many of these verbs:

> *Give thanks* to the Lord, *call* on his name;
>   make known among the nations what he has done.
> *Sing* to him, *sing* praise to him;
>   *tell* of all his wonderful acts.
> *Glory* in his holy name;
>   let the hearts of those who seek the Lord *rejoice.*
> *Look* to the Lord and his strength;
>   *seek* his face always.
> *Remember* the wonders he has done,
>   his miracles, and the judgments he pronounced, . . .
> *Ascribe* to the Lord, O families of nations,
>   *ascribe* to the Lord glory and strength,
>   *ascribe* to the Lord the glory due his name.
> *Bring* an offering and come before him;
>   *worship* the Lord in the splendor of his holiness.
> *Tremble* before him, all the earth!
>   The world is firmly established; it cannot be moved. . . .
> *Give* thanks to the Lord, for he is good;
>   his love endures forever.
> *Cry out,* "Save us, O God our Savior;
>   gather us and deliver us from the nations,
>   that we may *give thanks* to your holy name,
>   that we may *glory* in your praise."
> *Praise* be to the Lord, the God of Israel,
>   from everlasting to everlasting
>   (1 Chron. 16:8–12, 28–30, 34–36).

Children can do all these actions with meaning and pleasure. A Contemplative-Reflective Model takes these actions seriously as ways to let children worship authentically and as ways to teach them the vocabulary and culture of faith.

Knowing Our God

Underlying all that has been said is the foundational value that the leaders of the ministry, regardless of the model being used, must also know the character of God and encounter him regularly. This *knowing* must be connatural knowledge of him as well as speculative. When I experience God and his ways through the Holy Spirit, I myself am letting Christ be formed in me (Gal. 4:19). Only then am I able to help the children in my ministry do the same. All the while, in the context of this personal experience, I can critically retrieve the theology and practices from Scripture and history that will enhance my ministry and the spiritual formation of the children in it.

Some time ago I was reflecting on why, after decades of ministry with children, I have embraced the Contemplative-Reflective Model in recent years as a vital approach for children. I identified unique characteristics in this approach that are interrelated and, I believe, necessary for the nurture and formation of children. The following is not a list to be read linearly but characteristics that interact with one another in encounters with God at the hub:

Encounters with God

Leading to

Developing a sense of awe and wonder

Leading to

Knowing his character and actions

Leading to

Knowing and being formed in the character of God's people

Leading to

Owning an identity as part of the people of God

Leading to

Engaging in service and mission

Envision these characteristics as a circle to which entry may be at any point. Each of the "leading to" phrases represents the work of the Holy Spirit and a need for some type of conversion—a new or renewed turning toward Jesus, a deeper way of allowing Christ to be formed within. They also highlight the fact that as I create ministry opportunities, the Holy Spirit is the one who leads the child, and I need to get out of the way. Different church traditions may tend to emphasize some characteristics more than others, maybe even neglecting some. A balance, however, is ideal. Some denominational traditions emphasize the "knowing" characteristics, often in a cognitive way, and neglect the aspects relating to "encounters" and awe and wonder. Other traditions may tend to do the opposite. Still others may diminish the importance of service and mission. Balance happens when every characteristic is intentionally present for all ages of the faith community.

Characteristics of the Contemplative-Reflective Model

Not surprisingly, no two children's ministries are identical, and a Contemplative-Reflective Model of children's ministry used in one setting may look different from another. In spite of those differences, common qualities are evident in the child and in most contemplative environments. The thoughtful work of Cavalletti observed and named the following characteristics of the child in such an experience:[56]

- *Joy*—deep, peaceful serenity that is evident in children's posture, focus, and contentedness in being in the setting.

- *Dignity,* ensuing from the ability to have a personal relationship with God, accompanied by wonder, amazement, freedom, and independence.

- *Awe and wonder,* flowing from awareness of the presence of God through a visual symbol that draws the child to a responsive activity and contemplation.[57]

---

56. Sofia Cavalletti, *Discovering the Real Spiritual Life of Children.*

57. Referencing public educator Eliot Eisner once again: Eisner feels that much of what we teach and how we teach it undermines for the child the importance of wonder. He calls for environments and tasks that elicit wonder and stimulate the imagination. From "What Really Counts in Schools," *Educational Leadership* 48, no. 5 (1991), 81. He

Here are some of the characteristics of the environment:

- *Special space,* a space that communicates reverence, even mystery. Sometimes it is enough simply to remove shoes before entering the space.

- *Essentiality*—the elimination of frills and fluff because otherwise the young child may be lost in a cluttered, busy environment. "The spiritual life is to determine what is *essential.*"[58] Therefore, the child is the teacher, so watch the child's reaction and growth to determine what is essential.

- *Slow pace,* one that says, "There is no need to hurry here."

- *Quietness,* a calm atmosphere pervades because "someone might be listening to God."[59]

- *Worship,* a time that allows children to experience worship as both a noun and a verb.

- *Ritual,* a set order or pattern of activities that allows the children to sense dignity and reverence in order to "help them to know their own soul and provide or perfect the rituals and forms" that give meaning to their lives.[60] Some contemplative-reflective approaches follow the classic pattern of the early church: enter, prepare (call to worship), hear God's Word, respond, prepare for the

---

desires an education of "I wonder," instead of merely "I do," a context of vitality instead of insistence on the transmission of inert ideas. From *Education for Critical Consciousness* (New York: Continuum, 1973), 36.

58. Cavalletti, *Discovering the Real Spiritual Life of Children.*

59. From a training session for *Catechesis of the Good Shepherd,* level 1, at St. Barnabas Episcopal Church, Glen Ellyn, Illinois, June 1999.

60. Gertrude Nelson, "Christian Formation of Children: The Role of Ritual and Celebration," in *Liturgy and Spirituality in Context: Perspectives on Prayer and Culture,* ed. Eleanor Bernstein (Collegeville, Minn.: Liturgical Press, 1990), 117. Nelson adds that "for this to happen, we must protect children from the world's clamor and its call for them to fulfill their desires by buying 'stuff.' We must help them 'touch the places of life's mysteries and give them back meaning—not a sentimentalized meaning but a meaning that they will never outgrow.'"

feast (Lord's Supper), share the feast, receive a blessing, go out.[61]

- *Repetition,* the use of a pattern of words that may help the child learn the language and vocabulary of faith.

- *Experience* through active learning, described by some as "participatory knowing," which comes through appropriate activity or an active encounter that can inform the child for life, laying the foundation for cognition and further interpretation later.[62]

- *Liturgy* that is both individual and communal and may look different for different traditions. "The words, acts, and gestures point to the reality" that the faith community is celebrating and thus become "signs" through which "the reality is expressed and lived."[63]

- *Wonder statements* that invite the child to wonder or reflect deeply. Rather than asking content-type questions, the leaders make statements such as, "I wonder how it feels to be in the Good Shepherd's flock," or, "I wonder how it would feel to hear Jesus call my name." The challenge for leaders is to avoid responding to the statements themselves as if they were asking rhetorical questions. The developers of the Contemplative-Reflective Model entrust the Spirit of God to bring meaning to the story when the child is ready rather than tell the child what it means. Therefore, all the children will not "get it" at the same time; but when they do, they "own it" because it was their own insight.

Snapshots of Contemplative-Reflective Models

Space will not be taken here to describe in detail *Catechesis of the Good Shepherd* or *Young Children and Worship* or

---

61. Berryman, *Teaching Godly Play: The Sunday Morning Handbook,* 18.

62. Barbara Myers and William Myers, *Emerging Transcendence: The Church's Ministry and Covenant with Young Children* (Cleveland: Pilgrim Press, 1992), 4.

63. Cavalletti, *The Religious Potential of the Child,* 58.

Godly Play. All three are well-established models with extensive resources. The best source for information is www.cgsusa.org, Web site of the National Association of Catechesis of the Good Shepherd.

Sonya Stewart and Jerome Berryman's book, *Young Children and Worship,*[64] carefully presents a plan for setting up and executing their model in a church setting. Stewart's *Following Jesus*[65] does the same, presenting stories focusing on the Gospel of Mark. Berryman's *Teaching Godly Play: The Sunday Morning Handbook* is also a guide for his *Godly Play.* A search of the Web site for his Center for the Theology of Children provides a list of the additional resources he has developed.[66]

Following the pattern of Montessori education, minimal staffing is required for the above models when the staff is familiar with the model and has been adequately trained. These roles are essential: a greeter who sits at the door to welcome each child on her or his eye level and to prepare the child to enter the space; a circle person who is the storyteller but also sits in the circle to engage the children in appropriate conversation; and a general assistant who helps manage the resources, supplies for the feast, and helps with any disruptions that might occur.

Because of the thoroughness of the aforementioned resources, it may be helpful to consider ways those models have been modified. To do so, I would like to explain how my interest in Contemplative-Reflective Models has unfolded. It all began with my increasing awareness of the effectiveness of experiential learning and "participative knowing."[67]

A Bible-Time Museum. More than fifteen years ago we (church leaders and myself) began experimenting with how those active learning concepts might be used in a church setting. Drawing on principles from school field trips and from children's museums, we established a hands-on, Bible-Time Museum as the setting for Sunday morning learning. We wanted the children to be able to enter into the story, whether it was visiting in Esther's

---

64. Sonya Stewart and Jerome Berryman, *Young Children and Worship* (Philadelphia: Westminster/John Knox Press, 1988).
65. Sonya Stewart, *Following Jesus* (Louisville: Geneva Press, 2000).
66. For additional materials, see www.godlyplay.org.
67. Myers and Myers, *Emerging Transcendence,* 4.

court in Susa, walking through events in a New Testament village, or constructing the tabernacle during Moses' day. We developed a Sunday morning learning experience in which the children spent time doing authentic, contextualized tasks, hearing a first-person story about what God was doing in and through his people, and then discussing in small groups the implications of the story for life today. It was working well. The children loved what we were doing. They were engaged and focused. We still use this approach, constantly tweaking it for improvements, but with one significant change—the introduction of contemplative elements.

One Sunday, a visitor spent the time observing what we were doing. Later she came to me and said, "Scottie, the children have a wonderful time. They are learning. They have fun and enjoy themselves. But Scottie, when do they meet God?" I was startled. I did not realize what we had been omitting.

From then on we began to be intentional about contemplative activities. During the story time when all the children are together, we changed the type of music we used. We eliminated the camp-type music with wild motions—music that's just for fun or to "get the wiggles out"—and there was an immediate change in the children's behavior. As we introduced music that addressed God and directly related to the theme, the children became more settled and calm. We also began having a call to worship. With reverence we lit a Christ candle to remind us all that Jesus, the Light of the world, is present. Sometimes we had moments of silence. These simple changes, for the most part, also helped the small group leaders lead the children to be more reflective in their discussion time with the children. The vital experiential elements were preserved, but contemplation was added.

Assessment is one of the biggest challenges about a contemplative-reflective approach and experiential learning in general. A common question is two-pronged: What are the children learning, and how do you know that is happening? It seems many people, parents and staff alike, assume that only speculative knowing is true learning. An accompanying concern is that if the learning cannot be objectively evaluated then learning has not happened.

These issues are difficult to address directly because of the pervasive power of the assumptions present in traditional schooling. Helping children encounter the Lord Jesus and fall in love with him—in other words, the making of disciples—is virtually impossible to assess objectively without simply quantifying behaviors. There is a measure of validity in observing behaviors, but it easily falls into the legalistic categories of the religious behaviorism of the 1940s and 1950s. It seems more important to watch for transformation in the children—for attitude changes, for reports that their faith sustains them during the week, for an increasing love for God's Word, and for a desire to pray and to listen to God. After all, this is what children's ministry is all about.

Research on the Contemplative-Reflective Model

After observing *Catechesis of the Good Shepherd* and *Young Children and Worship/Godly Play* many times, I became curious how young children who only had experience in a preschool-type learning setting would respond to a contemplative environment. With some graduate student assistants, we melded principles from the *Catechesis* and *Godly Play* models, also adding elements of our own. For ten weeks on Wednesday mornings, we had two hours with children ages four and five in groups of fifteen to twenty. These children had no experience in a contemplative or a Montessori environment. We chose a nine-week curriculum written by graduate students based on attributes of the Good Shepherd. Through the parable of the good shepherd, a story that profoundly satisfies the young child's hunger for relationship with Other, according to Cavalletti's extensive research, the young child is struck that the shepherd calls the sheep by name. The basic story presentation was taken from Cavalletti and Berryman/Stewart, but we developed it into nine distinct presentations.[68]

Because we did not have a designated room for this experience, each week we set up the environment. This included screen-

---

68. We found that by focusing on the same story, e.g., the good shepherd, for several weeks, the children went deeper into the story than if a different story is presented each week.

ing off the toys normally used in that room, setting up an altar by covering a game table with purple cloth, creating a prayer corner on one side of the room and a praise corner in the other, and preparing a variety of materials that the children could chose to use to respond to the story. Much of the room setup looked like the instructions in the published resources mentioned earlier.

Once the room was ready, we leaders prepared ourselves by spending time in prayer for the morning and for the children. We placed our shoes outside the door as did the children as they arrived. Each child was greeted by the doorkeeper and invited to select a rhythm instrument. Early arrivers could then work on a mural of the good shepherd or sit on a large tape circle on the floor and visit with me.

The first week the children arrived in typical preschooler fashion—exuberant, high energy, curious. One boy looked behind all the screens hiding the toys, underneath the altar cloth, and inside the boxes of supplies. But that happened only the first week. Much of that first session was spent preparing the children for this two-hour weekly experience.

We helped them realize that in this special space we move slowly and speak softly. We explained these actions to the children and rehearsed them together. We practiced walking around the circle and making motions to God. Then we showed them how to use the materials for a response to the story they would hear. These materials included tangram blocks, colored pencils, watercolor paints, tempra paints, clay, shapes to trace with crayons, and sand. We had two trays of each. We showed the children how to prepare the materials as well as clean up after themselves, closely following Montessori's principles. We also explained what to do if they chose to "work" in the praise corner where they could use a headset to listen to appropriate praise music, the prayer corner where they could be curtained off to listen or talk to the Good Shepherd alone, and the book corner where all the books related to the Good Shepherd. In addition the children could choose baskets that contained materials with which they could retell the story. A different basket represented each of the nine stories about the Good Shepherd that were presented after the fashion in *Young Children and Worship*.

We established a ritual using the instruments to greet each child. With guidelines clearly spelled out, the children used the instruments appropriately. The weekly routine continued as we talked about each item on the altar and also lit the Christ candle. Next we sang praise songs to God—songs such as "Praise Him, Praise Him, All You Little Children," "Oh, How I Love Jesus," and "This Is the Day That the Lord Has Made." Sometimes we used the instruments as we sang and walked around the circle. Other times we passed out streamers so the children could make beautiful motions to God as they sang. Occasionally we used our bodies as percussive instruments to clap, snap, or slap.

Each week the story presentation followed the time of greeting, lighting the Christ candle, and singing praise to God. After the story, one at a time, the children were asked what work they would like to do in order to make or do something for the Good Shepherd or to listen to what he wanted to say to them. If a child had not decided, we asked them again a few moments later. This procedure, not original with us, enabled the children to select and prepare their materials in an orderly fashion.[69] If a child finished one type of work, after putting it away properly, he or she would come back to the circle where I would ask what work they would like to do next. Forty minutes was allotted for this response work.

The attentiveness of the children to their work during this extended response time was remarkable. Occasionally younger children meeting at the church on the level above us would run noisily overhead. The children never even looked up or asked if they could go play too. The boys' work choices were particularly surprising. Invariably they were the first to choose the reflective or reenactive work. They would select the basket materials to retell the story to themselves over and over. They would also select the praise corner. Surprisingly, no girl chose the prayer corner until about week 8, but boys spent time there every week.

---

69. For a complete explanation of how to begin a similar approach, see Berryman's *Teaching Godly Play: The Sunday Morning Handbook*.

One morning a boy, four and a half years old, emerged from the prayer corner and said, "God touched me." He couldn't explain what took place but restated, "God just touched me." Another youngster spent six or seven minutes sitting in the chair that was curtained off, and then he got down on his knees, putting his face in his hands on the floor and stayed in that position several more minutes. (I was aware of this because I could see him under the curtain.)

Next came the "feast" or snack time followed by more music around the circle. Then, to prepare for the children's departure, we developed a liturgy of light. With a little apprehension and many precautions in place, we passed the light of Christ from the Christ candle to each child by giving them a small tea light candle in a clear plastic glass. (We had to warn one child once about appropriate, safe behavior with a lighted candle.) We watched a look of awe come over each child as she or he received the light. We reflectively sang "This Little Light of Mine" and reminded the children that Jesus said that *he* is the light of the world (John 8:12), followed by his statement that *we* are also that light for the world (Matt. 5:14).

We established a dismissal ritual using the candles by calling each child forward one by one. With great care and reverence, he or she carried the small candle forward, placing it around the Christ candle on the altar. The children were able to see the light grow stronger as more and more candles filled the altar. This became a symbol to them of the power of the faith community gathered. After saying good-bye, each child received a blessing as they departed this special space.

Parents told us that on Sundays their child wanted to come down to "God's class" rather than attend the regular preschool Sunday school class. One mom was sick on a Wednesday. When her son realized what day it was and that he was going to miss his special class, he became so upset that she got out of her sickbed and brought him. It became obvious to us that this form of a Contemplative-Reflective Model was meeting some deep needs of these young children.

As I write this, I am doing follow-up work on this ten-week research project. I am interviewing as many of the participating children as still attend that church. Though the interviews are not yet completed, I am finding that some of the children remember remarkable details about the experience a full two years later, which is one-third of their lifetime. Some can describe the stories and the insights they received. Not surprisingly, others remember little except that they got to paint or that there were candles. The responses of the children through their actions and attitudes have shown me that the Contemplative-Reflective Model brings noteworthy responses from children when they as well as the environment have been carefully prepared for such an experience.

Older Children and the Contemplative-Reflective Experience

Although I have less experience with upper elementary children, they, too, seem to respond reverently to appropriately created contemplative experiences. I have observed the third level of *Catechesis of the Good Shepherd,* intended for nine to twelve year olds. The curriculum calls for the children to work with the time line of God's story, to grasp the significance of the various genres of Scripture, and to work with the Hebrew alphabet. At the same time, while in a contemplative context, they are also involved in leading some of the liturgies and rituals of the morning.

In a contrasting environment, every Sunday morning for thirty minutes, I meet ten to twelve fifth-grade girls under a dimly lit stairwell using camping lanterns in order to see to read. In this special "private" space, we speak quietly because of the smallness and intimacy of the space. We discuss and apply the Bible story we have just seen presented through drama, about God and his character. We share struggles and pray for one another, but we have few rituals. We are just simply being together with God. The girls respond eagerly to this time.

I have also found upper elementary boys responding well to a contemplative environment. In the spring of 2005, a special space was created for all the church's fifth graders to give them an overview of redemptive history. Because the structure of the time was to be different from that to which they were accustomed, the leader met with the fifth-graders in the hallway to prepare them to enter the space. Using a somewhat hushed tone, she asked everyone to remove their shoes before entering the room. She hoped they would sense God's presence, and taking off one's shoes in a public space feels humbling. She explained what they would experience and then led the group in prayer. She wisely divided them into smaller groups of six or eight, each with an adult leader, and had them enter in a staggered fashion, several minutes apart. (Since the group was large, it would take only one or two children to disrupt the mood, making a sense of awe and wonder difficult to attain.) These young preteens were initially uncomfortable by what was happening, so they entered the room rather giggly and whispering loudly.

The leader had carefully prepared several stations for the children to visit in sequence. It began with watching a DVD of the wonders of God's creation. Then there was a man portraying Abraham who brought to life for the children the covenant that God made with Abraham. That station was followed by one that was an artistic depiction of the new covenant, one that required solemn observation and reflection. Next came two people giving testimony to the power of the Holy Spirit to work in people's lives—one person portrayed a contemporary of Paul; the other was a modern-day teen telling her story. The next station displayed collages of sin as it can be seen in today's world. There was a lighted candle in the center of this display representing Jesus, the light of the world. The collages captured the children's attention. The last station was eschatological and called for the children to respond artistically to a reading of Revelation 5.

Though the room was glaringly lit by fluorescent lights and most of the stations were self-guided, the fifth-graders became more and more enthralled as the experience unfolded. They asked deeply reflective questions and became focused and reverent. It was remarkable to me that six weeks later, as a group, the children could recall what happened at the stations, and they remembered the meaning of each station.

The Contemplative-Reflective Model for a Single Sunday School Class

It is possible for a Sunday school teacher or a small church to introduce contemplative elements for children without establishing a complete atrium or an environment such as Stewart and Berryman suggest. A reflective environment can be enhanced by implementing just a few of the characteristics of a Contemplative-Reflective Model listed earlier. It might be through a reverent ritual to welcome and bless the children or to dismiss them. It could be as simple as removing shoes before entering the room. Or it might be through a symbol such as a Christ candle or piece of art that, with guidance, could help the children reflect. Any of these practices must include an age-appropriate explanation so they are not empty rituals, devoid of meaning.

The use of "wonder" statements would be the easiest to implement. Rather than using typical questions suggested in published curriculum, the teacher can guide the children to enter the story by helping them "wonder" about key aspects of the story, especially in the ways the story centers on God or the Lord Jesus. "I wonder how . . ." or "I wonder if . . ." or "I wonder what might be the reason . . ." Of course, the more characteristics of the Contemplative-Reflective Model that can be introduced, the greater the effectiveness may be.

Biblically, theoretically, and experientially, I have seen the Contemplative-Reflective Model bring responses from children that no other form of children's ministry has in my forty years of working with children and youth. A key factor for this difference, I believe, is the nature of the environment. It does not try to emulate a school, nor does it employ fast-paced, staged productions. I don't think that the change is within the children but in our assumptions about children. It is certainly not the only model that should be used, but I am convinced that it needs to be a key part in the spiritual formation of the children in our children's ministries.

My work with Contemplative-Reflective Models in recent years has brought some surprising outcomes. Before we began the research project with preschoolers, we were told by the church staff that two or three of the children should not be expected to do well in this type of environment because they exhibited short attention spans, disruptive behavior, and hyperactivity. That was true for the first session each child attended, but their behavior changed within a session or two. It was as if they needed an environment that provided less stimulation than usual, one that enabled them to slow down internally. This observation supports Damasio's hypotheses that relational and emotional responses should not be hurried so that these responses can be connected to cognitive processing.

One summer recently we were invited to minister to at-risk children through a local Christian outreach center. We prepared a Contemplative-Reflective Model using the nine weeks of sessions about the good shepherd. When we explained our plans to the staff, we were told that at-risk children did not do well when things were quiet or silent because their minds would fill with difficult or scary thoughts. Since this type of approach had not been used in this context, we asked permission to try it for the summer. Permission was granted, and the results were what we hoped for. At the end of the nine weeks, we asked some of the older children what they thought. One girl said, "When it is quiet, I feel God better." After the session that emphasized that the Good Shepherd knows the names of the sheep, we asked the children to respond by writing their names beautifully on small stones. Many of the children carried those stones in their pockets all summer.

The Contemplative-Reflective Model seems effective in a wide variety of settings when the leaders and the environment are carefully prepared. Experiences that encourage internal dialogue, connatural learning, or emotional connectedness seem critical for the spiritual formation of children given the research presented. These findings have significant implications for curriculum development. Children need settings where narratives are shared, as well as settings for personal reflection.

The Contemplative-Reflective Model is not intended to reach out to masses of nonchurched children. While experiencing this approach, young children, though usually wordless, "speak loudly through their attitudes and bodies."[70] Older children become more reflective as they contemplate symbols or enter into the story. The model is intended to help children fall more and more in love with the Lord Jesus Christ—to develop disciples who want to obey and follow him the rest of their lives.

We need to approach Scripture with the child in mind. As we assess the ministries of the church, we must remember the child. Give the essentials in word and materials; then step aside letting the Holy Spirit bring the child to the Lord Jesus to live together in relationship. What if we formed ministries with God's view of the child in mind? What if we considered the child among us as Jesus did in Matthew 18? What would it look like if we enabled children in our churches from their earliest years to encounter God in ways that become the very fabric of their lives? What if, as they reach early adolescence, they have become eager learners about the God who made them because they have experienced him? What if . . . ?

Responses to the Contemplative-Reflective Model

Response by Gregory C. Carlson and John K. Crupper

Before moving to some specific areas of agreement and difference, we'll give attention to some general observations. First, the fact that there are different approaches to the spiritual formation of children ought not to be surprising. Throughout the history of Christianity, there have been multiple approaches to spirituality. In his excellent overview, *Streams of Living Water*,[71] Richard Foster outlines six different spiritual traditions that are present within the Christian faith. They are the contemplative

---

70. Cavalletti, *Discovering the Real Spiritual Life of Children.*
71. Richard Foster, *Streams of Living Water: Celebrating the Great Traditions of Christian Faith* (San Francisco: Harper San Francisco, 1998).

tradition, the holiness tradition, the charismatic tradition, the social justice tradition, the evangelical tradition, and the incarnational tradition. Each of these has played an important part in the larger history of the Christian church. Each has its advocates and its well-known historical figures. Each of these traditions has made significant contributions to Christian spirituality, and each has weaknesses when isolated from other traditions.

In light of the historical reality of these six streams, the contemplative-reflective approach advocated by Dr. May stands within the larger tradition of what Foster identifies as the contemplative stream of Christian spirituality. In this sense, what this model is advocating is grounded in a long tradition within the church. This is something that cannot necessarily be said for some other models. Second, the essence of Christian spirituality is not something that can be isolated within one model only. The Instructional-Analytic Model is going to stand firmly within the evangelical stream highlighted by Foster; the Contemplative-Reflective Model is based in Catholic, Episcopal, and Lutheran faith traditions. Each of these models can learn from the other, but any attempt to isolate the locus of Christian spirituality solely within one stream is probably nothing more than *hubris* in operation.

While we believe that the Contemplative-Reflective Model highlights some significant needs in children's spiritual formation, we should see it as an addition to the base provided for us in the Scriptures. Our concern is that we keep children's spiritual formation as a Christian endeavor, focusing more upon those aspects that are uniquely oriented toward Christ. We look to the Scriptures as our standard for life and practice, not experience. Experience is shaped by the Bible.

In some sense we are faced with the typical "which came first—the chicken or the egg" quandary. Issues of theological emphasis may lead to varying approaches of spirituality, which in turn may lead to clustering with like-minded people. These may subsequently lead to larger groupings around commonly held perspectives.[72] The same could be said for the reciprocal

---

72. Historically, I have in mind denominations. This is still a reality, though we find ourselves in an increasingly postdenominational setting.

approach. That is, varying approaches to spirituality may lead to varying issues of theological preference. The point being that on any given Sunday morning there will be "high church" Episcopalians gathering for the liturgy and Eucharist, while just down the street the "low church" Baptists will gather for gospel music and the Lord's Supper. No doubt these two worship experiences will be different. One can also be certain of two other facts: both congregations are sincere in their commitment to enter into relationship with the Holy God, as well as the fact that their approach to nurturing children in the faith is also going to be quite different.

We share agreement with the Contemplative-Reflective Model in a number of areas. First, those of us who come at children's spiritual formation from an Instructional-Analytic Model also see the Scripture teaching that children are able to speak (use language), think, and reason (1 Cor. 13:11). In this sense we have much to learn from the Contemplative-Reflective Model. Many of our children's programs are far from reverential, and the constant barrage of impulses does not seem to help in developing this interior life.

Second, we do see human beings as spiritual beings. Spirituality is not simply a component part of human experience. God did not breathe the breath of life into Adam and say, "Well, now, there's a spiritual part." No, the Bible states that "man became a living being" (Gen. 2:7).

Third, the Instructional-Analytic Model also wants children to learn connaturally as well as speculatively. We want children to enter into a life-changing experience with God through the Lord Jesus Christ. We want them to learn about God. Any division between subjective and objective knowing is artificial at best. A rote learning of content is not in view. It is the words of God lived out in life. If I'm going in for brain surgery, I want my neurosurgeon to have both experience and factual knowledge.

Fourth, we agree that the spiritual nurture of children should be intentional and thoughtful. The Contemplative-Reflective Model clearly comes at its practical implementation through thought and careful reflection. So too does the Instructional-

Analytic Model. There may be instances in both models where some children simply copy outward activity without wrestling with the deeper philosophical base and methodology. Such an approach does not accurately represent either model. In Michael Anthony's taxonomy, both the Contemplative-Reflective Model and the Instructional-Analytic Model are aligned on the same axis with regard to how we learn about God. Both models agree that this is facilitated through reflective observation.

Fifth, we would see many of the techniques of teaching as valuable tools for learning. Our learning is focused on understanding the Word of God more than on delving into the fickle nature of humans; but the ideas of repetition and routine, telling the story (although I would prefer to be guided by Walsh's, James's, or the Haystead's understanding of the story over Cavalletti's or Buber's),[73] an emphasis on healthy families, and engaging in service are important; and we affirm them.

While we might agree with the Contemplative-Reflective Model in a number of areas, that is certainly not to say that we agree with it completely. There are several areas where we beg to differ. One such area of difference is the emphasis that is placed on meditation. Meditation is said to be the basis for the contemplative model. However, the Scriptures refer to meditation upon the Scriptures as the base, not the inner nature of a child. The Instructional-Analytic Model grounds itself on the Bible's repeated emphasis on instructional elements. Furthermore, while the chapter does make reference to biblical material, most of these references are to Jesus' *relationship* with children and to specific children mentioned in the Bible. Second Timothy 3:15 is quoted concerning Timothy's knowing the Holy Scripture from infancy. How did Timothy come to acquire this knowledge? We would contend it was through instruction and the example of his mother and grandmother (2 Tim. 1:5). Paul immediately follows the 2 Timothy 3:15 passage with four specific instructional applications of the Scripture: teaching, rebuking, correcting,

---

73. John Walsh, Christian Storytelling Network president; Steven James, *The Creative Storytelling Guide for Children's Ministry* (Cincinnati: Standard Publishing, 2003); Wes and Sheryl Haystead, *Bible Skills for Better Teaching: Helping Kids Make the Connection* (Ventura, Calif.: Gospel Light, 1999).

and training. A thorough word study of teaching and knowledge along with their related forms in the Old and New Testaments will give a solid foundation for the importance of knowing. Scripture is the basis of the child's spiritual development, not his or her nature.

Looking again at the taxonomy in the introduction of this book, it is evident that there is a clear area of difference between the Instructional-Analytic Model and the Contemplative-Reflective Model. While both models line up together on the "learning about God" axis, they are at opposite ends of the axis that focuses on how we experience God. The Contemplative-Reflective Model, with its preference for connatural, subjective knowing views feeling as the primary means for experiencing God. The Instructional-Analytic Model, on the other hand, views this happening primarily through cognitive reasoning or thinking. It's probably good not to push the taxonomy beyond what it's intended to do. The Instructional-Analytic Model would agree that subjective knowing is important, and this chapter acknowledges the importance of objective knowing as well. The root issue is where one begins. The Instructional-Analytic Model would say that the starting place is the revelation about God in his Word— his nature, his character, his activity. This objective knowing sets in place the conditions for moving to subjective knowing. Young Samuel indeed experienced God (1 Sam. 3) but only after he was instructed by an adult.

There is a fundamental theological watershed in the two positions. Genesis 1:26–27 tells us that God created human beings in his image. Genesis 3, along with Romans 3, tells us of the disastrous and far-reaching effects of the fall.[74] While the *imago Dei* is not obliterated in the fall, there is certainly sufficient scriptural evidence to indicate that humanity's propensity is to turn away from God, not toward him. We would disagree with the quote from Benedict Groeschel concerning the idea that the individual becomes aware of possessing a "spark of the Divine" via some increasing awareness of an internal spiritual craving. This concept is certainly not supported in biblical revelation. One would have

---

74. And, obviously, many other passages could be cited as well.

a hard time squaring it with Romans 3:11, which clearly states "there is no one who understands, no one who seeks God." The heart has dispositions that do not lead us to God but rather away from him. Jeremiah 17:9 affirms this: "The heart is more deceitful than all else and is desperately sick; Who can understand it?" (NASB) When does a child develop a deceitful heart? It is present in a child's nature.

The Bible is also clear in its call for a radical change in the human heart through conversion and new birth. According to Paul, only then can one truly understand spiritual things (1 Cor. 2:14-ff). Jesus said to Nicodemus, as he sought to understand what Jesus was telling him, "You must be born from above" (see John 3:3 NRSV). In response to the practitioners offered as examples in the Contemplative-Reflective Model, we would have to judge the sentiment as well intended but lacking biblical support and precedent.

Above, we affirmed the aspects of 1 Corinthians 13:11 (speaking, thinking, and reasoning) in a child's spiritual development. However, we must emphasize here that Paul said when he became a man, he "put away childish things" (1 Cor. 13:11 KJV). Jesus gave us a picture of the child as an illustration of humility and dependency, childlike but not childish.

Another troubling area is the notion that "the Contemplative-Reflective Model is not intended to reach out to masses of nonchurched children." One must ask, what then is to become of the "masses of nonchurched children"? The Instructional-Analytic Model clearly sees the conversion of the human heart which takes place when persons place their faith in Jesus Christ (*sola fide*) as the first step in the Christian life. Preliminary nurturing of the spiritual soil is clearly important, but what would one say to a farmer who only tilled the soil but never got around to planting any seeds and reaping a harvest? Given this framework, the Contemplative-Reflective Model becomes, at best, an important tool in helping provide a balanced development of the Christian spiritual life. By the chapter's own admission, it cannot serve as a strategy for evangelism. Any model which is effective only with small groups of churched children fails as a strategy for fulfilling the final commands of our Savior (Matt. 28:18–20; Mark 16:15; Luke 24:47; Acts 1:8).

In closing, we appreciate the Contemplative-Reflective Model's commitment to the development of the child's spiritual life. We are not in disagreement about the necessity of this. Nor would we disagree with the validity of the model to build upon the foundation that is laid by knowing Scripture. Further, we would acknowledge that the commitments that drive this model provide a necessary balance within the larger scheme of things. Our ultimate disagreement comes in what we see as a failure to enter into serious engagement with the Scripture as the primary means by which we go about guiding children in their knowledge of God (both connaturally and speculatively) through his Son, the Lord Jesus Christ.

Response by Trisha Graves

I found the chapter on the Contemplative-Reflective Model interesting and enlightening. As the author Dr. Mays states, this model of ministry is "unfamiliar to many" and seems to be practiced less in the region where I minister. Personally, this particular model was the least familiar to me, so it was fascinating to become acquainted with the theological and philosophical concepts of the Contemplative-Reflective Model and how they're implemented. While the Contemplative-Reflective Model of spiritual formation has been thoroughly explained in other noted books, Dr. May gives an understandable and practical explanation of this model and how it may be used within the realm of children's ministry. Being historically linked with the Montessori movement, the Contemplative-Reflective Model of spiritual formation has a great deal of historical and empirical research to support its methods and claims of effectiveness.

Dr. May gives some wonderful examples of situations where the Contemplative-Reflective model provides insights and spiritual encounters between children and God. She also provides some excellent arguments as to why some of the concepts within this model should be carefully examined and quite possibly included within the children's ministry context. While the values of helping children to encounter God and contemplate who he is in their lives are both worthwhile outcomes, one has to wonder if it's possible for a child's entire sense of spirituality to be built on these principles alone.

Let's start by reviewing one of the definitions from the introduction of this book: "In its Christian sense, 'spirituality' is about the process of renewal and rebirth that comes about through the action of the Holy Spirit, which makes us more like Christ. It's about spiritual growth and development and includes the development of just about every aspect of our life of Christian faith."[75]

First, one must have renewal and rebirth through the Holy Spirit. While Dr. May shows that this model allows the Holy Spirit to guide the child into a relationship with the Lord Jesus, it appears that the renewal and rebirth that Dr. May speaks of involves more of a child's ongoing faith process of discovery versus a personal decision of faith and ongoing spiritual growth.

According to the previous quote, the formation of spirituality in children should also encompass every aspect of a child's Christian faith and thereby transform that child more and more into the image of Christ. While I don't question this model's ability to have a profound impact on a child's spiritual development, I'm not convinced that the Contemplative-Reflective Model is able to be used as the sole method for the ongoing spiritual formation of children. Nor do I believe that it's versatile enough to be used in a variety of settings. As much as Dr. May broadened my perspective of the contemplative-reflective approach through this chapter, the model seems limited in its ability to lead children to a saving knowledge of Jesus Christ, offer ongoing experiences that influence their spiritual transformation, and then develop them into young disciples of Christ.

Before I critique some of the other concepts, let me first highlight what I perceive to be strengths of the Contemplative-Reflective Model. This particular model emphasizes a child's inherent desire to be a spiritual being and is predicated on the conviction that children have an innate ability to learn. Dr. May gives many

---

75. Alister McGrath, "Beyond the Quiet Time," in Barry Callen, ed., *Authentic Spirituality: Moving Beyond Mere Religion* (Grand Rapids, Mich.: Baker Books, 2001), 218.

excellent examples of people in the Bible that "all had encounters with the Holy as very young children or as yet unborn children," and she also aptly describes the value that Jesus himself placed on children. I firmly believe that if churches and parents today held this same value of young children that the Bible holds, we would see a new emphasis and more priority placed on children's spiritual formation. However, many churches, senior church leaders, and even parents today deny the ability of children to have meaningful and life-changing encounters with God. The precedent that those within the Contemplative-Reflective Model place on "helping children encounter God in ways that result in a sense of awe and wonder—to help them consider things of God with continued attention" is in my opinion one of the outcomes to be desired for all models of children's spiritual formation. How the Contemplative-Reflective Model and the Pragmatic-Participatory Model, which I represent, interpret such "encounters" with God and children "giving continued attention" may differ, yet the goal of helping children to experience God as real and awesome are desirable outcomes of both models.

The purpose of the Contemplative-Reflective Model overall is a positive one in that it seeks to "assist children [to] find the quiet place within themselves to sense the presence of God and hear his voice." Like adults many children long for a deep relationship with the Lord. I would agree with Dr. May that children often desire a relationship with God, one that may be characterized as sensing his presence through the Holy Spirit and hearing his voice speaking to them personally. As a child from an unchurched home myself, I remember looking for things of spiritual significance and desired to be in God's presence, so I often asked to go to church on holidays or attend with friends or relatives. Also, as Dr. May describes in the section on "Children in Scripture," I agree that the Bible is relevant to children and that God does desire to speak to us and lead us through his Holy Spirit (Hab. 2:2; Ps. 46:10; John 10:27). Where we may differ in opinion would be how the relevancy is communicated to children, and a different perspective might believe that God is able to speak in settings other than a contemplative environment.

Those that operate within the Contemplative-Reflective Model also hold a high regard for the child being a significant part of the faith community. Within the faith community of those that practice the Contemplative-Reflective Model it is believed that children more "readily realize the power and vitality of the spiritual." Agreeing with Dr. May, it is my experience that when children are held in high regard and when they are treated as a valuable part of the faith community, they are more able to partake in all that the church offers and are able to experience firsthand the power of God through his people. The body of Christ is how God carries out his plan on earth to reveal his love for humankind (1 Cor. 12:12–27), and it is a powerful concept for a child to witness as well as experience firsthand.

It also would be agreed that the "charity and the security of a reasonably healthy family," as Dr. May points out, is also vital in helping children to witness God and see a godly life lived out. "The Christian spirituality of children is nurtured through openness to the Holy Spirit as mediated by life within the faith community." However, from my perspective, as strong and important as the family (Deut. 1:31; 6:4–9; 11:18–21; 21:18–19) and faith community might be in the spiritual development process, the faith community does not replace a child's need to make a personal decision to accept Christ as Lord and Savior (John 3:16; Rom. 14:12). The faith community can help to nurture, model, witness, and provide opportunities for a child to learn and serve; but it cannot take the place of a child's need to experience personal conversion and personal belief in God (Rom. 10:9–10; Acts 16:30–31). If one's conversion was solely dependent on the faith community and the corporate practices within such a community, it would negate the ability for a child of an unchurched family to accept Christ and have a significant walk with Christ out of the context of the faith community.

Another important principle of the Contemplative-Reflective Model is worship. We both would agree that worship is a powerful time to allow children to respond to God and what the Holy Spirit may be doing in the child's heart or mind. The description of how children might respond to God based on 1 Chronicles 16 describes many different actions that children can take to worship authentically. Those that practice the Pragmatic-Participatory Model or the Media-Driven Active-Engagement Model would argue that the "doing" or active participation in worship helps children to respond to God. On the other side of the spectrum, Dr. May describes that the Contemplative-Reflective Model provides worship and liturgy as a quieter time to reflect as well as provide times for children to feel a sense of "belonging, feeling welcome, secure, having quietness, understanding, meaning, and connecting with God." While I personally do believe that worship with children can and should involve quiet reflection, it seems to me that the Old Testament demonstrates a variety of expressions for worshipping God. Some involve dance, singing, and corporate praise in addition to more reflective expression.

It is also interesting to note the role that the environment plays in the context of the Contemplative-Reflective Model. While those that practice a Pragmatic-Participatory Model would agree that the characteristics of the environment are important in helping to create a welcome and secure place to meet God, the environments of a children's ministry that practices a Pragmatic-Participatory Model versus a Contemplative-Reflective Model differ greatly. As I examine both types of environment, it seems that there may be a time for both within the context of a children's ministry setting. While all children may desire many of those senses listed above, must they all be achieved through the quiet, reflective worship setting? Or might different personality styles or learning styles be able to sense those same feelings of belonging, security, and welcome through structured group activities, relationships with other children, familiar upbeat worship songs, and consistent volunteers?

Dr. May provides some practical characteristics that should be noticeable within the Contemplative-Reflective Model and the environment in which the model is implemented. The listed characteristics of a contemplative-reflective environment seem to offer straightforward and practical ways to help implement a Contemplative-Reflective Model of children's spiritual formation. Yet it seems that many of these characteristics of joy, dignity, awe, and wonder in a child might be subjective in nature and not necessarily achieved only by practicing the Contemplative-Reflective Model. How can joy be measured by deep, peaceful serenity in a child's posture? Are children really able to show "dignity" through their wonder, amazement, freedom, and independence? How can a teacher know if the awe and wonder is really "flowing from awareness of the presence of God through visual symbol"? The given characteristics and their definitions are positive outcomes, yet it seems that given the different personality, cognitive abilities, and learning styles of children the outcomes may look different depending on the child.

The innate differences in children is one of the main reasons that I have difficulty in seeing this model as being highly effective in a variety of settings. While it may work in a smaller church setting with highly skilled and trained leaders, how does the Contemplative-Reflective Model work in a large church setting where there are more than one hundred children in one grade level alone? When there are large numbers of children, is this model able to adequately reach the various personalities and learning styles. Also, addressing the volunteer factor, it seems that it might be difficult to find adult leaders that would be trained and knowledgeable enough to facilitate such experiences. I can see how within the Montessori school environment a practitioner of such a model would be successful in guiding students and relating experiences back to a child's spiritual development. If you are from a large church, how do you train volunteers so as not to interfere with the contemplative approach? Plus, how is such a model implemented among a group of children, some of whom may only attend church for a little over an hour on a sporadic basis?

I enjoyed the examples that Dr. May gave of boys responding reverently to the Bible story they just heard and the at-risk child who was able to feel God better when it was quiet. While I agree that those examples are real and meaningful encounters with God, I question if it is possible for all children in such a setting to have such meaningful encounters if their personality or learning styles aren't attributes of a more reflective-contemplative style.

While I can see the value in "connatural knowing" and would equate this with the value of "biblical relevance" within the Pragmatic-Participatory Model, it seems that a great deal of emphasis is placed on the connatural knowledge regardless of the age or spiritual development of a child. I can see the connatural knowing being used in the infant and early toddler years (and even maybe preschool ages) to lay a foundation or groundwork for further spiritual growth and knowledge. Yet it seems that at some point in a child's cognitive or spiritual growth the speculative knowledge and a more directed approach of learning Bible knowledge might help children process and organize their thoughts and beliefs within the context of their own spirituality. I hold to the belief that the cognitive-development levels of children indicate that children are more literal in their thought processes and are limited in their attention span as well as perspective.[76]

Because of a child's developing cognitive abilities, it is important for an adult or leader to help guide the learning as well as help a child learn to apply God's Word to different circumstances they might encounter in their own lives. I agree with Dr. May that the teacher must model experiencing God's Word intimately. Yet I view the role of the teacher as imperative in not only helping a child by explaining biblical concepts beyond a child's understanding but also providing guidance and challenging children to see the relevance of God's Word and helping them see how they might apply it to their daily lives. Giving children the opportunity to discover, experience, and wonder about God's Word may help to articulate feelings and attitudes about God; however, without the guidance or framework that a teacher would be able to provide the systematic truth of Scripture is not clearly communicated. If children are able to create their own meanings of Scripture, how does one maintain the accuracy and content of the truth of the Bible.[77] These areas cause me to question this model's ability to provide ongoing spiritual transformation and/or disciple making of believing children. Many models

---

76. James Pluddemann, *Nurture That Is Christian,* ed. James C. Wilhoit and John M. Dettoni (Grand Rapids, Mich.: Baker, 1995), 51, 55.

77. Perry Downs, "An Introduction to Christian Education," *Teaching for Spiritual Growth* (Grand Rapids, Mich.: Zondervan, 1994), 163.

provide some type of desired outcomes and learning scope and sequence for what a child is to know and be exposed to before a child graduates from a children's ministry. It would be helpful to know the objectives and desired outcomes within the Contemplative-Reflective Model and how those are measured.

It also would be interesting to note if the level of spiritual experiences of children varies among different regions of the country. Recently our church had a guest Bible story teacher come to present a special Bible lesson to our elementary children. He has presented dramas and Bible lessons in various parts of the country as well as internationally. After teaching the group, he remarked how much more difficult it was to gain the respect and capture the attention of this group of children than when he had presented in other areas of the country. While that might be even more reason to teach the children about respect and reverence in church, it also points out the major differences of children within the cultures. This guest teacher had to change the lesson that worked so well in other regions of the country and use other teaching methods during his subsequent presentation times in order to capture the attention of the children. Children in different regions respond differently, and what might be effective in teaching a fourth grader in the Midwest may look different to a fourth grader in Southern California. Dr. May admits that this model is "not intended to reach out to masses of nonchurched children," yet other limitations of this model may need to be explored more fully.

There are several references to children "learning the language of faith" in this chapter. The Contemplative-Reflective Model is described as "children coming to know and experience God's redemptive story intimately to provide the language for their faith and relationship with God." Since this is to be the "focal point of all that is done," I see several mentions of the value in having a child learn the language of faith or having a desire to meet God. Yet what I don't read in this particular description is when a child is given the wonderful opportunity to make a choice or decision to possess a personal and saving faith in Jesus Christ.

Overall I think the Contemplative-Reflective Model is helpful in that it expands one's thinking regarding the cognitive capacities of children and the need to address children who will have significant encounters with God if given time and specific opportunities, including silent times of reflection and contemplation. Dr. May helps children's ministry leaders realize that contemplative elements can be introduced in different ways and that different church traditions tend to emphasize some characteristics more than others. I could see how some concepts could greatly enhance a child's ability to learn and make the Bible real in their own lives. By including "I wonder" statements during a small-group time following the Bible story, children can be given opportunities to respond in "awe and wonder" to the things they are discovering. Allowing children opportunities to retell the story, or respond emotionally, can help capture a child's heart and mind. Providing certain programmatically organized plans and repetitive phrases can help create security and a sense of belonging. Using active learning within a smaller group setting can help children better understand the biblical concepts being taught. Definite characteristics of this model can help influence a child's spiritual formation. My opinion, however, is that these contemplative concepts must be integrated with cognitive development theory as well as learning styles of children in order for the model to be most effective in allowing the Holy Spirit to bring about ongoing spiritual growth and transformation in children.

Response by the KIDMO Team

Author Scottie May presents a compelling case for the Contemplative-Reflective Model. This is a model of ministry for which she has a great deal of experience. The author's formal academic training in Christian education, her reading of contemplative writers, and her own experience in children's ministry have come together in a rich model for children's ministry. This model is built on the work of writers and practitioners such as Montessori, Cavalletti, Berryman, and Stewart. The model presented as a whole is solid. It is pointed out, however, "There is no perfect model of ministry with children, but our gracious God is at work in lives and in ministries in spite of flawed approaches and human shortcomings." This critique, consequently, will affirm much of the core of this model; it will focus on some of the difficulties of execution of the model as well as offer some minor corrections on the author's presentation.

The Contemplative-Reflective Model requires a minimum of three trained adults to prepare the environment and do the ministry. The author notes that these roles are "essential." The environment is prepared ahead of time with various stations for activities and contemplation. A greeter sits at the door and welcomes the children into the room. A "circle person" tells a story and helps the children engage in conversation and activity. An assistant helps to manage the resources, supplies food for a "feast," and helps with control. The story is the essential element of the model, with the children responding to the story either through activity, reflection, and/or prayer. Dr. May has been involved in the execution of this model for many years with a good deal of success. It would be intriguing to have some longitudinal studies of the Contemplative-Reflective Model and of the other models of ministry proposed in this book as well.

On what basis should we assess the Contemplative-Reflective Model? To be honest, though the title scared me, we were sympathetic to most of what we read. The term "Contemplative-Reflective Model" invoked in me an image of children sitting in rows of chairs with possibly a Bible and a notebook in hand, waiting quietly for extended lengths of time for the Holy Spirit to impress something upon them. The model presented, however, offers far more interactive engagement. While contemplation is certainly part of the model that Dr. May offers, the model is much larger than that. It's a richly constructed environment that involves multifaceted educational components. This may be one of the model's greatest strengths, but it also may be one of the model's greatest weaknesses.

Probably the biggest challenge to the model that Dr. May presents is finding people who are qualified and willing to be involved in this type of ministry. According to Dr. May, the practitioners for the Contemplative-Reflective Model must know four qualifications: (1) We must know the child. (2) We must know the story, and that story must be the center of all that is taught. (3) We must know the culture and the context. (4) We each must know our God. We would also hope that all children's workers would have knowledge of God. That's probably assumed. But do they have the rest of these qualifications? This would require biblical literacy, some developmental psychology, and knowledge of contemporary culture. The author herself has a PhD in Christian education. She is clearly more qualified than the average Sunday school teacher. The author's own experience in teaching the Bible to undergraduate students has exposed her to the dearth of biblical knowledge that is coming from many of today's large churches. Thus we argue that it would be difficult for many churches to find people to run a Contemplative-Reflective Model program that possess the requisite qualifications.

Is this type of ministry scalable? A large multistaff church can afford to hire a person trained in the methods proposed, but how many children can this accommodate? Just what is the ideal child-to-staff ratio? The model seems to work well with small intimate groups since the teacher must address each student individually. Larger numbers of children, however, would require more teachers in order to maintain teacher-student contact. These additional teachers could be trained by one master teacher, but how would the logistics work? Would these helper teachers repeat the story? Would these helper teachers be able to engage the children in the same way the master teacher could? Or would the master teacher tell the story and have the helper teachers engage in the dialogue? Would it be possible for the master teacher to tell the story and have it reproduced for the helper teachers, possibly on videotape or DVD? If so, how is this model significantly different from the Media-Driven Active-Engagement Model presented in chapter 4? Both involve a story with an opportunity to reflect on the story.

Smaller churches simply don't have the resources to hire trained teachers. They must rely on volunteers. Thus in both large and small churches capable volunteer teachers must be found. This is probably the biggest drawback to the proposed Contemplative-Reflective Model.

Two issues require more substantive comment: the author's use of brain research and her discussion of children and spirituality. The author cites a 2004 *Discover* article on brain research by Steven Johnson in which he summarizes the recent work of Antonio Damasio on the speed of neural transmissions in the brain. Damasio's argument is complex and will not be repeated here. Essentially, as the brain develops, parts associated with cognition develop a myelin coating, and processing speed is improved. This allows for both faster rational decision making and for more complex types of reasoning. Emotional responses, however, are located in the amygdala, a more primitive part of the brain which controls many of the more basic human functions, including the classic fear/flight response. The neurons in the amygdala do not develop the myelin sheath, and the speed of reaction does not change. Normal decision making requires both reason and emotions. Damasio suggests that as the pace of society increases, there is an increasing risk that the emotional elements of decision making will not be able to keep up with the rational. Damasio concludes: "The risk of emotional neutrality becomes greater and greater as the speed of cognition improves."

I would like to take issue with how Dr. May uses Damasio. She concludes: "The implication is that as we develop, we may rely more and more on cognition, and then we risk losing our emotional and moral connections regarding decisions we make. Electronic technology and media enable children to multitask with greater speed with what appears to be increased efficiency, but if Damasio is correct, that speed comes with the price of short-circuiting emotional connections."

Two things need to be noted about the author's conclusions. First, Damasio is discussing the reasoning process in adults and young adults. The myelin sheath which is necessary for advanced signal processing in the brain is not fully formed until early adulthood. Thus the data are not relevant for children. Children are simply physiologically incapable of advanced reasoning, moral or otherwise. Their brains have not developed sufficiently. Thus May's conclusion simply cannot be made based on the data. No empirical studies suggest that exposure to technology or media have any adverse impact on moral reasoning.

Second, the author connects "emotional" with "moral" in regard to moral decision making. A more rational approach to moral reasoning is not something bad to be avoided. Moral reasoning is typically a combination of both rational and emotional thought as Damasio and all current brain research acknowledge.

The second substantive issue where we disagree with Dr. May regards one of the Contemplative-Reflective Model chapter subsections, "Children and Spirituality." In this section the author notes, "The spiritual nature of the child is one of the prime considerations of this model." As stated, the topic of spirituality is "complex and multifaceted." Several different definitions of spirituality are discussed, from Christian spirituality to a universal spirituality. The professed understanding of spirituality appears to be rather ephemeral or mystical in nature. I would like to propose a more concrete understanding of *spiritual.*

In the writings of Paul, particularly Galatians, activity of the spiritual can be categorized as indicative-imperative. The believer, the person of faith, is one who possesses the spirit (the indicative). As a result, he/she is instructed to walk by the spirit (the imperative). Thus Paul instructs the Galatian Christians, "If we live by the Spirit, let us also be guided by the Spirit" (5:25 NRSV). The activity of the Spirit is expressed in tangible ways. Paul uses agricultural metaphors to describe this activity. Thus one can plant things of the Spirit (6:8) and harvest things of the Spirit (6:8). The agricultural product of the Spirit is, metaphorically speaking, fruit. Paul gives a representative list of this fruit: love, joy, peace, patience, kindness, generosity, faithfulness, gentleness, and self-control (5:22–23). The list is not a complete list of all the fruit but a representative list. Paul, like first-century philosophers, used virtue and vice lists to convey moral teaching. Paul used many of these lists, no two of which are alike. Thus items on the list and things like them describe what a "spiritual" person would look like. A "spiritual" person would show love, be kind, be generous, be patient, etc.

Dr. May suggests that the spirituality of children "is nurtured through openness to the Holy Spirit as mediated by life within the faith community. It is strengthened by corporate uses of Scripture, forms of prayer, hymns, ritual and sacraments, retreats, and the cycles of the liturgical year which includes feasts and celebrations." While the KIDMO team affirms the value of all the above aforementioned, more emphasis needs to be placed on the planting of seed if we really want to emphasize the spiritual. If one asks in most evangelical churches how one becomes more "spiritual," one will usually get the response, "Read the Bible and pray." While we affirm both of these disciplines, we would also suggest, sow to the Spirit. If one wants to reap a certain kind of fruit, one must plant that same kind of fruit seed.

The proposed Contemplative-Reflective Model and the Media-Driven Active-Engagement Model proposed elsewhere in this text have several significant elements in common. One similarity in particular is improved upon within the Media-Driven Active-Engagement Model. The writer states, "A value of the Contemplative-Reflective Model is to be able to enter into the story so that it is real and comes alive for them rather than only knowing about it in an informational way." The Media-Driven Active-Engagement Model recognizes this and helps the children enter into the story and make it real and alive.

In conclusion, the author makes a compelling case for what she calls a Contemplative-Reflective Model. The model has much to commend it. The personnel resources required for a successful execution of the model could make it difficult for many churches to execute successfully. Thus occasional use would be recommended. This model could be especially attractive at certain times of the liturgical year such as Christmas and Easter. A properly executed program could be used more frequently. The contemplative-reflective approach described in this text uses much more activity than the title of the approach would suggest. Children, like adults, have different ways of learning. Probably the best solution is to offer varied approaches to suit the various learning styles. As we have already noted, "There is no perfect model, . . . but our gracious God is at work in lives and ministries in spite of flawed approaches and human shortcoming." Loving teachers, who pour on the "seed," will go a long way toward helping our children grow into disciples of Christ, regardless of the model used.

CHAPTER 2

Instructional-Analytic Model

GREGORY C. CARLSON AND JOHN K. CRUPPER

But as for you, continue in what you have learned and have become
convinced of, because you know those from whom you learned it, and
how from infancy you have known the holy Scriptures, which are
able to make you wise for salvation through faith in Christ Jesus.
2 Timothy 3:14–15

You would expect an introductory Bible verse from the contributor discussing the Instructional-Analytic Model. As we seek to understand a model of children's spiritual formation in Christian context, we must depend on an application of the living Word of God. To create spiritual growth and obedience in children using the teaching and application of the Bible is the thrust of this verse and this chapter.

Definition of Terms

If a meaningful dialogue between people is going to take place, it must be based on terms that both sides agree on. In the event that it might not be possible to agree on the various terms used in this discussion, at least each author should put forward his/her definitions so the participants have a basis for understanding how each concept is being used. With that in mind, I'll advance the definitions of the various critical terms that I'll be using in this chapter.

Instructional-Analytic Model. This is defined as God working through the instruction of his Word and human agency whereby he creates an environment where the young person comes to know Jesus at an appropriate age and then grows in that relationship. This environment features four dimensions: Scripture memory, biblical instruction, a graduated award system, and a systematic structure for training.

Instructional Element. God gave us his Word. It is living, powerful, and the foundation of what an individual needs to know and trust in order to develop a relationship with Christ. The response to the focused instruction of the Word of God is the essential distinctive and starting point for spiritual formation in a child's life, according to this model.

Relational Element. Knowing and living in Christ is the outcome of the instruction cited above. It is not a rote set of ideas that is being proposed by this model. Rather, the real-time relationship that a child would have with the Lord of creation is in view here. Jesus' work on the cross is the basis for drawing a child into that relationship. The regeneration of one's life is based on the foundation of Scripture. Human agency is viewed as a child's parents, ministry leaders, and the body of Christ (local church) which models the Christian faith and shepherds children in the development of their spirituality.

Evangelistic Element. The Instructional-Analytic Model has a primary emphasis on leading a child to Christ. In view of the regenerative work of the Holy Spirit, the washing of the new birth is essential. "He saved us, not because of righteous things we had done, but because of His mercy. He saved us through the washing of rebirth and renewal by the Holy Spirit" (Titus 3:5). The washing of the Scriptures is an essential component of the spiritual formation process. "Just as Christ loved the church and gave himself up for her to make her holy, cleansing her by the washing with water through the word" (Eph. 5:25b–26). This is the most important aspect of spiritual formation.

It is my contention that the salvation of a child is the foundation and guide for a child's spiritual formation. Therefore, children's workers should have this in view as they work with children. "The most significant step in spiritual formation is receiving Jesus Christ as Savior. There is no specific age at which this step is accomplished. Cognitive development, one's view of God's holiness contrasted with the child's recognition of her own sinfulness, the clarity of the presentation of the plan of salvation, and the working of the Holy Spirit all contribute to an intelligent and life-changing acceptance of Christ as Savior."[1]

This is the fundamental issue! We have the capacity to understand the reality that there is a God prior to the new birth experience (Rom. 1:19–20), but anything done previous to this experience should be seen as preparatory (1 Cor. 2:6).

Developmental Element. Some critics of this model say that children are being forced to perceive, think, and act like adults. Appropriate levels, intensity, or capability are acknowledged. Paul said, "When I was a child, I talked like a child, I thought like a child, I reasoned like a child. When I became a man, I put childish ways behind me" (1 Cor. 13:11). We must teach children according to their age level, whether in speech, thinking, or reasoning. As Richards states, "We are not to try to force children into adult modes of learning or into modes that demand cognitive processes beyond their abilities. Instead it is our task to translate the great truths of Christian faith into terms that can be both understood and experienced by boys and girls as they grow up in the Christian community."[2]

It seems practical and necessary to use what the Lord has allowed us to discover in the social science fields of education, psychology, and sociology. But when a conflict arises, we must err toward scriptural understandings. Fowler describes how we

1. Robert Clark, "Spiritual Formation in Children," *The Christian Educator's Handbook on Spiritual Formation,* ed. Kenneth O. Gangel and James C. Wilhoit (Grand Rapids, Mich.: Baker Books, 1994), 242.

2. Lawrence O. Richards, *A Theology of Children's Ministry* (Grand Rapids, Mich.: Zondervan, 1983), 123.

should be seeking to "remodel" our educational endeavors but not to "remodel the foundation": "How do we mold a children's ministry that is centered and balanced? . . . Scripture must be the main focus, and then relevant application will follow."[3]

Scriptural Foundation. In the past evangelicals have held a high view not only of the inspiration of the Bible but also of its authority. We base a child's spiritual formation on the truths revealed in the Bible. The Holy Spirit uses Scripture to set the standard for what the child should be experiencing. The Scripture then becomes the means that the Spirit uses to activate faith. Faith is then guided by the truth of the Word of God. To draw upon any other source for the foundation is to limit the Holy Spirit's work. "I see the Bible as God's declaration of his character and ways, his love letter to the people he sent his Son to redeem, and his blueprint for how to live life with wisdom, purpose, faith, love, and hope."[4] Scripture not only is the content of our ministry with children; it also guides and informs our practice. It also guides and informs our understanding of the teacher-learner process, goals, and evaluation.

Old Testament Teachings on Children's Spiritual Formation

The innocence of Adam and Eve could be compared to the description that many have for the nature of children today. However, even when positive incentives toward a free and open relationship with God existed, people chose wrongly, sin marred character, and salvation became necessary.

Noah's sons then show us an example of undisciplined "natural" development. Genesis 9:21–25 describes a sordid affair of drunkenness and lewd behavior. Left to their own devices, people are enslaved to their fallen nature. Under such circumstances they need discipline to keep them in check. The actions of Shem, Ham, and Japeth revealed how far people fell from knowing God and his will for their lives.

---

3. Larry Fowler, *Rock Solid Kids* (Ventura, Calif.: Gospel Light, 2005), 42–43.
4. Kenneth Boa, *Conformed to His Image: Biblical and Practical Approaches to Spiritual Formation* (Grand Rapids, Mich.: Zondervan, 2001), 68.

Here we see the Lord placing a strong emphasis on family as the means of spiritual blessing. The promise to Abram found in Genesis 12:3 was, "And in you all the families of the earth shall be blessed" (NKJV).

Abraham is commissioned by God to the purposes God intended. Genesis 18:19 states, "For I have chosen him, so that he will direct his children and his household after him to keep the way of the LORD by doing what is right and just, so that the LORD will bring about for Abraham what he has promised him." The word *direct* or *charge* has a forceful impact when you consider that Abraham and Sarah were responsible to direct the activities of their household. This speaks to the purposes of spiritual formation being fairly directive from the adults that are involved.

The story of Hagar and Ishmael found in Genesis 21 reveals a wonderful biblical truth that God hears the petitions of a young child who at the age of thirteen cries out to him. Indeed, he hears the prayers of the young child.

The worship by sacrifice of Abraham and Isaac shows the marvelous mix of spiritual formation in the life of young Isaac. He trusted his father and the Lord to provide a sacrifice.

In Exodus 12–13, the Lord provides direction on the methodology of the parents and other adults in Israel to instruct the younger generation. They were to organize events so that the works of the Lord would be recited. In fact, the children were to be prompted to ask, "What do you mean by this service?" (Exod. 12:26 NKJV). The consecration of the feast of unleavened bread—using experiential methods to prompt memorizing and review of the law—was to be for this purpose: "This observance will be for you like a sign on your hand and a reminder on your forehead that the law of the LORD is to be on your lips. For the LORD brought you out of Egypt with his mighty hand" (Exod. 13:9). Notice that the law was to be on their lips! This implies that the words of Scripture should be memorized and reviewed creatively. The giving of the Ten Commandments seemed to be for the purpose of remembering the "words the Lord had commanded" (Exod. 19:6–7).

The same trend can be noticed in the commands found in Deuteronomy. The national mandate was to be a people who were taught the "statutes and judgments" (Deut. 4:5 NKJV) of the Lord "that you may fear the LORD your God, to keep all His statutes and His commandments which I command you, you and your son and your grandson, all the days of your life, and that your days may be prolonged" (Deut. 6:2 NKJV). The great *shema* passage further clarifies, "And these words, which I command thee this day, shall be in thine heart: And thou shalt teach them diligently unto thy children" (Deut. 6:6–7 KJV). The passage continues with lifestyle-oriented teaching, but it begins by having the *words* in their heart and then *teaching diligently!*

David also gives us an important window of understanding regarding infants and what happens to them should they pass away. David's first child with Bathsheba passed away in spite of significant prayer on David's part. The servants were concerned that the king would do himself harm upon hearing of the child's death. However, they were surprised by David's behavior and asked him about it. David's response: "While the child was alive, I fasted and wept; for I said, 'Who can tell whether the LORD will be gracious to me, that the child may live?' But now he is dead; why should I fast? Can I bring him back again? I shall go to him, but he shall not return to me" (2 Sam. 12:22–23 NKJV). David expected to see his son in heaven! This verse has been a comfort to many parents in bereavement.

Josiah, who became king at age eight, was trained to be tender toward the words of "the Book" so that when they were found in his eighteenth year, he responded with appropriate zeal, repentance, and obedience (2 Kings 22).

Jehoshaphat commissioned the teaching of the Scriptures throughout the land during his reign as king. "They taught in Judah, and had the Book of the Law of the LORD with them; they went throughout all the cities of Judah and taught the people" (2 Chron. 17:9 NKJV).

Jehoiachin was young and before the Lord was found to be evil. "Jehoiachin was eight [some translations say eighteen] years old when he became king, and he reigned three months and ten days in Jerusalem, and he did evil in the sight of the LORD" (2 Chron. 36:9 NASB). Whether eight or eighteen, the child's nature is referenced as being evil. This has significance for the children's worker or parent in relation to spiritual formation. We cannot assume that a child's nature is "innocent" when the Bible indicates that even young children are capable of sin. Therefore, direction and discipline as well as instruction should be blended to foster a positive learning environment.

During Nehemiah's revival there was extensive emphasis on teaching "the Book of the Law of Moses." The practice was to read, then explain to "all who were able to understand" (Neh. 8:2). This is similar to the progression of teaching that is expected from the children of Israel as portrayed in Psalm 78. There in the generational teaching that was to happen, the psalmist bases his instruction on the commands of God.

> For he established a testimony in Jacob, and appointed a law in Israel, which he commanded our fathers, that they should make them known to their children: That the generation to come might know *them, even* the children *which* should be born; *who* should arise and declare *them* to their children: That they might set their hope in God, and not forget the works of God, but keep his commandments (Ps. 78:5–7 KJV).

Job's children, perhaps most of them grown, were a concern in regard to having an inclination toward sin. "When a period of feasting had run its course, Job would send and have them purified. Early in the morning he would sacrifice a burnt offering for each of them, thinking, 'Perhaps my children have sinned and cursed God in their hearts.' This was Job's regular custom" (Job 1:5).

David seemed to think that children should have on their lips the praise of the Lord: "From the lips of children and infants you have ordained praise" (Ps. 8:2). In Psalm 25:7 David speaks of the responsibility of even a young man to know and apply a relationship based on truth: "Remember not the sins of my youth and my rebellious ways; according to your love remember me, for you are good, O LORD." David proclaimed that he had been taught since his youth, "Then our sons in their youth will be like well-nurtured plants, and our daughters will be like pillars carved to adorn a palace" (Ps. 144:12). All of these verses describe a robust and powerful spiritual formation during the days of one's youth. David's psalms also reveal his extremely high regard for Scripture and its place in one's spiritual formation, e.g., Psalm 19 and Psalm 119. "Wherewithal shall a young man cleanse his way? by taking heed thereto according to thy word. With my whole heart have I sought thee: O let me not wander from thy commandments. Thy word have I hid in mine heart, that I might not sin against thee" (Ps. 119:9–11 KJV). This familiar verse describes a young man being kept from sin by treasuring God's Word in the heart.

What can be said of Solomon's influence on our understanding of spiritual formation? The wisdom of Proverbs is especially relevant. Following are selected proverbs that deal with the importance of instruction:

The proverbs of Solomon son of David, king of Israel: for attaining wisdom and discipline; for understanding words of insight (1:1–2).

Listen, my son, to your father's instruction and do not forsake your mother's teaching (1:8).

My son, if you accept my words and store up my commands within you (2:1).

My son, do not forget my teaching, but keep my commands in your heart (3:1).

My son, pay attention to my wisdom, listen well to my words of insight (5:1).

My son, keep your father's command, And do not forsake the law of your mother. Bind them continually upon your heart; Tie them around your neck. When you roam, they will lead you; When you sleep, they will keep you; And *when* you awake, they will speak with you. For the commandment *is* a lamp, And the law a light; Reproofs of instruction *are* the way of life (6:20–23 NKJV).

My son, keep my words, And treasure my commands within you. Keep my commands and live, And my law as the apple of your eye. Bind them on your fingers; Write them on the tablet of your heart (7:1–3 NKJV).

Cease listening to instruction, my son, And you will stray from the words of knowledge (19:27 NKJV).

My son, eat honey because *it is* good, And the honeycomb *which is* sweet to your taste; So *shall* the knowledge of wisdom *be* to your soul; If you have found *it,* there is a prospect, And your hope will not be cut off (24:13–14 NKJV)

The Preacher sought to find acceptable words; and *what was* written *was* upright—words of truth. The words of the wise are like goads, and the words of scholars are like well-driven nails, given by one Shepherd. And further, my son, be admonished by these. Of making many books *there is* no end, and much study *is* wearisome to the flesh. Let us hear the conclusion of the whole matter: Fear God and keep His commandments; For this is man's all (Eccles. 12:10–13 NKJV).

The prophet Isaiah indicates that he and his children are a counterbalancing antidote to the worship of false gods (Isa. 8:18–19). He then concludes with an appeal to test all factors of national life with the words of the Scriptures: "To the law and to the testimony: if they speak not according to this word, *it is* because *there is* no light in them" (Isa. 8:20 KJV).

Hezekiah praises the Lord for the healing he received. Then he goes on to describe the resulting cascading impact that a parent can have: "The living, the living man, he shall praise You, As I *do* this day; The father shall make known Your truth to the children" (Isa. 38:19 NKJV). Notice the father makes known something of substance—the faithfulness of God and the firmness of the truth.

Observe the Lord's interaction regarding the ministry call of Jeremiah the prophet:

> "Before I formed you in the womb I knew you, before you were born I set you apart; I appointed you as a prophet to the nations." "Ah, Sovereign LORD," I said, "I do not know how to speak; I am only a child." But the LORD said to me, "Do not say, 'I am only a child.' You must go to everyone I send you to and say whatever I command you. Do not be afraid of them, for I am with you and will rescue you," declares the LORD (Jer. 1:5–8).

Jeremiah was set apart for service from the womb. This is not a unique occurrence; it happened in the life of Samson (Judg. 13) and in the New Testament in the life of John the Baptist (Luke 1). The prophet also was a young man, but the Lord did not allow the ministry to diminish because of that fact.

Daniel seems to be an example of a young child who had the knowledge of the Lord on his heart. He purposed in his heart not to sin. I think it is instructive to note that even at this young age Daniel and his friends could choose to serve the Lord in the face of overwhelming obstacles. Someone taught them the knowledge of God (Dan. 1:4) so that when it came to a decision of heart and mind, Daniel was ready.

Hosea shares the word of the Lord with his children in the midst of a difficult family circumstance (Hos. 2). The children were involved; there was expectation that they would have at least some understanding in the middle of their pain and that they were still valuable to God.

The last command of the Old Testament is focused on the instruction of the words of Scripture. "Remember the law of my servant Moses, the decrees and laws I gave him at Horeb for all Israel. See, I will send you the prophet Elijah before that great and dreadful day of the LORD comes. He will turn the hearts of the fathers to their children, and the hearts of the children to their fathers; or else I will come and strike the land with a curse" (Mal. 4:4–6 NIV). The fathers and children will have heart obedience when the Spirit of the Lord is heard and heeded.

Here is a list of principles from Old Testament teaching.

1. Children's nature in the Old Testament could be described as bearing the marks of *imago Dei* and yet possess a fallen nature.

2. Adults, and most specifically parents, are responsible to be directive in shaping the spiritual lives of the children they influence.

3. Children are capable of normal spiritual disciplines like prayer, understanding the Scriptures, worship, praise, and service.

4. The role of the teacher is to prompt the next generation to have the law of the Lord on their hearts and lips.

5. Another role of the teacher is to model having the words of the Lord on their own heart, then ensuring that they are taught through a variety of means.

6. The predominant mode of instruction to the child is via the family in the Old Testament.

7. Specific teaching of the Scriptures occurred in every era after it was written. This was often true in the impact of teaching from one generation to another.

8. We cannot assume that a child's nature is "innocent" when the Bible indicates that even young children are capable of sin. Direction and discipline as well as instruction should be blended to foster a positive learning environment.

9. The eternal state of young children seems to be that they go to heaven, should they die. The God of all does justly in saving a child. He does this on the basis of his mercy and the provision of the Son.

The Proverbs give ample evidence that the instruction between parent and child:

- Is strongly based on intentional instruction.

- Comes from the "law," "commands," and/or "words" of the parent, which are the words of the Lord!

- Results in "words" that are on/in the heart. Not to know these commands by heart is to lack the sufficient basis of wisdom.

- Has severe consequences if disregarded. Immorality, a shortened life, and generally an unwise and unsafe lifestyle are perpetuated when one strays from the "words of knowledge."

- Has great profit in finding and keeping the words of wisdom in one's life when based on the commands of God.

- Can become so bookish that the main reason for learning—the fear of the Lord—is missed. Application should always be in view when teaching the Scripture.

10. Children are important in the public honoring of God. Isaiah seems to indicate that they can be signs along with their parents and should adhere to the standard of God's words.

11. Jeremiah's call to ministry speaks of the early training to have children know how to interact with the word from the Lord.

12. Children can be expected to obey the truth of God. Decisions from the heart, well thought out, can be expected from a child. Dare to be a Daniel!

13. God's Spirit must quicken the words of his truth if families and children are to be restored from the heart.

New Testament Teachings on Children's Spiritual Formation

Jesus. When the Lord demonstrated his love for us, he sent his Son. A child was born. He grew in normal ways. As a young child growing up in Sunday school and children's church, I thought that Jesus had an accelerated life. That's how I describe it today. Back then I thought that Jesus was born at Christmas. Then maybe around January of the next year, he showed up with his parents at the temple. Then late in February or early March he started his ministry. Jesus chose his disciples, healed people, and had trouble with the Pharisees in April. Later that same month, he was crucified, buried, and resurrected. High-speed growth for the Son of God was the thought process in my young mind.

Children's spiritual formation may be suffering from a similar malady today. Expectations almost seem like a child should be having a concept of God, an awareness of sin, an appreciation of the cross, and a deep faith within months, if not weeks, of teaching. How significant that the Lord's way to demonstrate the perfect man was to send a baby. No "hurried child," the Lord Jesus was growing in normal childhood fashion according to Luke 2:40: "And the child grew and became strong; he was filled with wisdom, and the grace of God was upon him." This portends a rather normal if not obscure and uneventful growth. Jesus perhaps experienced the normal scrapes and bruises physically (yet no broken bones—Ps. 34:20 and John 19:36). May we also assume that he grew in other ways? "And Jesus grew in wisdom and stature, and in favor with God and men" (Luke 2:52). Yes, Jesus grew socially; he matured at presumably normal rates, or at least there were no perceivable supernatural factors demonstrated that Jesus' neighbors were able to pick up. Note the amazement of those from Jesus' home town:

> Coming to his hometown, he began teaching the people in their synagogue, and they were amazed. "Where did this man get this wisdom and these miraculous powers?" they asked. "Isn't this the carpenter's son? Isn't his mother's name Mary, and aren't his brothers James, Joseph, Simon and Judas? Aren't all his sisters with us? Where then did this man get all these things?" And they took offense at him. But Jesus said to them, "Only in his hometown and in his own house is a prophet without honor." And he did not do many miracles there because of their lack of faith (Matt. 13:54–58).

But the question remains, how should we think about the *spiritual* development of the Son of God? In Hebrews 5:8, Jesus is described as learning obedience. This obedience came through the things which Jesus suffered. Shortly after this amazing statement in this passage, the writer continues with an application for all: "We have much to say about this, but it is hard to explain because you are slow to learn. In fact, though by this time you ought to be teachers, you need someone to teach you the elementary truths of God's word all over again. You need milk, not solid food!" (Heb. 5:11–12). Notice that the elementary truths of God's *Word* were necessary for the expected obedience of these immature adults. Can we expect children to be able to know deep obedience without the teaching of the Word of God? I think not.

Yes, I equate spiritual formation with obedience to God as guided by God's Word. John 17:17 states, "Sanctify them by the truth; your word is truth." Sanctification is spiritual formation in the best sense. This sanctification comes via the word of truth. To think that character development can happen without the guidance of the Scriptures seems to be making secular the spiritual processes that cause a child or anyone to be formed in Christ. What other source can one find which will provide the substance and motivation for spiritual growth? To depend on an innate ability within the child is to deny the fallen nature of people. When Paul writes that "all have sinned and fall short of the glory of God" (Rom. 3:23), there does not seem to be a special exemption for a child. In addition, the consequence of sin is spiritual death (Rom. 6:23).

Jesus' Teaching. Children served as examples of a variety of spiritual formation attitudes in Jesus' teaching. Servant leadership and greatness in the kingdom have a child to emulate.

Children are lauded by our Lord Jesus for their sincere faith. Remember that Romans tells us that "faith comes from hearing the message, and the message is heard through the word of Christ" (Rom. 10:17).

> He called a little child and had him stand among them. And he said: "I tell you the truth, unless you change and become like little children, you will never enter the kingdom

of heaven. Therefore, whoever humbles himself like this child is the greatest in the kingdom of heaven.

And whoever welcomes a little child like this in my name welcomes me. But if anyone causes one of these little ones who believe in me to sin, it would be better for him to have a large millstone hung around his neck and to be drowned in the depths of the sea (Matt. 18:2–6).

Notice that the adult is called to *become* like a little child. Such a perspective is humbling; it is being open, having single-focused faith. Watching a new mom guide her son toward confidence shows how reliable the object of trust is in a young child's life. Viewing a young father's impact on his young daughter even when he is teasing shows how respected children think their parents are. It is an awesome trust, needing the guidance of the Scriptures.

Jesus displayed anger when adults hindered children in their access to spiritual experience. The disciples were not spiritually sensitive to the desires of Jesus and actually were sharply rebuked when they became a spiritual hindrance to them. The touch of the Lord Christ was sought.

People were bringing little children to Jesus to have him touch them, but the disciples rebuked them. When Jesus saw this, he was indignant. He said to them, 'Let the little children come to me, and do not hinder them, for the kingdom of God belongs to such as these. I tell you the truth, anyone who will not receive the kingdom of God like a little child will never enter it.' And he took the children in his arms, put his hands on them and blessed them (Mark 10:13–16).

Mark then continues with a discussion of how to inherit eternal life. Our Lord directed the scribe to the commandments to show how impossible it is to receive eternal life without this childlike faith (Mark 10:19).

The shepherding care of our heavenly Father is contrasted as being even greater than the normal parental concern for a child. "If ye then, being evil, know how to give good gifts unto your children, how much more shall your Father which is in heaven give good things to them that ask him?" (Matt. 7:11 KJV).

The importance of learning the Scriptures is also portrayed in the life of our Savior. In Luke 2:50 the young Jesus was found in the temple asking questions and listening. What a positive example. The methodology of submitting to the instruction of the elders from the Word of God is a model for all children (and adults also).

Paul. The apostle Paul, when standing before King Agrippa, testified of living since he was a child according to the teaching of the Scriptures. These Scriptures were instrumental in leading Paul to the place where the Holy Spirit could convict him of the promise the Lord Jesus can fulfill (Acts 26:4–6).

A key verse to understand the developmental nature of children's spiritual formation is found in 1 Corinthians 13:11: "When I was a child, I talked like a child, I thought like a child, I reasoned like a child. When I became a man, I put childish ways behind me." The ability to think, reason, and speak seems to have at least two stages—childhood and adulthood. These characteristics are initiated in childhood and change over time. Children's workers should nurture this development as they work with young children.

Paul gives us an interesting model of spiritual formation when he says that its beginning is similar to childbirth. "My dear children, for whom I am again in the pains of childbirth until Christ is formed in you" (Gal. 4:19). The word *formed* seems to indicate that a child should be morphed to become more like the Master.

Observe the limitations of teaching the law in Paul's description to the Galatians:

> What I am saying is that as long as the heir is a child, he is no different from a slave, although he owns the whole estate. He is subject to guardians and trustees until the time set by his father. So also, when we were children, we were in slavery under the basic principles of the world. But when the time had fully come, God sent his Son, born of a woman, born under law, to redeem those under law, that we might

receive the full rights of sons. Because you are sons, God sent the Spirit of his Son into our hearts, the Spirit who calls out, "Abba, Father" (Gal. 4:1–6).

The tutoring of the law should lead to a free and open paternal relationship. "Fathers, do not exasperate your children; instead, bring them up in the training and instruction of the Lord" (Eph. 6:4). This is a critical verse for the spiritual formation of children! First, it is the parent's responsibility. So many church ministries for children suffer from a parent "drop-off" mentality. There is also a warning not to exasperate or make your children angry. Too many times adults are insensitive to the nurture and instruction of children. Notice the balance! On the one hand there is training, nurturing, or instruction of a child. On the other, the warning or instructional dimension is emphasized. Training in God's Word must have a relational aspect.

Paul's relationship with Timothy gives us some great insights regarding the place of the Word and spiritual growth. Paul described Timothy as his "child in the faith" (see 1 Cor. 4:17). As interesting as this is, Paul's reminders to Timothy about his spiritual heritage deserve our focus. "When I call to remembrance the unfeigned faith that is in thee, which dwelt first in thy grandmother Lois, and thy mother Eunice; and I am persuaded that in thee also" (2 Tim. 1:5 KJV). Generations were involved in the shaping of Timothy's life. And what was the content of their influence? Clearly it was the Scriptures.

"And that from a child thou hast known the holy scriptures, which are able to make thee wise unto salvation through faith which is in Christ Jesus. All scripture *is* given by inspiration of God, and *is* profitable for doctrine, for reproof, for correction, for instruction in righteousness: That the man of God may be perfect, thoroughly furnished unto all good works" (2 Tim. 3:15–17 KJV).

John. The *Scriptures* are the source of teaching children about salvation. The apostle John describes a spiritual stage model in 1 John 2:12–14:

I write to you, dear children, because your sins have been forgiven on account of his name. I write to you, fathers, because you have known him who is from the beginning. I write to you, young men, because you have overcome the evil one. I write to you, dear children, because you have known the Father. I write to you, fathers, because you have known him who is from the beginning. I write to you, young men, because you are strong, and the word of God lives in you, and you have overcome the evil one.

A child in the faith becomes a youth by overcoming the evil one, becoming strong, and having the Word of God live within. We dare not miss this last characteristic. The application of God's words is the basis that provides the strength to overcome temptation. This verse signifies that young people must have the Scriptures in their lives.

Here is a list of principles from New Testament teaching.

1. Jesus' example of normal growth sets a progressive pattern for all children in emotional, social, mental, and perhaps spiritual growth (Luke 2:52).

2. Jesus was called upon to "learn obedience." This obedience comes to our lives via a teaching of the Word of God (Heb. 5).

3. Spiritual formation is a sanctification which happens by the word of truth.

4. The faith of a child, simple in the best way, is indicative of the kind of faith adults should possess.

5. The Lord's primary concern that children have access to spiritual leadership and experience is evident.

6. A child's faith is in many ways the model for all.

7. At a young age Jesus modeled learning the Scriptures.

8. Children should be morphed as they grow.

9. Adults are responsible to instruct children, and children are responsible to learn. This is a key part of the spiritual formation process for children.

10. The Scriptures are the source of the content for teaching regarding salvation.

11. The way a child becomes strong and grows is by knowing the Word of God.

Philosophical Rationale for the Instructional-Analytic Approach to Children's Spiritual Formation

What is the philosophical rationale for the Instructional-Analytic Model? Every local church search committee looking for a pastor/director of children's ministry should ask, "What is your personal philosophy of children's ministry?" Unfortunately, most candidates don't know how to answer this question. To make matters worse, most committees barely know what they're asking. In an effort to inform both search committees and candidates, I will outline the seven key elements of a philosophy of educational ministry and review their implications for the spiritual formation of children.

Purpose. The purpose of spiritual formation in the Bible is to bring a person into conformity to Christ. "For those God foreknew he also predestined to be conformed to the likeness of his Son" (Rom. 8:29a). Conformity to Christ necessitates that a child will come to receive the gift of eternal life at an appropriate time. Spiritual formation has a momentous beginning: The salvation of a person! In the life of a child, that "event" may be a months-long process of faith with no personal knowledge of when that event occurred. Or this may be a remembered time, reviewed often by the child, and renewing the life. In any case the Bible indicates that eternal life (and the formation that accompanies it) begins with the act of receiving Christ. "Yet to all who received him, to those who believed in his name, he gave the right to become children of God" (John 1:12). Any person can know that he or she has a relationship with Christ. "And this is the testimony: God has given us eternal life, and this life is in his Son. He who has the Son has life; he who does not have the Son of God does not have life. I write these things to you who believe in the name of the Son of God so that you may know that you have eternal life" (1 John 5:11–13).

Often people are made to doubt childhood decisions. We should again let the Bible guide the thinking of a young person. At a young age my oldest son believed in Christ, and essentially, he has never doubted it. Another of my boys trusted Christ at age four, again at ages five, seven, and nine. He later reaffirmed his salvation as a middle-school student and perhaps several times since. In other words the individual personality of the child makes us avoid cookie-cutter formation and continues to call for Scripture to guide the spiritual formation of the child.

Conformity to Christ implies that his life is being lived out through the child's life. This is true for adults also. Paul was greatly concerned for the Galatians. He was in doubt that they had received salvation at all and felt like he was "in labor" spiritually all over again: "My little children, of whom I travail in birth again until Christ be formed in you" (Gal. 4:19 KJV). We know that this purpose is an ongoing process in the life of a person after salvation. But does it have implications before the regenerating work of the Spirit? Yes. A mother shared her concern with me after a seminar: "I'm so concerned that I lay the proper foundations for my child! Can you tell me specifically what they are?" I asked how old her child was. "Five," was her reply. I prompted her to think of all the wonderful truths she could share about the character of God, about his creation, about his love and care. I urged her to continue to teach the Bible; it is the source for knowledge about God. But I cautioned her that she need not push her child toward salvation but let the foundations set. Here is the tension that we feel: not rushing, not slacking, but ready when the child is ready. How are we to know God's purposes? Conformity to Christ in the life of the child goes back to the idea of that child coming to know Christ as their personal Savior. Foundational truths learned through God's creation are not excluded, but Scripture interprets and guides those experiences, perceptions, and emotions.

Conformity to Christ implies that we who teach be careful to view children's spiritual development in an integrated manner with other areas of their growth (e.g. physical, emotional, intellectual, social, etc.). To know what a child is capable of thinking, reasoning, and comprehending requires skill. Putting young children in a place where they have to grapple with abstract concepts is expecting too much. I remember sitting with a Boys Brigade group of which one of my sons was a part. The novice teacher was pulling items out of a paper sack to describe God. "How is God like a candy bar?" I'm sure it made sense to the teacher, but he clearly did not understand the cognitive reasoning ability of a young child. (Some of us adults were struggling too!)

Conformity to Christ is not a simple process. "The purpose of Christian life is for us to know God personally and become more like Jesus Christ, a complex process. We must also learn to work with God through the Holy Spirit to discover how we can help children develop spiritually in total personality structure."[5]

In saying that Scripture focuses our spiritual formation of children, we are not saying we exclude other avenues of learning, but Scripture is at the core. At a seminar I was conducting, a participant began to explain in rather lengthy detail how narrow she felt my viewpoint was. She described how a child's personality should be shaped so that the young person was aware of nature, conservation of resources, the wonder of a flower or a sunset, and the overall sense of awe in experiencing our world. Her further concern was that relationships with others could be hindered if we "pushed" a child to be thinking only about Jesus and God. She seemed to think that if we learned only what was in Scripture we would not develop the whole personality of the child. I sought to explain that Scripture is the core of a proper understanding of all of life. The Bible gives us the ability to interact with experiences, theology, and religious traditions without being at a helpless impasse of individualism. "We must begin by being utterly convinced that there is a biblical perspective on everything—not just on spiritual matters."[6] A key issue here is

---

5. Clark, "Spiritual Formation in Children," 234.

6. Nancy R. Pearcey, *Total Truth: Liberating Christianity from Its Cultural Captivity* (Wheaton, Ill.: Crossway Books, 2004), 44.

that we not compartmentalize a child's spiritual life away from all other aspects, that we see the Bible and our relationship with Christ as foundational rather than as a segment of our lives to be held in balance with others.

Secondary goals and aims such as those mentioned are important, but they pale in relation to the scriptural message. That is why an emphasis on knowing, memorizing, studying, obeying, and proclaiming the Scripture takes priority over any other study, discipline, endeavor, or experience. Values, however lofty, not leading us to Christ and the Christ life will eventually be found to be little more than the rearranging of deck chairs on a sinking ship. On the other hand, the living out of the Christ life should not be limited: "The aim and substance of spiritual life is not fasting, prayer, hymn singing, frugal living, and so forth. Rather, it is the effective and full enjoyment of active love of God and humankind in all the daily rounds of normal existence where we are placed. The spiritually advanced person is not the one who engages in lots and lots of disciplines, any more than the good child is the one who receives lots and lots of instruction or punishment."[7] The Scriptures bring us to Christ and to experiencing his love.

Conformity to Christ necessitates a regeneration in him. To say that a child can be fully shaped without the spiritual core being born from above is to deny the power of transformation. Socialization may occur. Conformity to righteous standards may occur. Protection from adverse happenings and outcomes may occur. Personality development may occur. But spiritual formation is eventually hindered and lost if salvation is not presented and received. This presentation is learned not from things created but from things revealed. That means salvation is known from Scripture. People can participate in eternal life without sound personalities, as tragic as that may be. People can participate in eternal life without understanding or appreciation of God's creation, as dull and boring as that existence may be. People can participate in eternal life without harmony and strength in their relationships with others, as heartbreaking as that would be. But they cannot participate in eternal life without the work of

---

7. Dallas Willard, *The Spirit of the Disciplines: Understanding How God Changes Lives* (San Francisco: HarperSanFrancisco, 1991), 139.

the Holy Spirit in salvation. The question is, how should/could a child experience eternal life? Through faith. Jesus describes it as "childlike" (Matt. 18:1–4).

In the life of a child, care should be used to avoid two extremes. One extreme is when a salvation decision was made; and on the basis of that moment, nurture and growth become undervalued. An overzealous Sunday school teacher prided herself that all the children in her class were never promoted to the next without "coming to the Lord." It seemed to me that a child was only a notch on her spiritual belt. Spiritual nurture, continued scriptural explanation of the Christian life, and shepherding of relationships did not seem to matter. This extreme fails because spiritual formation is a process, not simply an act or decision.

The other extreme is never to present salvation through faith. The doctrine of salvation is the major matter of the Christian life, even for a child. A college-aged young person came and wondered about her salvation. She said she was raised in a church where she grew up thinking she was a Christian. Yet now she wasn't so sure. There had never been a time in her life that she could remember when she had believed in Christ for her salvation. The lack of assurance was causing her doubt. Even with a loving family and instructing church workers, her relationship with Christ was not one of confidence.

The purpose of spiritual formation then is to guide the child toward becoming like Jesus. Children are not naturally like Jesus because they are born with a sin nature. There is no age where children are given an old sin nature; they are born with it. That is why the purpose of conformity to Christ is most directed toward the spiritual regeneration of a young person. "Therefore the Law has become our tutor *to lead us* to Christ, so that we may be justified by faith" (Gal. 3:24 NASB). The word for *tutor* is the word used to describe the trusted slave that was in charge of the family children, to educate and to train. My contention is that the teaching of the Bible to pre-Christian children and youth should lead them as soon as they are ready to a faith in Christ. This faith results in progressive sanctification not unlike the formation in adults. This formation is a process of increasing glory: "But we all, with open face beholding as in a glass the glory of the Lord, are changed into the same image from glory to glory, *even* as by the Spirit of the Lord" (2 Cor. 3:18 KJV).

Content. The second element of the teacher-learner process is perhaps the crucial area of focus for the Instructional-Analytic Model. The Bible is the content of education which prompts spiritual formation in children—not reflection (contemplative-refection), experience (pragmatic-participation), or activity (active-engagement). This model views that learning the Bible will create an educational situation where reflection, practice, and obedience occur. Our statement purposes that the foundation is the Bible; and reflection, experience, and activity then result—not vice versa. While deep appreciation for the methodologies of each of the other views makes the Instructional-Analytic Model thrive, the view must insist that biblical content have top priority.

Catherine Stonehouse describes Ted Ward's model of how God has revealed himself.[8] Based on this model, she makes several helpful suggestions.

Ward's Model of Divine Self-Revelation

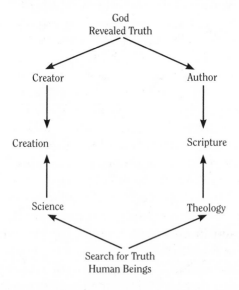

<hr>

8. Catherine Stonehouse, *Joining Children on the Spiritual Journey: Nurturing a Life of Faith* (Grand Rapids, Mich.: Baker Books, 1998), 14–15.

1. The tension of God revealing and mankind searching for truth may be felt in working with children. How experienced is the search for creation truth in a child's life? There may be wonder, excitement, even partial understanding; but you would not want to have your next airplane flight based on the piloting of a child or to have a group of youth have the chemistry classroom all to themselves. Nor would it seem wise to remove adult influence from the search of Scripture.

2. When interpretation of creation and interpretation of Scripture conflict, we should attempt to "check" our methods of understanding. "Christian developmentalists have an absolute metaphysic but a relative epistemology. They believe that there are unchanging and reliable absolutes in the universe (absolute metaphysic), and yet at the same time they acknowledge that one's perceptions of God and the world are conditioned by one's own mental structures and experiences (relative epistemology). The developmentalist is not a skeptic but recognizes the conditional nature of all our perceptions."[9]

3. When those interpretation checks still result in conflict, the revelation of the Bible must take precedent. "We cannot simply borrow from the results of secular scholarship as though that were spiritually neutral territory discovered by people whose minds are completely open and objective—that is, as though the Fall had never happened."[10]

Environment. What is the best environment for learning? The other models in this book have much to teach us about where and how children learn best. Most Christian education experiences seek to have the cleanest, most up-to-date facilities and techniques possible. However, looking at the learning situation from new viewpoints could be valuable. Are there opportunities for reflection, active play, quiet thinking, and relational sharing? Sometimes being tied to buildings or methods holds us back from the learning that is possible. The reader should observe that great spiritual formation can occur with the simplest of methods and in outdated and nonmodern surroundings. Note

9. Jim Wilhoit, *Christian Education and the Search for Meaning* (Grand Rapids, Mich.: Baker Book House, 1986), 81.

10. Pearcey, *Total Truth*, 46.

that Jesus did most of his instruction outdoors. Certainly camping for children and youth ministry has not diminished.

Biblically there seem to be examples of home, church, and marketplace-type settings where learning occurred. Some would criticize children's ministry as having gone entirely to a fortress mentality. This may be true, but most children's workers teach the Bible with as much enthusiasm, diligent preparation, and creativity as they can muster. It has become too easy in some quarters to memorize Scripture by rote, be too heavily involved with extrinsic motivation and lazy in our motivation of children to know the Bible in more than a heady way. Our learning environment should be as bright, beautiful, interactive, and fun as possible.

1. *Home.* Perhaps the greatest missing element in Christian education in our day is the home. Many Bible-related ministries have started a renewed interest in training parents and others in the family to pick up the role of discipleship. A home is a natural place to learn Scripture. Everything from the pictures and plaques on the wall to the books on the shelves can signify the importance of this learning setting. Too many times our media usage is not focused on learning the Bible but rather undermines it. Television, computer, music, and other media should help us focus on learning the Scripture. The home can redeem the time children have available with good results. "Give it back!" could be the remedy for the concern that we have taken the parent out of the equation of learning.

2. *Church.* The respect for and ubiquitous presence of the Scriptures is an undeniable factor in the environment of the early church. "They devoted themselves to the apostles' teaching and to the fellowship, to the breaking of bread and to prayer" (Acts 2:42) indicates that the early church was committed to studying Scripture. Too often we in Christian education become known as "people of the program" instead of "people of the Book." The public reading of Scripture, the recitation of memorized passages, and the common knowledge of biblical story have all fallen on hard times.

3. *School.* Adults are becoming increasingly reluctant to call their Bible studies on Sunday morning "Sunday school." The whole idea of going to school on another day of the week doesn't make kids' day either! Unfortunately, the confusion and frustration with schooling impacts the perspective of the education of the church. And this carry-over attitude is sometimes justified because the extreme experimentation, confused delivery, and mixed message priorities have taken their toll when passed from the educational sector to the church. However, the gathering of the family members to learn together and the specific tutoring of children and youth are noted in the biblical literature. School, or more specifically, a learning environment, was obvious whether at home, synagogue, or temple. Today the debate about the best place to conduct religious instruction (e.g. home, Christian, private, public, or Sunday) continues. What is obvious is the need for a variety of structures and learning situations.

Methodology. Methodology can be divided into approach and methods.

1. *Approach.* So many voices are vying for the right to set the educational agenda for children. My contention is that we let the Bible set and guide our educational means as well as our ends. "For Christian educators this would require the use of the most updated approaches and technologies in the light of the recent research and developments and trends. It would also require a critical and careful analysis of every particular cultural context before an educational agenda could be proposed."[11]

To align our educational work with the biblical plumb line is not easy. Too often we have bought into the humanist idea that we are the authority over Scripture instead of Scripture being the authority over us. As Mullholland put it, "You are the 'victim' of a life-long, educationally enhanced learning mode that establishes *you* as the controlling power who seeks to master a body of information that can be used by you to advance your own purposes."[12]

11. Robert W. Pazmino, *Foundational Issues in Christian Education,* 2nd ed. (Grand Rapids, Mich.: Baker Books, 1997), 163.

12. Robert M. Mullholland Jr., *Shaped by the Word: The Power of Scripture in Spiritual Formation* (Nashville, Tenn.: The Upper Room, 1985), 21.

The methods we use sometimes seem not to connect. We don't see Scripture lived out in our homes, churches, and communities so we substitute character development, values education, spiritual experiences, or even spiritual disciplines. All of these cannot replace obedience to the instructions of God found in the Bible. "Routine aspects of life we need to redeem are of varying kinds. Some arise because of pressures placed upon us by our society; others stem from regular activities in which we are involved. Quite specific questions are raised in the areas of work and leisure, and the central features of modern life bring other issues to the fore."[13]

2. *Methods.* What specific methods would the person holding to an Instructional-Analytic Model suggest? While openness to the wide variety of methods from any of the other views is evident, special focus is upon what the Scriptures reinforce: read, study, and memorize the Scriptures.

Read the Scripture. Many Evangelical churches are found to be lacking in the area of reading Scripture. We have forgotten the first part of 1 Timothy 4:13: "Until I come, devote yourself to the public reading of Scripture, to preaching and to teaching" (1 Tim. 4:13). We seem to be so wrapped up in children's ministry in doing the last two aspects described by the verse that we don't do the public reading.

Study the Scripture. You would expect this from someone who works for AWANA, wouldn't you? Our institutional verse is: "Study to shew thyself approved unto God, a workman that needeth not to be ashamed, rightly dividing the word of truth" (2 Tim. 2:15 KJV). Approved Workmen Are Not Ashamed is where AWANA Clubs International derives its name. Being diligent with the Scriptures is not just an academic pursuit or a Sunday pursuit. It is the need for every child, youth, and adult. The Bereans of Paul's day demonstrated it well: "Now the Bereans were of more noble character than the Thessalonians, for they received the message with great eagerness and examined the Scriptures every day to see if what Paul said was true" (Acts 17:11).

Memorize the Scripture. The Instructional-Analytic Model of children's spiritual formation views Scripture memory with

13. Robert Banks, *Redeeming the Routines: Bringing Theology to Life* (Wheaton, Ill.: BridgePoint Books, Victor Books, 1993), 71.

esteem. Psalm 119:9, 11 is often referenced: "How can a young man keep his way pure? By living according to your word. . . . I have hidden your word in my heart that I might not sin against you." Memorizing verses of the Bible puts them within the life of the child where the Holy Spirit can use them for transformation. Of course, some do not view Scripture memory with this lofty purpose in mind. "Most of our pupils are not memorizing scripture the way we'd like them to because they see no need to do so. They are not searching the scriptures because they don't see the difference it will make in their own lives; they don't see the relevance of doctrine to life."[14]

All of our contemporary instructional methodologies cannot be found in biblical usage. There were no video data projectors, color printing presses, or computers in Jesus' day. However, that doesn't mean we shouldn't make use of every instructional resource available to us for the purpose of teaching the Scriptures. We also need to be careful that our methods do not distort and distract from the message. "Good instructional aids enhance the presentation of essential content. When aids draw too much attention to themselves, however, they lose their usefulness."[15]

The Nature of the Learner. This is also a major difference between the instructional-analytic view and others. We would emphasize an interactive balance between the *imago Dei* (image of God) and the fallen nature of people. Stonehouse described the seemingly innate seeking after God: "Adults who listen to children attentively and know them well . . . believe children are sensitive and responsive to God. Evidences of profound spiritual experience in early childhood come from many sources."[16]

However, the Bible describes a fatal spiritual flaw: sin—both the principle of sin in a person's life and the practice of sin through the way a person lives. This becomes obvious. No one seems to have to teach a child to be selfish and say, "Mine!" No parental curriculum renders toddlers resistant to authority or

---

14. Lois E. LeBar with James E. Plueddemann, *Education That Is Christian* (Colorado Springs: Chariot Victor Publishing, 1995), 142.

15. William R. Yount, *Called to Teach: An Introduction to the Ministry of Teaching* (Nashville, Tenn.: Broadman & Holman Publishers, 1999), 68.

16. Catherine Stonehouse, *Joining Children on the Spiritual Journey: Nurturing a Life of Faith* (Grand Rapids, Mich.: Baker Books, 1998), 128.

rude. The shift of a young person, sweet and innocent, can amazingly, suddenly become uncontrollable, sassy, or sullen. How does one account for this—the fall of humans into sin? "There is both 'good news' and 'bad news' from the Fall, if we can use those trite phrases. The 'good news' is that we humans never fully lost the image of God from Eden. But everything else is 'bad news.' God's image became severely twisted and distorted by the first sin."[17]

Like a vessel being shaped, the pre-Christian child should be taught the foundational truths of knowing God, Jesus, and the meaning of the cross. The conscience will be shaped to acknowledge sin, both in practice and principle. "Parents and teachers are to train up a child in the way he *should* go, not the way he *would* go, for the bias of inbred sin, strengthened by actual sin, tends to direct his actions in the downward way."[18] But as we gain in the ability to answer some of these developmental questions about children, we know that there are appropriate times or sequences for the spiritual formation of our children. This means that we need to discover how we can best teach the Bible to our children.

Because of the work of the Holy Spirit in regeneration, the child has a fresh ability, or "new option" for obeying God from the heart. Whereas, before conversion, we can only guide and tutor the child toward spiritual things (Gal. 3:24–25), when a child is regenerated, there is the potential to be conformed to Christ, even at whatever developmental stage the person may be. This then results in an interactive journey with Scripture as the road map. As Boa states: "I have discovered that while everyone has a world view, a philosophy, a set of pre-suppositions about life that they hold by faith, few people are aware of it. Of the few who can express their fundamental assumptions about human existence, only a fraction have thought through the logical implications of these assumptions. And of this small fraction, only a handful have contrasted these logical implications with the way they live."[19]

---

17. Ronald T. Habermas, *The Complete Disciple: A Model for Cultivating God's Image in Us* (Colorado Springs: NexGen, Cook Communications, 2003), 82.

18. Lois E. LeBar, *Children in the Bible School: The HOW of Christian Education* (Old Tappan, N.J.: Fleming H. Revell Co., 1952), 164.

19. Kenneth Boa, *Conformed to His Image: Biblical and Practical Approaches to Spiritual Formation* (Grand Rapids, Mich.: Zondervan, 2001), 68.

Some would say that early childhood conversion is not good, even dangerous. A Bible college youth ministry professor once said to me, "I instruct my students not to present the gospel to children. I think it's wrong to force kids to accept Christ before the age of twelve or thirteen." I thought he was kidding. But then the leading editor of a Christian publishing company chimed in, "Our research has discovered that many of the kids who accept Christ at a young age need to have a renewal or recommitment during their teen years."

My response is to ask any group of Christians how many of them believed in Christ before age ten. Usually, a majority of hands will go up. To take away this window of opportunity from a child seems unconscionable to me. Barna concludes, "Parents must start the spiritual training of children when they are young. Waiting too long produces unfortunate outcomes for parents and children."[20] The fact that many teens in their adolescent years need to have a renewal of faith should not surprise us. There will always be a need for ongoing spiritual formation. No one is satisfied with a "one prayer and you're done" approach to spirituality development. George Gallup Jr. reminds us to be "mindful that teens should be regarded not as pathologies waiting to happen, but sparks of joy to be developed and nurtured."[21]

The Role of the Teacher. What is to be the role of the teacher in this process of a child's spiritual formation? A teacher is to be a guide, model, catalyst, and shepherd. The Word of God becomes the teacher's road map, the standard of the model, the active ingredient in life-change reaction, and the staff of the shepherd's hand. "Students are not passive raw materials on an assembly line. Rather they are active pilgrims on a difficult journey. People who help pilgrims must know both the needs of the pilgrim and the map of scripture, which shows the pilgrim where to go and how to get there. Pilgrims don't study the Map merely to learn information. They don't memorize verses merely to earn badges or bubble gum."[22]

---

20. George Barna, *Transforming Children into Spiritual Champions* (Ventura, Calif.: Regal Books, Gospel Light, 2003), 82.
21. George Gallup Jr. in Timothy Smith, *The Seven Cries of Today's Teens* (Nashville, Tenn.: Integrity Publishers, 2003), 5.
22. LeBar and Plueddemann, *Education That Is Christian,* 135.

Wilhoit's fourfold view of teacher options in Christian education may prove instructive. The Romantic (Teacher as Gardener),
Transmissive (Teacher as Technician), and Developmental (Teacher as Coordinator) views all have their applications.[23] There are
times when each of these roles may be necessary. However, life-
change in the lives of our children would seem to necessitate the
fourth option which is the Transformational (Teacher as Guide)
model. Seeking to view the teacher as guide curbs the dual dangers of the Instructional-Analytic Model: simple behavior conformity and "knowing is enough."

If a teacher seeks only to modify behavior, then it is certainly
possible to make a child conform to the standards in the learning
situation. This kind of teaching, however, most often results in
a cycle of guilt and pressure where the student cannot leave the
"greenhouse environment." This may be the reason some youth
who have awards for years of Scripture memory can go away to
college and "lose their faith." The teacher's role is to use discipline to cause the student to learn, not just to be rewarded for
behaving in a certain way with no heart change.

Some who agree with the Instructional-Analytic Model err
when they teach for a gain in knowledge rather than a true heart
change. They may quote, "God's word will not return void" (Isa.
55:11) but not recognize that Jesus said the seed of the word could
be snatched away and become unfruitful (Luke 8:11-12). We cannot be satisfied with simply teaching for a gain in knowledge,
but we must teach for obedience. "Anyone, then, who knows the
good he ought to do and doesn't do it, sins" (James 4:17).

Summary of Several Cognitive/Emotional
Development Issues

1. *Learning by Heart.* With an emphasis on Scripture memory, it seems wise to describe this intended outcome of the activity
in children's ministry. It is not to learn only by rote. The Bible
seems to say one should "learn by heart." "And these words, which
I am commanding you today, shall be on your heart" (Deut. 6:6

---

23. Jim Wilhoit, *Christian Education and the Search for Meaning*, 61–96.

NASB). When children learn only by rote, they have not learned enough. Our children should be encouraged to go deeper. Few children's ministry leaders are satisfied with simple rote learning, although the practice seems widespread.

2. *Age of Accountability.* Lois LeBar informs us regarding this important concept in her classic work:

> It is often said that children are responsible to God after the age of accountability. What is that age? The church has sometimes assumed it to be the age of twelve, when the Jewish boy became a "son of the law." Until twelve, therefore, it formerly neglected the child and allowed him to stagnate spiritually. May not the age of accountability vary with individuals and with environmental conditions? May not the age of accountability be considerably lower in our day in cities than it was previously on isolated farms?[24]

3. *Competition.* Because of the variety of methods mentioned above and because of the nature of the student cited earlier, this view purports that a level of competition is an effective tool of discipline. Care should be taken to avoid the extremes of "win at all costs" and not allowing less skilled children to achieve. Team games should be fun for all and not just for a few talented and athletic individuals. Adult supervision and guidance should ensure the elimination of overcompetitiveness. Competition that focuses on improvement and task accomplishment is the nature of the competition in ministries that use it, not comparison to others in their level of accomplishment.

4. *Awards/Incentives.* Based on the nature of the student, we espouse that the accomplishment of desirable outcomes can and should be recognized. These awards should be tied to meaningful accomplishments, achievable by effort on every student's part, not just a select few. In addition, the achievement of these rewards should be guided by the teacher or parent. The older the student, the less emphasis should be placed upon the incentive. Youth and adults should learn for the joy of learning, realizing that even adults learn more effectively when there is fair

---

24. LeBar, *Children in the Bible School,* 175.

assessment and reward. "When we believe we will be reinforced for learning something, we are more likely to pay attention to it and mentally process it in an effective fashion."[25] However, care should be taken to ensure that mastery of material is in view and not just performance.

Programmatic Design of the Instructional-Analytic Model

An example of the Instructional-Analytic Model is the ministry of AWANA Clubs International. Nearly a million kids participate in AWANA Clubs across North America. But certainly AWANA is not unique in its programmatic design. Aspects of the Instructional-Analytic Model may be observed in the core values of a number of similar organizations that minister to children and youth. Two such programs are Child Evangelism Fellowship and Pioneer Clubs.

Child Evangelism Fellowship has as its stated purpose to evangelize boys and girls with the gospel of the Lord Jesus Christ and to establish (disciple) them in the Word of God and in a local church for Christian living.[26] Child Evangelism Fellowship personnel describe "personal, individual ministry with more than five million children each year" worldwide.[27]

Pioneer Clubs also embrace Scripture as God's Word and the authority for all aspects of life. It is the core of everything Pioneer Clubs does and the tool they use to introduce children to Jesus Christ and to disciple them. A primary goal of their curriculum is to help children use, understand, and apply the Bible in daily life.[28]

The Historical Development of AWANA

AWANA Clubs International, originally known as the AWANA Youth Association, officially came into existence in 1950. The

---

25. Jeanne E. Ormrod, *Educational Psychology: Developing Learners,* 5th ed. (Columbus, Ohio: Merrill Prentice Hall, 2006), 333.

26. "Purpose," http://www.cefonline.com/about/purpose.php, 1.

27. Reese Kauffman, "Note from the President," http://www.cefonline.com/about/index.php, 1.

28. "What Is Pioneer Clubs?" Pioneer Clubs Core Values, http://www.pioneerclubs.org/corevalues.htm, 1.

roots of AWANA, however, can be found several decades earlier, going back to the 1920s.[29] In the spring of 1922, Evangelist Paul Rader arrived in Chicago, and on June 18 the doors of the Chicago Gospel Tabernacle opened to a crowd of six thousand. What was to be a six-week crusade turned into an eleven-year ministry. Rader, who during his career also served as pastor of the historic Moody Church and as president of the Christian and Missionary Alliance, left an indelible mark on Christian ministry. Rader's influence on those who served around him during the Tabernacle days led to the forming of ministries such as HCJB Radio, the Slavic Gospel Association, New Tribes Mission, and Youth for Christ. One of the young men around Rader was a young, gifted musician named Lance "Doc" Latham, who was to become the cofounder of AWANA.

With thousands pouring into the Tabernacle, Rader tapped Lance Latham, along with Clarence Jones and Richard Oliver, to lead outreach to children and youth. Jack Eggar notes, "Tabernacle Scouts was the name of the first Tab children's ministry. Lance, Clarence and Richard became the directors, or 'Scoutmasters,' to a growing number of boys and young men. The club grew so rapidly that it became necessary to divide up into age groups."

Not to be outdone, Virginia Highfield, who was to become Lance's wife, began a club program for young girls.

In 1933, Rader resigned as pastor of the Tabernacle. As Lance and Virginia sought God's will for their future, they felt God's call to plant a church on the north side of Chicago. Thus was born the North Side Gospel Center. Lance and Virginia's commitment to minister to children became the heart of the Center. The motto for the newly planted church was, "If you want to do a work for eternity, reach boys and girls for Christ."[30]

One of the families that moved from the Tabernacle to become part of the newly planted North Side Gospel Center was a family by the name of Rorheim. Their fifteen-year-old son, Art,

---

29. Sources for AWANA's history are Robert L. Moeller, *AWANA: God's Miracle* (Streamwood, Ill.: AWANA Clubs International, 2000) and Jack D. Eggar, *Great and Mighty Things* (Streamwood, Ill.: AWANA Clubs International, 2004).

30. Eggar, *Great and Mighty Things,* 18.

was soon to come to the attention of Latham, and in the mid-1930s, Latham invited him to become the leader of the Center's youth activities. Art accepted the invitation and thus began a life-long relationship that would continue to grow until Latham's death in 1985.

Latham, the son of a Presbyterian minister, had a formative impact on the development of AWANA. Having memorized the Gospel of John, Romans, and James by age seven, Scripture memory was a significant part of Latham's life. As Latham developed his philosophy of youth ministry, four other principles were to be combined with Scripture memory to form the core of his approach. These five core values were to become the foundation of AWANA's design for ministry to children and youth.[31] They are:

1. Scripture memory
2. The gospel of the grace of God
3. Leadership development
4. Doctrinal integrity
5. Good, wholesome fun

Early Beginnings. These principles were to become ingrained in Art Rorheim as Latham mentored him as a young man. As the ministry of the North Side Gospel Center got under way, Latham looked to Art for leadership in the area of youth ministry. Initially he served in a volunteer capacity, and then at age twenty-five he became the Center's full-time youth director. Building on the philosophical base developed by Latham, Rorheim became the creative force behind the organization and development of the nascent AWANA Club.

Working with what was at hand in a time of limited economic resources, Art discovered a box at the bottom of an unused elevator shaft in the store that had been converted to the North Side Gospel Center. In the box were hundreds of beanie caps in four distinct colors: red, blue, green, and yellow. From this came the colors that have become so much a part of AWANA. In order

---

31. Moeller, *AWANA,* 14.

to bring order to the gathering of the many children coming to the Center's youth program, Rorheim developed the now familiar AWANA Game Square.

By the close of the 1940s, other churches had begun looking to the AWANA ministry for help in beginning their own youth ministry. Because of these requests for help, consideration was given to developing a formal organization to help meet these requests. In 1949, Lance Latham, Art Rorheim, and several other leaders met to begin the process of starting such an organization. In 1950, the AWANA Youth Association came into existence.

Program Elements of AWANA

From its initial focus on a club for boys ages eight through ten, the AWANA ministry has grown today to include programming for children and youth, boys and girls from preschool through high school. Each age group club has a specific name. They are:

Cubbies. Cubbies are preschool children. The AWANA curriculum for these children (two years before kindergarten) is built on two premises:

- Young children can and should receive spiritual training.

- Home is the primary place for spiritual training.

The Cubbies curriculum features two handbooks written in a fun, storybook style that appeals to preschoolers. The handbooks contain twenty-four Bear Hug sections along with six optional special-day sections. Each section combines basic Scripture memory with parent-child activities to help a child grasp a simple biblical truth. Two extra-credit handbooks containing additional memory verses and character-building activities are also available.

Before starting a handbook, newcomers to Cubbies are taken through an introductory brochure that gives parents and children a brief overview of the program and presents God's plan of salvation at a preschooler's level.

In addition, all memory verses are presented at a level appropriate for three- and four-year-olds. For example, John 3:16 reads, "For God so loved the world, that He gave His only Son . . ."

Sparks. The Sparks program is for children in grades kindergarten through second grade. The Sparks curriculum builds on the material taught in our preschool club. The aim of the curriculum is to take youngsters a step deeper into God's Word while giving unsaved boys and girls regular opportunities to hear the gospel and come to faith in Jesus Christ. After being immersed in solid foundational teaching at the preschool level, boys and girls frequently come to an understanding of their need to trust Christ as their personal Savior while in Sparks.

Sparks curriculum is comprised of three handbooks. Each handbook communicates spiritual truths through memory verse drills, crafts, activities, and review of key doctrine, Bible facts, and verses. All three handbooks follow a nature motif, starting with Skipper and ending with Climber.

The theme of the first handbook is "Jesus in the past." The second book's theme is "Jesus in the present." The theme of the third book is "Jesus in the future." Before working in a handbook, newcomers to Sparks complete an entrance booklet that introduces them to the program and begins teaching them basic biblical truths.

Truth & Training Clubs, or T&T, are designed for children in grades three through six. Each of the four handbooks in our Truth & Training clubs investigates four questions. Eight answers from the Bible are provided for each question. Children will learn all eight answers to each of the questions and verses to back up these answers. The handbooks also include Bible studies and activities that allow children to delve into the subject matter.

Besides this curriculum, children can complete more challenging extra-credit sections throughout each handbook to earn special awards. Before beginning work in a handbook, newcomers to T&T must complete a short booklet that explains God's plan of salvation.

Trek 24–7. Trek 24–7 is a two-year (with an optional third year) curriculum aimed at students in middle school and junior high. AWANA equips and challenges junior-high students with a thorough Bible curriculum. Young people learn to follow Christ in their daily lives through memory verses, in-depth Bible study and application, relevant stories, missions and service projects, and character lessons.

The junior-high curriculum begins with a brief booklet that introduces newcomers to the program, explains the gospel message, and teaches basic Bible truths. It is free for them to take home, so it becomes a gospel tract for the whole family.

The junior high program meets the needs of teenagers at three different levels.

- First level (Come See) targets unsaved youth.

- Next level (Come Follow) helps young or nominal believers grow in their faith.

- Final level (Come Serve) trains committed teenagers for leadership, ministry service, and a deeper walk with God.

Young people are given opportunities to put their faith in action by getting involved in service projects and serving their church. One such program plugs youth into assistant leadership roles in younger-age AWANA clubs.

Journey 24–7. The senior high program is called Journey 24–7. This recently revised curriculum is tailored for students at all spiritual levels. Your church's most committed Christian teenagers will be taken on an in-depth journey through God's Word through our Journey 24–7 study manuals. Students will also complete one elective study manual each year.

Journey 24–7 curriculum has it all: relevant twenty-first century content, a strong emphasis on life application, thorough apologetics and our trademark Scripture memory—invaluable ingredients for character-shaping discipleship. These materials are challenging yet meaningful to seekers, nominal believers, and fervent followers of Christ.

Our high-school program, Journey 24–7, features an energetic look, enhanced content, life application, and an emphasis on Scripture memory. These new materials provide youth pastors and leaders with relevant tools for in-depth, focused discipleship. They are challenging and thought provoking yet accessible to students from all spiritual backgrounds.

Common Club Elements

Each club is built around three main elements: small-group activities, large-group activities, and game time.

Small-Group Time. This program component focuses on communicating the message of the Bible to children and youth. It also involves Scripture memory as a key element. During this time children work through a planned sequence of material in handbooks. The material is age appropriate.

Large-Group Time. Also known as Lesson or Council Time, this is a flexible, large gathering that can be used to present a Bible story or teaching. Usually this includes a presentation of the gospel; however, this time is not specifically structured and provides the individual church with the opportunity to include the components they deem important.

Game Time. The AWANA game square provides maximum opportunity for children to get involved, no matter what their athletic ability. They unleash their energy while learning teamwork, sportsmanship, and other character traits through their participation.

In addition there are a large number of additional elements involved in making an AWANA club successful. They are detailed at www.awana.org.

Why AWANA Works

To say that AWANA works is not to imply that the other orientations discussed in this book do not work. Suggesting that other approaches to the spiritual formation of children that are currently employed, have been employed in the past, or may be employed in the future are of lesser value or effectiveness would be narrow-minded at best and egotistical and self-absorbed at worst. Clearly the Christian faith has been communicated to children and communicated effectively before any of the theorists/practitioners writing in this volume came along. In the context of our varying commitment and perspectives, we can learn from one another and support one another in the large task before us of giving a positive answer to Westerhoff's now-famous question, "Will our children have faith?" Having said that, we will now look at why AWANA works, not why other approaches do or do not. The answer to why AWANA works is as simple as looking at the five core values developed by Lance Latham on which AWANA has based its approach.

1. *AWANA works because it takes Scripture seriously.* The Old and New Testaments have been informing the faith community of Christianity for two thousand years. The historic weight of testimony within the Christian community is that in the Scripture is to be found the unique communication from God regarding his purposes and his guidance for those who choose to enter into covenant with him. AWANA stands in that tradition in saying that we believe that the Scripture is vital for our understanding of God, ourselves, and the world around us. We believe that it is vital for children to learn Scripture; come to know the God of Scripture through his only, unique Son; and begin to order their lives according to the Scripture.[32]

We would not deny that spirituality is a rich component of human experience or that spiritual formation is a complex process in which a multiplicity of approaches is helpful. Human beings are, as the psalmist says, "fearfully and wonderfully made" (Ps. 139:14). We are complex creatures capable of a rich relationship with our Creator. A variety of methodologies may be profitably employed in the development of this relationship. The crucial question, however, is, "On what do we base spiritual formation?" Is the fundamental base for the road map guiding the

---

32. It should be noted that AWANA does not believe that rote memory is the ultimate goal here. We are not so shallow in our understanding of the Scripture as to believe that the mere repeating of memorized words holds great significance. Neither are we so naïve as to believe that there are not children going through our program who never move past rote memory. We are committed to seeing children and students engage the Scripture in serious contemplation which leads to life change.

development of one's relationship with the God revealed in the Scripture to be the Bible, or is it to be some other guide such as the latest educational theory or some subjective determination of the content of spirituality? Ultimately the issue being discussed in this volume comes down to epistemology and our understanding of revelation in the process of human knowing about God. Historically, the church has understood the Bible to be the revelation of God and, therefore, indispensable in knowing him and his purposes.

AWANA, and other proponents of the Instructional-Analytic Model, pursue the spiritual formation of children the way we do because of our firm belief that God has revealed himself and his purposes for us most clearly in his Son, Jesus Christ (Heb. 1:1–4) and that the clearest testimony that God has given to his Son is found in Scripture (John 20:31; 1 John 1:1–3). So we turn to the Bible as the bedrock for our understanding of God. Taking the Bible with the utmost seriousness, we endeavor to help children understand God's message to them and, in concert with the drawing power of the Holy Spirit (John 6:44; 16:13), come to faith in his Son, Jesus Christ, and thus begin the process of spiritual formation in which they are conformed to the image of Christ.[33]

2. AWANA works because it is committed to the central message of the Bible. The message of the gospel has always been central to the ministry of AWANA. It is central because it is a message of vital importance. Because of the vital importance of this message, AWANA approaches the spiritual formation of children as we do. We want children to be well adjusted, but the central message of the Bible is not about personal adjustment. We want children to develop positive character traits, but the central message of the Bible is not about developing character. We want to approach the spiritual formation of children with the best understanding of their growth and development possible, but this also is not the central message of the Bible. The central message

---

33. Historically, theology has understood this process to be sequential. Justification precedes sanctification. In the dimension under discussion here, sanctification can be seen as an ongoing process. Note Wayne Grudem's comment that "sanctification is a progressive work of God and man that makes us more and more free from sin and like Christ in our actual lives." *Systematic Theology* (Grand Rapids, Mich.: Zondervan, 1995), 746.

of the Bible is that humanity is alienated from a holy and righteous God because of sin and that this holy God has provided the *only* possible remedy for this alienation from himself and enslavement to sin. That remedy is through the life, death, burial, and resurrection of his Son who secured humanity's freedom from death and sin on the cross standing on a lonely hill outside Jerusalem we now know as Calvary. This act was completed, as the great evangelical theologian Francis Schaeffer used to say, in space-time history. It was a real event that secured a real change in humanity's relationship to God. It is the pivotal point of salvation history.

3. *AWANA works because it is committed to leadership development.* From the earliest days of the AWANA ministry, a core concern has been to raise up leaders. The AWANA ministry is committed to moving children from recipients of ministry in their earliest years to becoming leaders in ministry who give in service and mission.

As children progress through the AWANA program, they are encouraged to become Leaders-In-Training (LITs). In this capacity they are involved in working in younger clubs helping younger children in their learning and Scripture memory. While AWANA has stressed moving from passive recipient to active involvement in service because of the Bible's teaching on such, recent work done by the National Study of Youth and Religion (NSYR) has affirmed this.[34] Researchers "found a significant positive correlation between a religious commitment and civic volunteerism among U.S. high school seniors."[35]

4. *AWANA works because it is committed to doctrinal integrity.* In the longer view of AWANA's history, this has meant remaining faithful in stating the clear message of the gospel as presented in Scripture. While AWANA has developed an updated look and feel to its program materials, employed translations

---

34. This study can be found in Christian Smith, *Soul Searching: The Religious and Spiritual Lives of American Teenagers* (New York: Oxford, 2005). This study, now converted to a longitudinal study, was led by Christian Smith of the University of North Carolina, Chapel Hill.

35. http://www.youthandreligion.org/news/6-4-2002.html.

beyond the King James Version,[36] and provided options other than the traditional gray shirt uniform so identified with AWANA, the program has remained true to its commitment to begin with the Bible, which is at the heart of the Instructional-Analytic Model.

Thousands and thousands of children have come through the AWANA program. Certainly, many of them are not currently active in a local congregation or growing in their faith, but countless others are. Even those who are not currently actively living out the Christian faith remember their days in AWANA. Ask anyone connected with AWANA about their experience when publicly wearing clothing with the AWANA logo on it, and they will tell you about people of all ages spontaneously telling them about their memories of going to the club as children.

5. *AWANA works because it provides an opportunity for children to have fun.* Some of this fun happens in games where competition is a factor; much of it is not based around competition. Even where competition is involved, it does not have to be negative. I'm aware of one instance where a child involved in AWANA came in absolute last during the club's annual Grand Prix.[37] While the child was certainly disappointed, the experience led to the child and his father working together the following year. After spending time together learning how to build a winning car, the child took first place in the next year's race. Rather than being a negative experience, it was an experience that brought the boy and his father closer together.

Often AWANA and others who subscribe to the Instructional-Analytic Model come under criticism for the games and other fun components because they are seen as promoting competition or depending solely on extrinsic motivation for maintaining the child's involvement. While the research base is minimal, one recent study examining AWANA determined that these components, while present, were by no means central. The researchers noted:

---

36. Materials are currently available in the New King James Version (NKJV) and the New International Version (NIV), as well as the traditional King James Version (KJV).

37. The Grand Prix is an event where clubbers build race cars out of a pine block. This kind of event is also held by organizations such as Boy Scouts. It is also known as a pinewood derby.

Our research from interviews suggests that AWANA leaders in our sample of children generally are effectively promoting intrinsic motivation while de-emphasizing the importance of award achievement. This conclusion is congruent with our field notes we documented when at the AWANA sites. The milieu of the clubs did not highlight trophies, plaques, or other permanent mementoes of successful clubbers. In addition, although AWANA clubs did use extrinsic motivation through reinforcements, they were mostly low-key about them. . . . In sum, visitors or new clubbers would not appear to be drawn to AWANA based primarily on extrinsic motivators provided by the leaders of the club.[38]

As was seen earlier when program design was discussed, game time is only one component. AWANA provides a balance between times when the child is sitting, listening, participating, and having fun. Further, AWANA has constructed its fun component around physical activity rather than relying on a further dose of electronic media which saturates kids today.

Responses to Instructional-Analytic Model

Response by Scottie May

It's a delight to read Dr. Carlson's exposition of the role Scripture must play in our ministries and in the lives of our children if we desire them to be Christian. I laud him for the way he presents key texts to underscore the importance, the crucial nature, of teaching God's Word to children. His words reveal his passion for Scripture and his heart for children. They must serve as goads to all of us who minister with children. The Bible, God's story, is central to all we do in ministry with children. My hope is that this would indeed be true throughout children's ministry in any Christian context.

Dr. Carlson takes us through both testaments to demonstrate the importance of teaching God's Word. From Abraham,

---

38. Michael W. Firmin, Perry C. Kuhn, Jared D. Michonski, and Terra N. Posten, "From Outside-In to Inside-Out: A Qualitative Analysis of Childhood Motivation by Achievers in AWANA Programs," *Christian Education Journal* 2, no. 1 (1985): 94.

Isaac, and Jacob through the kings to the postexilic prophets and on into the New Testament, he guides us to see how God desires his people to engage in knowing God's instructions to his people. The focus on Jesus' coming to Earth as an infant and then growing and developing into an adult man is especially helpful for those of us who work with children, reminding us that though Jesus is fully God, he came to Earth fully human as well. The shift then takes us to Jesus' own view of children. Woven into this section is the reminder that children are sinful and, through a question that Dr. Carlson asks, the incongruous thought that someone might consider that the innate ability of the child is adequate for spiritual growth.

He shows us that the epistles also give instruction on the role of Scripture. Some of those passages clearly refer to the young, but it should be noted that the epistles written by the apostle John are less clear. In his first epistle John frequently uses the phrase "dear children" when he is clearly addressing all the recipients of his letter. Therefore, the position that 1 John 2:12–14 describes a "spiritual stage model" should be held tentatively.

I don't find the word *morph* to be helpful when describing the transforming work of the Holy Spirit in a person's life. As I see it, we humans are responsible for creating an environment, including content, that facilitates spiritual formation, but only the Spirit of God can bring about transformation. The word *morph,* a currently popular media special effect and superhero-type toy, seems to reduce the divine action of God to a creative gimmick, though I know this is not what Dr. Carlson intends.

Evangelical Christian churches are noted for being "people of the Book." This chapter emphasizes that and rightly so. For evangelicals it is at the core of who we are and what we do. But throughout the chapter there is a tone that seems to imply that the other models do not see it the same way. I will say more about this later, but I was assuming (which is always dangerous to do) that all four models in this book are being used in evangelical churches. Therefore, the focus would be on the "delivery system" of the Scripture rather than on the place of Scripture itself.

I also want to affirm the strength of the scholars Dr. Carlson cites as he describes the Instructional-Analytic Model. Lois Le-Bar, Catherine Stonehouse, and Jim Wilhoit, among others, have long respected careers in the field of Christian education, making their words worthy of serious consideration.

That being said, it appears that Dr. Carlson is arguing that *instruction* in Scripture is *the* means to spiritual formation. If that is indeed the case, then that position seems to be in opposition to much of the writings and testimony of Christians throughout the centuries of church history. Certainly, instruction is *a* means of formation, but I question if, as presented here, it is *the* means. In conjunction with that, we would do well not to equate the word *school* with the word *education*. To *educate* (from the Latin *educo*) means "to draw out or to lead out." Regarding children's ministry, I like to think of education as leading children from a state of not knowing Jesus into one of knowing him. In other words, I want to facilitate educating children *into* the Lord Jesus Christ, more so than simply teaching *about* him and his Word. Schooling is simply one means of educating, though an important one. From my experience with children, the more school-like ministries are, the more children seem to compartmentalize the learning (just like learning the state capitals). That learning often has little impact on their lives.

In the "Definition of Terms" section, Dr. Carlson presents a wide-ranging approach to the terms he defines. The definitions, which are without citations supporting them, seem to be written to sustain the model, especially from AWANA's perspective. This is most evident in the definition of the evangelistic element. He writes, "The Instructional-Analytic Model has a primary emphasis on leading a child to Christ." That statement begs the question of whether that definition is true for the model or inherent in AWANA. I wonder then whether AWANA is being treated as synonymous with the model. Dr. Carlson also states that "he [God] creates the environment" that includes among other things "focused instruction of the Word of God." It is interesting to me that this explanation is in contrast to the Deuteronomy model of education that places instruction about the things of God (as taking place) in natural settings, in the context of all of life. This may be due in part, as Dr. Carlson notes, to the abdication of many Christian parents of their crucial role in the spiritual formation of their children, leaving it instead to church programs.

Surprisingly absent from the entire chapter is the analytic aspect of the model as contained in its title. My understanding of Kolb's theory of learning styles (see the introduction) is that the cognitive activity of analysis is the key identifier of that style. Yet an explanation of that activity appears nowhere in the chapter except in the title. I wonder why that might be.

I also wonder how much cognitive development is necessary for a child to have a *salvific* relationship with Jesus Christ. Several times Dr. Carlson refers to cognition and other aspects of development. What does that mean for the person who is mentally or socially disabled, such as severe autism or Down syndrome? How does this model work for these children? I am grateful that answers to questions like these are not up to me or my theological system but up to our loving, gracious God.

The reader would have been well served if practical tips had been included for using this model on how to be a "teacher as a guide." How does one avoid the "dual dangers" of conformity and content acquisition? If we are to teach for obedience, how do we do that within this model? How do we encourage children to "do deeper" rather than be "satisfied with simple rote learning"? What is the teacher to do? "Mastery of the material" can also bring conflicting purposes for volunteer teachers if the ultimate purpose of a ministry is Christian formation of the child. For the Christian traditions that adhere to an age of accountability, it would have been helpful to guide the reader as to its relevance to the model.

Another area of concern for me is the implicit message sent about programs using the Instructional-Analytic Model. Although each of us has areas of specific expertise and bias (Dr. Carlson is on staff at AWANA headquarters), it seems that an imbalance favoring AWANA is glaring. Child Evangelism Fellowship and Pioneer Ministries each receive a few lines of text while AWANA is discussed over several pages. The bias becomes more evident in phrases such as the "Journey 24–7 curriculum has it all" and the reasons "AWANA works." AWANA works for some, even many children, but it certainly does not work for all children. No model or ministry does.

In seeking to make AWANA and other instructional–analytic programs distinct, Dr. Carlson notes that the Bible is "the fundamental base" rather than "the latest educational theory or some subjective determination of the content of spirituality." He seems to fail to recognize that AWANA is also shaped around educational theory that directs the manner in which they teach the Bible. AWANA also uses subjective determination in choosing the content of Scripture to be memorized. Isolated verses are memorized around doctrinal topics rather than blocks of Scripture that would keep the verses in context for the learner. (For example, Romans 3:34 is separated from 3:24.) In saying that, I don't mean to imply that is wrong, but it is important to recognize that the *content* is objective truth. How we read and interpret it, how we teach it, how we organize it, and how children receive it are not. An explicit, guided, analytic process (which looks a lot like contemplation), in addition to the instructional process, would strengthen children's ability to live out and obey the texts that are taught.

That leads me to respond to the role of incentives and awards in the Instructional-Analytic Model in general and in AWANA in particular. I affirm the importance of Psalm 119:11, and, as Dr. Carlson states, God's Word can keep us from sin when we *treasure* it ("treasure" is one of the Hebrew meanings for the word that also is translated *hid*). But from my experience, which is supported by a plethora of research, when extrinsic incentives are involved, it is often the award that is treasured more than the task or content that is learned. One source that cites data from more than six hundred academic research projects is *Punished by Rewards* by Alfie Kohn.[39] Though not a Christian book, it deserves attention by all those who assume incentives bring intended results. Short-term results or compliance should not be equated with long-term life change. The literature on this

---

39. Alfie Kohn, *Punished by Rewards* (New York: Mariner Books, 1999).

topic is too vast to be discussed in this venue, but it behooves all of us who are involved in the formation of children to be Christ followers to investigate thoughtfully the implications noted by these researchers.

It may be helpful here to go back to the introduction to revisit David Kolb's model of experiential learning that Kolb sees as having four components: concrete experience, reflective observation, abstract conceptualization, and active experimentation. Concrete experience focuses on creativity and relationship through divergent mental processes, reflective observation on analysis of ideas through assimilating facts and concepts, abstract conceptualization on executing plans and strategies by converging ideas and theory, and active experimentation by motivating others and bringing about change through accommodation.

As Dr. Anthony notes, it is not possible to represent graphically complex concepts. Learning styles is one of those complex subjects because no person or ministry is purely one style but a blend of the four styles in differing degrees. As I see the Instructional-Analytic Model as described here, it's more focused on direct instruction than some other models but does not necessarily employ analysis. Yet from my observation this model views learners as assimilating content, hopefully converging or bringing the content together into a usable strategy or lifestyle change and also hopefully being able to accommodate this new knowledge into sustainable habits. It is not a pure model, as none of these is, according to Kolb's categories in his theory. Less explicit in the existing materials of this model is the divergent aspect of creativity in the context of relationship.

As the proponent of the Contemplative-Reflective Model, I see that model as focusing on the content (the Bible) in a diverging way within a relational, creative context. An instructional aspect is present through the biblical story, though the presentation mode looks quite different from what is demonstrated in AWANA. This assimilating aspect is present. After hearing the story, children are encouraged to diverge or create their response to the Bible story. This requires the cognitive activity of contemplation or prolonged attention. This prolonged response time also allows opportunity for convergence and accommodation to occur. I say this because, if I were presently a children's minister, I would use insights from Kolb's learning styles as well as biblical principles from Acts 2 to strengthen as much as possible every ministry I offer to children.

Care needs to be taken to help parents see that children do not need to be enrolled in a ministry that matches their learning style but to help parents wisely discern the ministries that meaningfully address various types of learning styles and forms of spiritual formation.

Response by Trisha Graves

Gregory Carlson's perspective on the Instructional-Analytic Model gives a thorough argument for Scripture being the central foundation of any ministry to children. Many Old and New Testament references are given in his presentation that reflect how a model for children's spiritual formation must be grounded and based on Scripture. Speaking for the Pragmatic-Participatory Model, we agree with the instructional-analytics believing strongly that a ministry to children must be based on "an application of the living word of God."

Those within the Pragmatic-Participatory Model also hold to the same belief that the central message of the Bible is "that humanity is alienated from a bold and righteous God because of sin and that this holy God has provided the only possible remedy for this alienation from himself and this enslavement to sin." Dr. Carlson states, "To think that character development can happen without the guidance of the Scriptures seems to be making secular the spiritual processes that cause a child or anyone to be formed in Christ." Basing a model of spiritual formation on anything but the foundation of Scriptures would be for me negating the purpose of a Christian ministry to children. Within the Pragmatic-Participatory Model all teaching is from God's Word and is the basis for any ministry to children. Comparing the Instructional-Analytical Model and the Pragmatic-Participatory Model, it is the *means* by which the material is taught that differs, not necessarily the *material* itself.

The instructional-analytic approach views Old Testament passages such as Exodus 12:26, 13:9, 19:6–7, and Deuteronomy 4:5 as proof that God's laws and commands are not only to be known by children but to be memorized. The literal interpretation of such passages regarding God's Word or commands gives the basis for a ministry where Scripture memorization is paramount to all other spiritual disciplines. Those that practice the Pragmatic-Participatory Model would agree that there is great value in children having God's Word memorized as Dr. Carlson references Psalm 119:11, "I have hidden your word in my heart that I might not sin against You." However from our viewpoint, more important than memorizing God's Word is that children might understand and comprehend the Word of God and know how his living and inerrant words are relevant to their lives so that they might better be able to obey his Word. We believe that the understanding of God's Word comes through experiencing it and through being able to see its value and worth as we learn to weave it into our lives. Dr. Carlson assumes that the only thing one can do is to "know" the Bible and be able to recite it back. The Scriptures speak of "hiding God's word in your heart" (Ps. 119:9), but how does one who is "fearfully and wonderfully made" (Ps. 139:14) attain a knowledge of Scripture? Is rote memorization the only method, or might memorable experiences based on God's Word or thought-provoking questions applying God's Word also be effective means for a child's spiritual formation? While it is clear that "Scripture remains the main focus" of Dr. Carlson's model, this particular essay doesn't seem to address how the "relevant application will follow."[40] Dr. Carlson speaks of the danger of the instructional model that "knowing is enough." Yet in this particular essay, little evidence is given that shows how "teaching for obedience" or change in heart is achieved, so one must surmise that Bible study and memorization are the sole methods used within this model.

In addition to both models realizing that the fundamental base for spiritual development must be the Bible, there are many other commonalities between the Pragmatic-Participatory Mod-

---

40. Larry Fowler, *Rock Solid Kids*, 42–43.

el and the Instructional-Analytic Model. We both agree in our belief that even young children have the capacity to understand God's holiness and recognize their own sinfulness. The focus given to the early childhood child is an important aspect of both models because of the philosophy and biblical beliefs that those ages are when foundational truths can be taught to help ready them for a faith in Christ. A strong belief within both models is that children need to be given opportunities to make decisions to receive Jesus Christ as their Savior. There also is commonality among both models that evangelism and outreach to children are important elements within any children's ministry paradigm. The Instructional-Analytic Model also holds to the value that the Old Testament teaches that "the family is to be the predominant mode of instruction to the child" and aptly addresses this value by providing activities and Scripture recitation that require parental participation and support. The cognitive abilities of the different ages seem to be addressed by providing separate curriculum for different age groupings and adjusting the awards structure to meet the developmental needs of children as well. Volunteer development is held in high regard for both models.

Both models also speak to the value of the relational element. In the description of the Instructional-Analytic Model, the modeling of Christian faith is based on the modeling of Scripture memorization that parents, ministry leaders, and the local church provide. There is little mention of how relationships within this model shepherd a child and help to meet the needs of individual children at varying points on the spiritual development spectrum. The focus on "guiding the child toward becoming like Jesus" is a worthy endeavor; however, there do not appear to be any program elements described here that speak to how else this might be achieved within this model.

In Deuteronomy 6, we are not only called to observe "the commands, decrees and laws the Lord your God directed" (v. 1) and "be careful to obey" (v. 3); we are also called to "love the LORD your God with all your heart and with all your soul and with all your strength. These commands . . . are to be upon your hearts. Impress them on your children. Talk about them when you sit at home and when you walk along the road, when you lie down and when you get up" (vv. 5–7). This speaks to our loving God with our whole beings and incorporating our knowledge and understanding of God throughout the many facets of our daily lives. It's the belief of the Pragmatic-Participatory Model that children must be guided and given opportunities to learn how to apply God's Word into their daily lives and the issues they are being faced with in their worlds. This passage doesn't merely speak of knowing God, but it speaks of a deeper understanding of God's Word that governs the way in which the Israelites were to live their lives. Dr. Carlson shares that AWANA "endeavors to help children understand God's message in concert with the drawing power of the Holy Spirit," yet further explanation needs to be given to show how this is achieved.

I agree fully with Dr. Carlson's assertion that "a key issue here is that we not compartmentalize a child's spiritual life away from all other aspects; that we see the Bible and our relationship with Christ as foundational rather than as a segment of our lives to be held with others." This statement gives value to helping children interpret and provoke thinking of how their spiritual lives are and can be incorporated into other segments of their lives. Given children's limited cognitive developmental abilities, children under the age of seven do not have the ability to apply logical thought to specific and concrete situations.[41] Children before this stage need help from adult leaders or need to be provided materials or experiences that might help them incorporate God's Word with other areas of their lives because it's a skill they can't yet do on their own.

It may be interesting to note that the church where I serve as children's pastor runs a successful weekday AWANA club program in addition to our weekend children's ministry. The Instructional-Analytic Model can complement the Pragmatic-Participatory Model and prove to be an extremely effective model for providing spiritual growth in children. At our church AWANA meets the needs of approximately 120 children based on a

---

41. Dennis Dirks, "Foundations of Human Development," in *Foundations of Ministry: An Introduction to Christian Education for a New Generation,* ed. Michael Anthony, (Grand Rapids, Mich.: Baker Books, 1992), 77.

weekend attendance average of 1250. From my vantage point our AWANA ministry is successful; it not only meets the needs of many families within our community, but it also attracts extremely committed and gifted volunteer leaders. However, I believe it is effective at our church because it works in conjunction with another model of ministry that occurs on the weekends. The weekend ministry helps to achieve understanding of God's Word, appeals to the broad personalities and learning styles of children while it also meets the needs for relevancy and life application for today's children.

While it is effective at helping children develop spiritually, the Instructional-Analytic Model seems to appeal to a certain type of child. Those that do well with structure are motivated by awards and enjoy the process of learning; they seem to be attracted to these types of programmatic methods. How are other learning styles engaged or encouraged to learn? While the games provide "maximum opportunity for children to get involved, no matter what their athletic ability," it does appear that game time would appeal to the kinesthetic learner. However, there is no mention of biblical application or the scriptural basis of these games although they do help to develop worthy attitudes of "teamwork," "sportsmanship," and "other character traits."

How are individual learning styles approached and taught within this ministry model? While this model holds a high regard for child evangelism and presenting the gospel to children so that they might accept Christ as their Savior, how are children who come from unchurched homes or have unbelieving parents reached? Are nonbelieving children or families drawn into the church through such ministries, or is it a model that is meant to focus on the child who comes more from a churched home? Is the Instructional-Analytic Model one that can be applied as a stand-alone ministry for a church which is looking for a weekend ministry format? Does it need to be? If this model can function as a stand-alone ministry by which spiritual formation occurs, how are other tenets of the faith accomplished such as worship, service, tithing, and baptisms? Acts 2:42–47 provides Luke's description of the vibrant early church. Worship, instruction, fellowship, and expression are all noted as a means of discipling early Christ followers.[42] While instruction is definitely achieved within this model, how are children taught to worship (Rom. 12:1–2), and how are children given opportunities to personally express their faith and respond to that which God is doing in their lives as young believers? It would be interesting to explore other programs or formalized Sunday school ministries that fall within this model. Spiritual formation doesn't always happen within the confines of an organized ministry program, and ministry models working in tandem with one another can help to bring about powerful transformation among children. I know many adults who as children were participants in AWANA, Child Evangelism Fellowship, and Pioneer Clubs; and because of their involvement in such ministries, they have a strong knowledge of Scripture and are still able to recite memory verses that were hidden in their hearts as a child.

Response by the KIDMO Team

Growing up in church, I participated in many Bible verse memory contests. The excitement of competition and the pursuit of prizes certainly got my attention. In fact, I am sure I read and reviewed more Scripture than I would have if left to do so solely motivated by my love for God and the value I saw in studying his Word. Let's be honest, how many of us, even now in ministry leadership roles, struggle with Scripture memorization when left to our own intrinsic motivations?

I remember vividly in the days leading up to the recitation deadline, reading and memorizing as many verses as I could. I set to the task with all the passion and enthusiasm one would have while memorizing information from a dictionary or phone book. In fact, it didn't really matter to me that I was memorizing the Word of God as opposed to any other book. My interest was not in the content or the Author but rather in the fame and fortune of walking away with the most valuable prize and the renown of the group, being proven as the best, the winner.

---

42. Robert Choun and Michael S. Lawson, *The Christian Educators Handbook of Children's Ministry* (Grand Rapids, Mich.: Baker Books, 1993), 24.

The final car ride to church was spent in frantic review, topping off my memorization storage tank with one last look at the most difficult verses. "I don't know what many of these words mean, but I am not going to let someone else say more of them in the correct order than I do." That was my prayer as I prepared my heart for morning worship. Numerous times my prayer was answered, and I went home triumphant. Everyone was happy. I was happy for having achieved my goal of victory and spoils. My teachers were happy because having recited so many verses, I validated all their hard work teaching me week after week.

More than a few decades have passed since those days, and I find myself serving in various ways to help children grow spiritually. I owe it all to the way my spirit was formed by engaging in the activities previously described, right? Well, not in the way you might think. I did not enjoy church all that much growing up. In that way, my childhood may have contributed to my choosing a career in children's ministry. I want to help children come to know Christ, grow in their relationship with him and others, and have them thoroughly look forward to their weekly church experiences. May God forgive us if, due to a poor presentation, we ever give children a negative view of him or his Word.

It is possible that I didn't really like going to church because my heart was more hardened than your average grade-school boy. It's also possible that my teachers were worse than your average church children's workers—that they were less prepared, less skilled, and simply did not care all that much. However, I don't think any of these were the case. My heart was no further from God than any average boy's. At a certain point in my life, I began loving and living for God, so God was able to reach me. Likewise, it was not the fault of my teachers. In fact, one of them in particular was instrumental years later in my spiritual development. He was the exception though, reaching me through his interest and personal interaction, not because of his classroom teaching.

My dislike had much more to do with the environment that was created. The children's environment was created by the model of ministry being used there, the Instructional-Analytic Model.

While much good has come to people as a result of ministries shaped by this model, more good could come to them if those same ministries adapted a different approach. I agree with much of what is written in the instructional-analytic chapter. A lot of people involved in ministry with children share some general common goals. However, many of the agreeable statements are general enough that people endorsing any of the models could have made them.

These statements and beliefs are also much more likely to be found in another of the models. For example, the author repeatedly espouses the idea that for effective training in ministry to happen, there must be a relational aspect to that training—that is, a relationship between the teacher and the student. I wholeheartedly support that idea. I would argue though, that in the Instructional-Analytic Model, if relationship does occur between children and their leaders that it happens almost by accident. The relationship comes simply as a result of prolonged exposure between the child and teacher, or it happens because the leader has actually deviated from the genuine practice of the model. No intentionality of relationship is built into this particular model of ministry. Certainly, an intentionality of dispensing information is present but through instruction, not modeled relationship.

Another key value of this model is its high regard for Scripture. I believe each model examined here has at its underlying core a belief that the Bible is the content upon which all ministries should be based. No one is questioning the importance or foundational aspects of the Bible in the role of children's spiritual formation. The key differences lie in the view of how best to teach the Bible to children and in which format they will best respond to the life-changing truths found in God's Word. It appears that because this model has more emphasis on Scripture memory, it implies it has a higher regard for Scripture in general. That is an erroneous assumption. In fact, the exact opposite argument could be made. One could say that because another model puts less emphasis on the quantity of verses learned, it allows for further thought on those select verses memorized, e.g., quality versus quantity. This further reflection could lead to more effective discussion with parents, church leaders, and friends. Quality discussion will then allow for targeted teaching on specific life application issues, which in turn leads to life change and spiritual growth.

Is it better to have children spend more time learning fewer verses but having those verses truly take root in their hearts and minds or to see how many verses they can recite and check off in a booklet? Kids participating in last-minute drive-to-church reviews, saying the words of some verses they do not understand, doesn't really give the Bible its proper place of importance. The children may receive a prize, gold star, or other affirmation, but then a few weeks later they have forgotten what the verse says. Is that really hiding God's Word in their hearts?

Scripture memorization is extremely important. But let's ask ourselves what it truly means to memorize the Bible. In other words, should it be the *means* or the *end*? The author of this chapter has stated that rote memory is not the goal of this model, but it seems that by remaining true to the instructional-analytic method, the outcome of rote memory is a high probability. In this model the act of memorizing Scripture is one of the most important aspects of spiritual formation. I agree that the Bible is of irreplaceable value in the development of one's faith. However, it is possible, and highly likely in this model of ministry, to memorize verses but see them render little if any change or growth in the life of the learner. Wasn't that much of the reason Jesus had such disdain for the scribes and Pharisees? They knew the Word of God but didn't practice it. Obviously, that is not the goal of any children's worker. However, when examining instructional-analytic practices, one could question if there is another result more widely achieved.

Isaiah 55:11 tells us that the Word of God does not return empty but accomplishes all God desires. That verse can be referenced as an explanation of the good that has come through churches based on this model. On the other hand, Matthew 13:19 states that if God's Word is not understood, it has no chance to take root because Satan comes and snatches it away. A danger in this model is that so much emphasis is placed on memorizing so many verses so quickly that understanding is severely undervalued. Emphasis is placed solely on the knowledge acquisition element of the cognitive domain while sacrificing the more important elements of synthesis and analysis.

Another key element of the Instructional-Analytic Model is a reward system. Exactly when are the children rewarded? Are they rewarded after evidence of growth? Are they rewarded after testimonies by parents, schoolteachers, or friends about the change they have seen in the life of the child? Are they rewarded for a lifestyle displaying true understanding and application of the Bible? No. They are rewarded simply for having said what is in the Bible. The true goal of using Scripture is to point kids toward the God who created them. The Bible exists to reveal God to us so we can worship him with our daily living. In 2 Timothy 3:16, Scripture refers to itself as "useful." Scripture is a tool. It's only useful after it's learned and lived out. Memorizing it with no further action should never be the goal. This model makes it easy to put the emphasis on the Scripture and stop short of attaining the outcomes for which Scripture was given in the first place.

If we all agree that our goal is to share with children what the Bible says so they can come to know Christ and live their lives according to his will for them, then I think we should also agree that if there are methods that can be used to give us an advantage in that process, such methods are worth serious consideration. Given the state of children's culture today, especially the way they spend their time consuming various forms of entertainment media, why would we choose to shape their time at church to look like a child's culture from decades ago?

Families have more options available to them when considering how to spend their time than at any other point in history. It is a considerable challenge just to get someone to walk through the doors of a church. On any given day they can choose from a myriad of activities to engage in around their communities, not to mention how many options are available to them without even leaving their home. Many of these options exist largely because of how often people choose to use media. Once we are able to overcome that challenge and get families to attend church, why would we choose to put ourselves at a disadvantage in reaching and teaching children by voluntarily ignoring some of the most powerful communication tools available to us today?

Ultimately, our task is to help kids enter into a growing relationship with Jesus. The church should not shun cultural advancements. In fact, the church should be at the forefront of cultural innovation. We are to be counter-cultural in areas where the culture is detrimental to a child's pursuit of God. Media is certainly not one of those areas. When the culture provides tools for us to use that can make us more effective in our task, we must use them and use them well. Some might argue that media in its various forms and the amount of time kids spend engaging in it is not good for them and contributes negatively to their development. However, media like any other form of communication is merely a tool. Tools inherently are neither positive nor negative. It is the use of the tools that makes the difference. What media communicates and how it's used is what determines its value. When used to communicate biblical content in a way that children respond to and enjoy, media engagement is clearly an option to be considered seriously.

CHAPTER 3

Pragmatic-Participatory Model

TRISHA GRAVES

Within the field of Christian spirituality, there are different ways by which people come to experience God and learn about him. The human capacity to be in relationship with God is not limited solely to adults. Mel Lawrenz proposes an excellent definition of Christian spirituality when he states, "Spiritual formation is the progressive patterning of a person's inner and outer life according to the image of Christ through intentional means of spiritual growth."[1] Children have the capacity to come to and grow in faith.[2] If one is to help a child grow more and more like Christ, how is this best achieved? Just like adults, children form a view of God by either experience or knowledge. The Pragmatic-Participatory Model is a ministry model that is dependent on a child's thought process that is formed through active participatory learning. This model is known for engaging the children in learning while using a variety of different methods to teach them with practical and relevant application.

---

1. Mel Lawrenz, *The Dynamics of Spiritual Formation* (Grand Rapids, Mich.: Baker Books, 2000), 15.
2. Ibid.

Ministry models that fit within this model feature a multifaceted approach that has a propensity toward choreographed singing, dramatic presentations of Bible stories, application-oriented games and discussions. Curriculum designed within this model helps to engage children's minds, encourage them to think and apply the practical and biblical concepts being taught. Often this type of programming is presented using some type of larger group creative program and then a smaller group setting that provides for reinforcement of learning and application. Children are encouraged to apply the Bible to their own lives through relevant lessons that make sense in their real worlds. The variety of methods used to teach and reinforce the Bible appeal to the broad learning styles of children.

The setting for this model of children's spiritual formation often includes both large-group gatherings and small-group discussions to meet the individual learning styles and needs of children. Using a mix of innovative and creative methods such as video, references to pop culture, games, and appealing worship music are ways to capture the child's attention and make the Bible come to life and become relevant to children of today's culture. There is a focus on the entire child's spiritual development and a strategic effort to reach children through a variety of activities and ministries within the realm of children's ministry.

The goals of this model are for children to discover and learn who God is, make a personal decision to accept him as their Lord and Savior, and continue to grow and walk by the Holy Spirit as they mature in their faith. Other values of this model are for children to experience God's love through committed and passionate volunteers and staff and, because of their fun experiences, to desire to invite their friends to church.

Old Testament Teachings on Children's Spiritual Formation

From the perspective of those churches that practice the Pragmatic-Participatory Model, the Old Testament contains several key passages that describe the significance of the family to God's people in the spiritual development of their children. Indeed, the Lord's first commandment to Adam and Eve in Genesis was to "be fruitful and increase in number; fill the earth and subdue it" (Gen. 1:28). God gave a nearly identical command to Noah after the flood (Gen. 9:1). Although Abram (later Abraham) and his wife had no success conceiving children, God made a covenant with him that his offspring would be as numerous as the stars (Gen. 15:5). The directive to use the family structure to populate the Earth reflects God's desire that children would be an important part of his plan for the world.

Positive references to having children abound throughout the Old Testament. One psalmist wrote that "sons are a heritage from the Lord, children are a reward from Him" (Ps. 127:3). Children are continually referred to as a reward (Gen. 30:18) or a "precious gift" (30:20) and are spoken of as evidence of being remembered by God (Gen. 30:22; 1 Sam. 1:11, 19) and being given "good fortune" (Gen. 30:11).[3] To be "fruitful" with children was to be a recipient of God's blessing (Gen. 17:16; 28:3; 49:25; Exod. 23:25–26; Deut. 7:13–14; 28:11; 30:9; Job 5:25; Pss. 127:3–5; 128:3–4).[4] It is evident through the stories of many families found in the Old Testament, particularly those who struggled to conceive, that children have immeasurable value to them and to God. For instance, Hannah struggled to have children and often wept "in bitterness of soul" (1 Sam. 1:10). She described herself to Eli, the priest, "deeply troubled" and in "great anguish." Because of her prayers, God remembered her, and she conceived Samuel.

Because of the value that God has placed on children, he clearly desires that they be raised with a full knowledge of him. In Deuteronomy 4:9–10, Moses relays one of God's directives from his encounter at Horeb when he received the Ten Commandments:

> Only be careful, and watch yourselves closely that you do not forget the things your eyes have seen or let them slip from your heart as long as you live. Teach them to your children and to their children after them. Remember the day

---

3. Roy B. Zuck, *Precious in His Sight: Childhood and Children in the Bible* (Grand Rapids, Mich.: Baker Books, 1996), 49.
4. Ibid.

you stood before the LORD your God at Horeb, when he said to me, "Assemble the people before me to hear my words so that they may learn to revere me as long as they live in their land and may teach them to their children."

God desired that his people not only remember his commandments but also teach them to their children and their children's children. Moses understood the importance of God's people having a full knowledge of God and a willingness to place their trust in him. He had experienced the negative consequences of having to wander in the wilderness because the people of God had continually rebelled against God's commandments and failed to trust him (Deut. 1:26–27, 32).

The Old Testament also presents several clear, straightforward principles for a family to consider in their efforts to raise godly children:[5]

- Parents should provide the primary nurturing and spiritual training for their children (Deut. 1:31; 6:4–9; 11:18–21; 21:18–19; Ps. 78:5–8).

- Parents must start the spiritual training of children when they are young and inexperienced (2 Chron. 13:7; Ps. 34:11; Isa. 7:15).

- Spiritual development in children is a continuous lifelong process (Deut. 6:7; 11:19; Prov. 22:6).

- Parents must introduce appropriate discipline into children's lives (Prov. 3:11–12; 13:1, 24; 19:18; 23:12–14; 29:15–17, 21).

- Parents are to introduce their children to appropriate behavior and traditions of the church as modeled by the church's patriarchs (Exod. 12:24–27; Num. 18:11; Deut. 15:20; 16:11).

- Spiritual transformation of children requires parents to pray and rely on God's power (Gen. 17:18; Judg. 13:8;

---

5. George Barna, *Transforming Children into Spiritual Champions* (Ventura, Calif.: Regal Books, 2003), 82–83.

1 Sam. 1:10–16; 2 Sam. 12:16; 1 Chron. 29:19; Job 1:5; Lam. 2:19).

- The basis for spiritual development is found in God's Word (Prov. 30:5; Pss. 19:7; 119:11, 89, 104).

- Responding to God in worship is one of the believer's most significant responsibilities (Gen. 8:20; 31:54; Deut. 16:11; 29:18; 1 Sam. 1:19).

- Parents can work in tandem with reliable spiritual partners to provide spiritual training for their children (1 Sam. 1:27–28; 3:1–10).

First and foremost, these passages express the importance of the parents' central role and responsibility for teaching the Word of God to children so that God's love could be passed from generation to generation of believers. Second, because of the magnitude of this task, God knew that parents would never be able to complete this assignment alone. Therefore, the church would have an important role to play in assisting parents in meeting their responsibility.

Not only can we glean the importance of nurturing the spiritual development of children from the Old Testament, but we can identify some of the specific methods that God has provided for us to use. The Pragmatic-Participatory Model in its various forms attempts to incorporate many of these specific methods, including the reading of God's Word, practical application, worshipping, praying, and modeling biblical values through individual leaders outside the family.

Children's ministries typically have approximately one to one and one-half hours a week (maybe more depending on the use of a midweek program) where they are in direct contact with children. This model attempts to use many of the concepts presented in the Old Testament to maximize this time and obtain the greatest possible spiritual impact. Naturally the structure of the program employed by each church using this model varies depending on that particular church's doctrines, values, and goals.

However, the overarching goal is for each children's ministry to bring each child to personal relationship with Jesus Christ.[6]

Although God conveys many elements that successfully contribute to the spiritual development of children throughout the Old Testament, there are no specific examples of God using children's ministry as it is known in any of its modern forms. Yet most churches using the Pragmatic-Participatory Model have developed the content of their programs based on many of these concepts from the Old Testament. As discussed below, several passages from the Old Testament contain the basic elements from which churches in the Pragmatic-Participatory Model have found support for their programmatic structure.

Teaching from Scripture

The Old Testament clearly identifies the Word of God as the primary source for spiritual truth. Scripture is perfect (Ps. 19:7); it is flawless (2 Sam. 22:31; Prov. 30:5); it can keep us pure and prevent us from sinning (Ps. 119:9–11); and it is eternal and stands firm in the heavens (Ps. 119:89). As the psalmist noted, "Your word is a lamp to my feet and a light to my path" (Ps. 119:105). As the foundation for spiritual truth, the Word of God takes the central role in the spiritual development of children.

The book of Nehemiah relays the story of the return of the Israelites from exile to Palestine. Because the temple had been destroyed and the Israelites had been taken captive and spread across the Middle East, they had not been able to observe many rituals and ceremonies that God had commanded them to perform. Through the leadership of Nehemiah, the Israelites were organized and rebuilt the walls around the city of Jerusalem. When the work had been completed and the people settled, the Israelites gathered to hear the high priest, Ezra, read from the book of the Law of Moses, which had not been done since before their exile: "Ezra the priest brought the Law before the assembly, which was made up of men and women and all who were able to understand. He read it aloud from daybreak till noon as he faced the square before the Water Gate in the presence of men, women,

---

6. Robert J. Choun and Michael S. Lawson, *The Christian Educator's Handbook on Children's Ministry* (Grand Rapids, Mich.: Baker Books, 1982), 41, 43.

and others who could understand. And all the people listened intently to the Book of the Law" (Neh. 8:2–3).

When Ezra read the Book of the Law to the people of Israel, he read it not only to adult men and women but to "all who were able to understand." The implication is that "all who were able to understand" includes those adolescents and children who possessed the mental capacity to understand the content of the Scripture being presented to them.

This passage reveals one of the most basic methods to assist in the spiritual formation of children—namely, reading directly from Scripture. Churches using the Pragmatic-Participatory Model vary in the degree to which they have children read or read to children directly from Scripture. This will depend on the goals and values that these ministries set for their programs.

When applying the lessons from these passages to the context of today's ministry to children, many programs within the Pragmatic-Participatory Model consider the ability of children not only to hear the Scripture being read to them but also understand and respond to it. Great care is taken to ensure that the Scripture being used for the lesson is something that is within the children's capacity to understand. Sometimes passages are too complicated for young children to comprehend, and they are saved to teach for an older group of children. On the other end of the spectrum, many passages and stories can easily be understood by children as young as two years old.

Practical Application of God's Word

As noted above, churches that employ the Pragmatic-Participatory Model seek to present Scripture in a way that can be understood by the children within the program. One way to accomplish this goal is to take God's truth and apply it in a way that is both culturally relevant and age appropriate.

As noted above from Deuteronomy, God desires his people to teach his Word to each generation. He later expands on this directive, describing how parents and others should teach children about God's truth:

> Love the LORD your God with all your heart and with all your soul and with all your strength. These commandments I give you today are to be upon your hearts. Impress them upon your children. Talk about them when you sit at home and when you walk along the road, when you lie down and when you get up. Tie them as symbols on your hands and bind them on your foreheads. Write them on the doorframes of your houses and on your gates (Deut. 6:5–9; see also Deut. 11:18–21; 32:45–47).

God challenges parents to be engaged in communicating God's truth both formally and informally and both in conversation and visually.[7] Many spiritual lessons are taught through interaction between parents and their children outside the context of a formal church or classroom setting. As suggested by Martha Aycock: "Most educators and theologians agree that the most effective way for children to begin to know and understand the truths recorded in the Bible is to live with adults whose lives express these truths. When they do, children catch the spirit of Christ long before they can read or understand it."[8]

Through the ongoing interaction between adults and children and the personal relationships that develop between them children see God's Word applied to their lives in real time at their level. The Pragmatic-Participatory Model seeks to create these opportunities for interaction so that children not only hear Scripture but also see it applied through the volunteers and staff who serve in the ministry. This application can be found in the use of activity stations prior to the service or interaction in small groups during discussions, role playing, or application-oriented games.

Worship

One of the most important responsibilities of parents in the Old Testament was to lead their children to love and worship the Lord.[9] Worship in the Old Testament took many forms. Noah,

7. Zuck, *Precious in His Sight,* 126.
8. Martha B. Aycock, ed., *Understand* (Richmond, Va.: John Knox, 1972), 115, referenced by Robert E. Clark, Joanne Brubaker, and Roy B. Zuck, *Childhood Education in the Church* (Chicago, Ill.: Moody Press, 1986), 381–82.
9. Zuck, *Precious in His Sight,* 114.

Jacob, and Job, acting as the priests for their families, each made burnt offerings to the Lord as an example to their children (Gen. 8:20; 31:54; Job 1:5). Noah and Isaac also built altars as visual reminders to their families of God's faithfulness (Gen. 8:20; 26:25). Joshua and the Israelites built memorials from stones on the west side of the Jordan River so that future generations would remember God's miraculous work in dividing the river (Josh. 4:1–7). Israelite families also observed Sabbath and other holy days, including Passover, the Feast of Unleavened Bread, Firstfruits, Pentecost, the Day of Trumpets, the Day of Atonement, and the seven-day Tabernacles.[10]

In particular, in Exodus 12:26–27, we are told that one of the purposes of Passover is to elicit questions from children about the meaning of the rituals. This inquiry would then provide parents an opportunity to educate the children about the miracles performed by God in order to free the Israelites and then give them an opportunity to respond in worship. An opportunity to respond in worship also occurred in response to the reading of the Book of Law when the Israelites returned from exile (Neh. 8:6). The Pragmatic-Participatory Model encourages children to engage in worship in response to God's goodness and holiness.

Prayer

The Old Testament contains many examples of powerful prayers that were answered by God. There are examples of parents who specifically prayed for their children. Job regularly offered burnt offerings for each of his ten children in case any of them had sinned in their hearts (Job 1:5). Abraham prayed for Ishmael (Gen. 17:18), and Hannah prayed that God would give her a son (1 Sam. 1:11, 27). David prayed publicly for his son, Solomon, to have a "wholehearted devotion to keep your commands, requirements and decrees" (1 Chron. 29:19).

Prayer for the children in our ministries should not only be offered up by volunteers and staff, but prayer must be modeled so that children will observe and understand its importance as a way to communicate with God. As stated by Eleanor Hance:

---

10. Ibid., 114.

"It is often said of children's learning that as much occurs when 'caught' unconsciously, or when 'sought' through the sense of need, as occurs when 'taught' directly. And this is certainly true of prayer. Fortunate is the child who from his earliest years hears sincere prayer in understandable words about meaningful concerns. Prayer is 'caught.'"[11]

By both relaying these stories of prayer from Scripture and modeling how prayer works, children will sense its importance from an early age.

New Testament Teachings on Children's Spiritual Formation

Age of Accountability

Focusing on the spiritual formation of children is vital. Children have the potential to become followers of Christ, and the church plays a significant role in introducing children to Jesus and then helping them grow more and more like him. In Acts 2:38, as Peter is witnessing to those who are not following God, he declares how they need to repent from their sin and call upon God to be saved. As Peter reminds them of the gift of forgiveness of sins and the gift of the Holy Spirit, he specifically includes believers of all ages. Peter states, "The promise is for you and your children and for all who are far off—for all whom the Lord our God will call" (Acts 2:39). Peter doesn't exclude children. In fact, he specifically mentions them in reference to whom the promise has been given. The fact that believers of all ages, including children, are able to receive the Holy Spirit, gives credence to the fact that children are capable of repenting and accepting forgiveness of sin, thereby fully experiencing Christ's saving power. God's Word can transform the lives of even the littlest ones, and nothing is more exciting than to see a child trust in Christ for the first time.

So at what age or period of life is one aware enough of God to respond to him? The Bible itself does not point to a specific age

11. Clark, Brubaker, and Zuck, *Childhood Education in the Church*, 432.

at which children are capable of conversion. Though there are many different viewpoints, the theological distinction of when the age of accountability occurs is important because it will determine the scope and purpose of a ministry to children.

The Christian gospel is based on John 3:16, "For God so loved the world that he gave his one and only Son, that whoever believes in him shall not perish but have eternal life." Most evangelicals believe Christian conversion includes belief in the gospel of Jesus Christ, recognition and repentance of one's sinfulness, and willful trust in Jesus Christ as Lord and Savior of one's life.[12] The common belief of many who practice the Pragmatic-Participatory Model is that all people, regardless of age, are sinful by nature and guilty before God. Children, because of their limited understanding, are not held accountable for this original sin until they reach an "age of discretion" or "age of accountability."[13]

Paul wrote in Ephesians 2:3 that we are "children of wrath" (NASB) and that we are all corrupt and sinful in God's eyes. While some churches and denominations believe that infants who die are condemned to hell unless they are baptized, many churches that use the Pragmatic-Participatory Model would believe that Scriptures teach the original sin of Adam is imputed to all mankind, thereby implying that an infant child is born into sin and will ultimately be accountable for that sin. In addition, infants and young children are covered by God's grace and atoning work on the cross until they reach the level of awareness and understanding when they are confronted with the decision either to accept or to reject the gospel message.

These conclusions are drawn by the New Testament passages that speak to the high value Jesus himself placed on children (Matt. 19:13; Mark 9:36; Luke 18:15). "The reference in Matthew 18:10 to angels guarding children clearly refers to God's special place for children in the kingdom."[14] Jesus himself taught that

---

12. Kevin Lawson, Ed.D., *Childhood Conversion in the Evangelical Church* (Lanham, Md.: Rowman and Littlefield, 2004).

13. Klaus Issler, "Biblical Perspectives on Developmental Grace for Nurturing Children's Spirituality," in Donald Ratcliff, ed., *Children's Spirituality: Christian Perspectives, Research and Applications* (Eugene, Oreg.: Cascade Books, 2004), 54–57.

14. Edward L. Hayes, "Evangelism of Children," in *Childhood Education in the Church*, ed. Robert E. Clark, Joanne Brubaker, and Roy B. Zuck (Chicago: Moody Press, 1986), 402.

to receive a child was to receive himself (Matt. 18:5; Mark 9:26; Luke 9:48). Jesus also gives stern warnings to anyone who leads children astray (Matt. 18:6–14; Mark 9:42; Luke 1:2). Given the strong value that Jesus holds for children, one must conclude that infants and young children are not to be held accountable for their original sin until they are mentally capable of making a decision of faith in Jesus Christ.

There will be a time when a child will eventually grow and mature, and there will be a time when a child is capable of believing in Christ. As Paul stated in Romans 14:12, "So then, each of us will give an account of himself to God," which would support the belief that even children must come to an understanding and belief of who Jesus is and what he did on the cross. Even among churches that operate within this model, the view on age of accountability varies.

Many believe that infants, although they have the inherent potential for sinning, still have a protected relationship with God. Furthermore, as Christ has come to seek and save that which is lost (Luke 19:10), it's within his power and responsibility to save them. At what point this relationship is broken and a child would be then held accountable for personal sin is not detailed in Scripture. A child's individual accountability begins when the child is old enough to sin consciously and deliberately.[15] The accountability also comes at the time when a child "is capable of understanding that Christ died for him and that he can be saved by placing his trust in Christ."[16]

Until children are capable of making a conscious and understandable decision to accept Christ, we must assume they are not saved. Given that there are no clear delineations within Scripture that point to an age of accountability, a ministry and its volunteers must commit to be alert to times in children's lives when the Holy Spirit is prompting and drawing them closer into a relationship with the Savior.

---

15. Ibid., 405. "Anyone, then who knows the good he ought to do and doesn't do it, sins" (James 4:17).

16. Zuck, *Precious in His Sight,* 240.

Evangelism of Children

Several studies have shown that childhood is a key time for conversion. The recent research by George Barna indicates that the probability of someone embracing Jesus as his or her Savior was 32 percent for those between the ages of five and twelve; 4 percent for those in the thirteen to eighteen age range; and 6 percent for people nineteen or older.[17] These statistics point to the important role of childhood evangelism in helping children to hear the gospel message. The likelihood of someone accepting Christ after the age of nineteen is slim and therefore gives much credence to children's evangelism.[18]

A century ago Starbuck wrote, "One may say that if conversion has not occurred before [age] 20, the chances are small that it will ever be experienced."[19] Although the times have changed drastically since Starbuck wrote that statement, childhood still remains the key time when individuals make decisions to become Christ followers. A ministry to children can have profound implications.

Given that a child's religious beliefs and worldview are basically formed before a child reaches the age of thirteen,[20] we have a compelling reason to share the good news of Jesus Christ with children. Many children's ministries realize the harvest is plentiful (Matt. 9:37; Luke 10:2) in regards to potential Christ followers among children; and, therefore, they will plan specific opportunities within the curriculum for children to hear the gospel message. Children, because of their nature to trust and believe, are at a prime time to understand and respond in faith. Yet it is essential that when conversion does occur there needs to be a conscious "turning from sin and a turning toward God" (Acts 9:35; 11:34–35; 26:20).[21]

Churches that practice the Pragmatic-Participation Model provide various times throughout the year for elementary-aged

---

17. Barna, *Transforming Children into Spiritual Champions*, 34.

18. Ibid., 34.

19. Edwin Diller Starbuck, *The Psychology of Religion* (New York: Charles Scribner's Sons, 1899), 28, as referenced by Zuck, *Precious in His Sight*, 19.

20. George Barna, "Foreward by George Barna," in Sue Miller with David Staal, *Making Your Children's Ministry the Best Hour of Every Kid's Week* (Grand Rapids, Mich.: Zondervan, 2004), 11.

21. Hayes, Clark, Brubaker, Zuck, *Childhood Education in the Church*, 402.

children to hear the gospel message presented clearly and respond in faith after being prompted by the Holy Spirit. Since the goal of each lesson is to teach children important biblical truths and help them become more like Jesus, the gospel message is not necessarily given at every weekly lesson. There is a balance in these ministries between reaching and preaching in order to evangelize the lost and grow up maturing child believers.

How convictions regarding childhood evangelism impact the way ministers apply their theology may vary a great deal in different denominations. Yet most agree that the gospel message should be presented in a way that is clear and understandable for children. When done correctly, these gospel messages are presented in a way that children feel free to respond to the Holy Spirit's prompting without feeling pressured by adults or other children.

In Willow Creek's Promiseland curriculum, the gospel messages are planned strategically throughout the year according to elementary age groupings. Due to developing cognitive abilities, the kindergarten/first graders hear the gospel presented in the spring of each year. The philosophy applied here is that younger kindergarten and first-grade children still need time to develop a deeper understanding of who God is before they are able to respond in faith. In the other ages the gospel is presented three times during the school year.

In addition to presenting the gospel message on weekends, children may be given opportunities to hear the gospel and respond at other key special events where evangelism of unchurched children is being emphasized. These opportunities may include events such as Vacation Bible School, camps, or other special events geared toward reaching children who do not yet know Jesus.

In the children's ministry at Mariners Church in Irvine, California, the gospel is presented at specific times of the year during the weekend children's ministry program. The gospel message is also presented to children during Mariners' Vacation Bible School, where approximately one quarter of the fifteen hundred children who attend are from unchurched homes. The gospel message is presented in a group setting where the children hear a story that explains who Jesus is and the significance of what he did for us on the cross. Children are then given an explanation of what it means to have a personal relationship with Jesus and an opportunity to ask him to be their "Forever Friend."

The groups of children are given a time of reflection and a time to respond in prayer quietly while a leader leads the group, specifically those who want to commit their lives to Christ. Later all children are asked to fill out a commitment card where they check off a box indicating whether they accepted Christ for the first time, had already made a decision prior, or want to think more about it. While it is always exciting to note the number of children who make first-time decisions for Christ, what is equally interesting is to see the number of children who mark the box that they want to think more about their decision. This illustrates an interesting component of conscious decision-making on the part of the children. To make the conscious choice to think more about accepting Jesus as their forever Friend or to check the box that one had already made a decision for Christ previously goes to support that children are cognizant of the decisions they are making and not merely giving in to any pressure they may feel.

Many churches who practice this model of ministry believe that presenting the gospel message is paramount to their ministry, and the number of children who make decisions for Christ is one of several measuring tools for evaluating the effectiveness of their curriculum and indeed the children's ministry program overall. The strong belief of many of these churches is that children have the capacity to come to Christ for salvation. There are no age constraints. As Jesus himself said, "Your Father in heaven is not willing that any of these little ones should be lost" (Matt. 18:14). Presenting the gospel and allowing children to respond to the prompting of the Holy Spirit is one of the most significant roles a children's ministry may have in impacting the future of Christ followers.

Baptism

For many who follow the Pragmatic-Participatory Model, childhood conversion is a key element in their children's ministry. Within these churches all would agree that one of the first significant events within a believer's spiritual walk with Christ is obeying his command of being baptized. Some churches require baptism for an individual to be a member of their congregation. For others baptism is a powerful testimony of a life transformed and provides an outward expression of an inner belief in Christ. As we learn in Matthew 28:19, we are commanded by Christ to be baptized as believers. Just as the early church practiced baptisms (Acts 2:38, 41), we as Christ followers within the context of our church body are to exercise the same rite. Baptism also acts as a central symbol of the Christian faith (Rom. 6) in that it identifies us as Christ followers (Acts 2:38; 8:16) and identifies believers with the church (1 Cor. 12:12–13; Rom. 12:4–5).

When it comes to childhood baptism, children too can be in line with the early church practice of being baptized following a decision for Christ. Children also are identified as important parts of the body of Christ as they celebrate this significant obedient step following their declaration of faith in Jesus Christ. While within this model there is an agreement as to the purpose and meaning of baptism, the age at which children are able to be baptized is not consistently agreed upon among these churches.

The common belief among most evangelical churches is that baptism is a public demonstration of obedience to God after one has accepted Christ as Savior. In the early church only believers who had placed their faith in Christ were baptized as a public testimony of their faith and identification with him (Acts 2:38; Rom. 6:3–4). The act of baptism itself does not save a person, so therefore a personal decision to follow Christ must precede the act of baptism (Acts 8:35–38).

For many of these churches, infants are not baptized as they are not yet capable of understanding or making a conscious decision to place their trust in Jesus. Instead, many of these churches provide the opportunity for parents to dedicate infants in a public church ceremony where the parents vow to teach and raise the child in a way that they might be able to understand and accept Christ as their Savior at an early age.

Although many of these churches believe that baptism is an important first step in a person's spiritual conversion and would agree upon its meaning, the viewpoints on the proper age for baptism vary greatly. For some churches, children of any age are able to make the decision to be baptized following a decision to accept Christ. For other churches there are some age limits set as to when a child's baptism can occur. The age range of churches which practice this model of ministry appears to be anywhere from six to twelve as to when a church may allow a child to be baptized. Willow Creek Community Church's stance on baptism is stated on their Web site:

> Because the symbolism of Baptism requires a more adult level of cognitive and developmental readiness, the Elders require that children be at least 12 years old to be baptized. Proverbs 20:25 issues a significant caution against the danger of making a vow before adequate knowledge, forethought and reflection have been given. In an effort to prevent young people from making a premature commitment that they may not fully understand, this minimum age has been established.[22]

Most churches that practice this model of ministry implement their age requirements because of the developmental learning abilities of a child. Even if a child may have made a decision for Christ at a young age of three or four, more often than not, children are encouraged to delay baptism until an age that they will be able to understand more of the symbolism and significance of the event which would also help them to recall the occasion as an adult.

The Scriptures do show that those who were baptized usually did so immediately following their conversion (Acts 2:41; Acts 8:35–38). Yet in most churches, baptizing children is usually done after some time has passed beyond the child's decision to become a Christ follower. Most churches offer a class to children who are interested in being baptized and require the child to be able to profess their testimony to a pastor or someone in

22. Willow Creek Church 2005, Willow Creek's Statement on Baptism. Retrieved September 1, 2005 from http://www.willowcreek.org/Baptism/WCStatement.asp.

leadership to ensure children have an understanding of the basis for their belief and baptism. During the baptism classes, children are encouraged to study what the Bible says about being baptized and be able to articulate what it means to be a sinner and trust in Jesus as their Savior. It is stressed to children that becoming a believer and choosing to be baptized is an individual decision and not something to feel pressured into by a loving parent, Sunday school teacher, or friend.

One of the most rewarding aspects of my job as a children's pastor is to hear children clearly articulate their love and faith in Jesus Christ and be able to point to a specific moment or date in time when they prayed to receive Christ as their Savior. There have even been times when parents who are not following Christ give permission for their child to be baptized. They cannot deny the fruit that they have seen in their child's life after a child has made a decision to accept Christ as their "forever Friend" at an event such as Vacation Bible School or other outreach event.

It is the desire of many of the children's ministries who operate under the Pragmatic-Participatory Model to fulfill the Great Commission within their own communities and to see children profess their faith and show their obedience in being baptized.

Service

Another strong belief within this model is that according to Scripture all believers are given gifts of service (1 Cor. 12:1–11). Gifts are given to believers, by God, in order to advance Christianity and to edify the church. Since children are capable of being Christ followers, they are members of the body of Christ and, therefore, are capable of possessing spiritual gifts. All followers of Christ, including children, are capable of serving and play a role in his kingdom. We see a perfect example of a child being used by Jesus in John 6:9, when a little boy offers his food to Jesus to feed the crowd. Jesus, the one who has dominion over the entire universe, could have used any adult man or woman to solve this problem. Yet Jesus used a young boy to feed the multitudes and to demonstrate his power and the value he placed on the potential of children.[23] In the Pragmatic-Participatory Model, children are often seen as playing an integral part of the ministry implementation.

At churches where the Pragmatic-Participatory Model is used, it is not uncommon to see children serving within the local church or outside community group helping those in need. Older elementary children are given opportunities to help lead worship, act in dramatic presentations of the Bible story, assist in puppet ministry, or even be active participants on short-term mission projects. Many times at such a young age, children are unable to recognize what spiritual gifts or talents they possess; however, serving within the context of the church or even the children's ministry allows children to explore a variety of gifts and to watch those gifts and talents be modeled by passionate volunteers and staff. In this particular model of ministry, children are allowed or given opportunities to serve fellow children or to be involved in the ministry to children.

Worship

The Old Testament gives many references to worship and the importance of personal and public worship as a means to show honor and respect to God. In the New Testament we are reminded of our role as believers to appreciate all that God has done for us and to worship him for his own glory (Eph. 2:4–10). As for those in the early church, worship was an integral part of their life as well as their faith community. In the first two chapters of Ephesians, Paul reminds us of the power of corporate worship and the affirmation of our hope. This emphasis on worship helps us to remember that even in the early church the gathering of the church body was not just simply to hear a message but also to worship corporately.[24] Paul's admonition in Colossians 3:16 provides a basis from which churches can structure a church service: "Let the word of Christ dwell in you richly as you teach and admonish one another with all wisdom, and as you sing

---

23. Miller and Staal, *Making Your Children's Ministry the Best Hour of Every Kid's Week*, 40.

24. Lawrence O. Richards, *The Teacher's Commentary* (Wheaton, Ill.: Victor Books, 1987), 916–17.

psalms, hymns and spiritual songs with gratitude in your hearts to God."

Not only did Paul direct the early church to teach and dwell upon the Word of God, but he gave them instructions to worship God in song with gratitude in their hearts. To apply Paul's teaching within children's spiritual formation, we see that in addition to teaching and encouragement, worship must be a vital part of becoming a fully devoted follower of Christ. If worship is not included in children's spiritual formation, they miss out on a unique opportunity to shift their hearts and minds away from themselves and to focus on the one true God.

Some may contend that children should participate in corporate worship services with adults. While this may meet a church's goal for having intergenerational worship, often it can interfere with children freely participating in worship and fully understanding the worship component. In Ephesians 5:19–20, Paul tells the church in Ephesus: "Speak to one another with psalms, hymns and spiritual songs. Sing and make music in your heart to the Lord, always giving thanks to God the Father for everything, in the name of our Lord Jesus Christ."

Worshipping through song is a way to communicate spiritual truths of who God is and what he has done in a child's life. Just as we would not expect children to communicate using words they do not understand, it is often difficult for a child to worship God through songs and words that have little or no meaning to them as children. Therefore, in worship, children need to be given opportunities to praise or honor God using songs and words they understand based on their limited knowledge or cognitive development.

Using age-appropriate songs or explaining meanings behind words of songs help children to enter into an experience where they can freely communicate to the living God. As children are able to focus on God in praise and adoration, they are able to discover more of who God is and experience freedom from those things that hold them back.

Philosophical Rationale for the Pragmatic-Participatory Approach

Cognitive/Emotional Developmental Issues

Studies have shown that children begin to absorb values as early as two years of age.[25] Therefore, a children's ministry often begins teaching children at the age of two and focuses its efforts on introducing children to Jesus and God through stories in the Bible. As children mature, the Bible is held as the authoritative written Word of God, and a ministry to children must be based on teaching the Bible. In the Pragmatic-Participatory Model, knowing about God and knowing God are important; however, the process in which children learn about God is done in a way where children are able to experience God and who he is (or could be) in their lives.

The philosophy behind the Pragmatic-Participatory Model is based on developmental theory. "Developmentalism declares that the valuable content of Scripture must be combined with an awareness of the age the child is in so as to match the teaching of content to the capacity of the child."[26] Jean Piaget, one of the original proponents of cognitive development theory, would argue that "there is distinct sequence to cognitive growth, and that at earlier stages many concepts simply cannot be grasped by young children."[27] Most churches who follow this model would agree for the most part with Piaget regarding the cognitive growth of children; however, there are exceptions to his theory. As recent research has shown, Piaget's theory underestimates children's abilities because the tasks he used to measure cognitive ability were far removed from children's real-life experiences.[28]

These studies go on to prove the importance of attaching biblical truths to real-life experiences as a means to teach

---

25. Barna, *Transforming Children into Spiritual Champions,* 100.

26. Julie A. Gorman, "Children and Developmentalism," in James C. Wilhoit and John M. Dettoni, eds., *Nurture That Is Christian* (Grand Rapids, Mich.: Bridge Point Books, 1995), 142.

27. Lawrence Richards, *A Theology of Children's Ministry* (Grand Rapids, Mich.: Zondervan, 1983), 59.

28. Study results referenced by Robert F. Biehler and Jack Snowman, *Psychology Applied to Teaching* (Boston, Mass.: Houghton Mifflin Company, 1997), 57–60.

children about God and his Word. "A child at the pre-operational stage (preschoolers, kindergarteners and most first and some second graders) can be given opportunities to describe and explain things through the use of artwork, body movements, role-play, musical performance and speech."[29] Applying this research to the Pragmatic-Participatory Model shows how learning and understanding can be improved with the addition of such activities as games, role plays, worship, kinesthetic movement, and discussions.

The developmental teaching of Erik Erikson gives credibility to the focus on age appropriateness and the reminder that a model of spiritual formation for children must take into account the lived experiences of a child in order to effectively influence spiritual growth.[30] Within the Pragmatic-Participatory Model, spiritual truths are taught in a way that addresses age-appropriate needs and meets the cognitive and emotional levels of the various children. Churches that follow the Pragmatic-Participatory Model provide children of different ages opportunities to experience the Bible and its content. Within this model there is a strong belief that the Word of God can be communicated meaningfully to children and that children are capable of developing and becoming more like Christ.

Within the context of this model, it is often understood that although the Bible is true and inspired by God, there are parts that might not be suitable for teaching children due to their developing cognitive and emotional skills. Often great care is taken to ensure that what is being taught is explained so that it makes sense to the child in that age group. Sometimes the Bible story may be paraphrased or translated into simpler words in order for it to be understandable to the child.[31]

The research of Piaget regarding child development also helps us to see that learning is a social activity. The social activity seems to be an important philosophy of the Pragmatic-Participatory Model. As stated by James E. Plueddeman, "Chris-

29. Robert F. Biehler, *Psychology Applied to Teaching* (Boston, Mass.: Houghton Miffin, Co., 1997), 59.

30. Les Steele, "The Power of Erikson," in Wilhoit and Dettoni, *Nurture That Is Christian*, 101.

31. Gorman, "Children and Developmentalism," 143.

tians should not need to be reminded that good education must involve the body of believers, the church. People develop as they interact with other people."[32]

The pragmatic-participatory approach to children's spiritual formation uses the social elements of learning to help children process and make sense of biblical truths being taught. The social interaction allows children to participate in the learning process and to apply God's Word through discussions and interactions with other children. Hearing other children vocalize their views in turn helps children to learn from one another. The interplay between children also helps them process verbally what they are learning and to attach the lesson to their own direct experiences. To relate a lesson to a child's direct experiences, a drama presentation might show the interaction between two children as they seek to make a wise choice based on a biblical truth. Other times discussion questions or a game in small-group time incorporates interaction between children and adult leaders.

This model of children's spiritual formation also relies on sequential learning. At each stage children learn and understand different insights, and those different stages of learning help to form the basis of the next stage. Curriculum that is written for the Pragmatic-Participatory Model may address certain points of a story at one age, and then at the next developmental stage it may address the same topic but with a broader and deeper comprehension required of the child.[33] Children are capable of building on the knowledge that they learn at different stages, and an effective ministry to children allows for sequential learning and developmental stages of children.

Piaget's third stage of cognitive development, known as Concrete Operational (ages seven to eleven), gives us a unique perspective on the learning abilities of the elementary-aged child and the developmental basis for this particular spiritual formation model (see page 29). As described by Plueddeman, "This elementary-school-aged child has the new capacity to use mental

---

32. James E. Plueddeman, "The Power of Piaget," in Wilhoit and Dettoni, *Nurture That Is Christian,* 59.
33. Gorman, "Children and Developmentalism," 143.

logic but is limited to situations that are real and observable."[34] At this stage hands-on learning and activities are instrumental in helping children expand their thinking. This stage is characterized by substantive and concrete elements that help children to make sense of their world.

In her chapter on "Children and Developmentalism" in *Nurture That Is Christian*, Julie A. Gorman gives credence to the importance of active participation and speculation in regard to children's spiritual development. "Hands-on experiences, concrete objects, and activities are vital when teaching concepts of spiritual truth. Pictures, drawings, clay, models, investigations, and drama help reshape and build new ways of understanding."[35] Experiences where children are able to interact with concrete representations of the spiritual truths they are learning help children understand concepts and grow in their knowledge and understanding of spiritual truths. Within this model biblical stories are often depicted by dramas, role plays, or for younger children even a puppet show. These dramatic presentations help a child form a basis of understanding because it brings the concept back to concrete, relevant situations in a child's life. Focusing on real-life application not only helps children apply the spiritual truths they are learning to their own lives, but it also provides a framework for children to understand that concept based on their stage of development.

Faith Development

The way children understand and experience their faith is important to examine when considering children's spiritual formation. Faith is a gift given by God (Eph. 2:8–9), and children are extremely open to the spiritual dimension in their lives. Strong evidence suggests that young children are capable of religious experience.[36] Because of their trust and innocence, they do not need convincing that faith in God is important. Their highly creative mind helps them to grasp those omnipotent characteristics

---

34. Plueddeman, "The Power of Piaget," 53.
35. Gorman, "Children and Developmentalism," 146.
36. Donald M. Joy, "Why Reach and Teach Children," *Childhood Education in the Church*, 12, referencing the study by Edwin D. Starbuck, *The Psychology of Religion: An Empirical Study of the Growth of Religious Consciousness* (New York: Scribner, 1906).

of God that even adults have trouble with. Yet it is evident that children, as well as adults, experience faith at different levels. A spiritual maturity occurs as people grow in their knowledge and love for God. James Fowler's faith development theory involves six stages of faith through which human progress (the other four stages relate to later periods of human development).

As described in stage one, "intuitive/projective faith" occurs during early childhood and is highly imaginative. Children of early childhood age are strongly influenced by images and stories, but their faith is not yet logical.[37] Even young children begin to assimilate experiences with their parents as reflections of the personhood of God. Children at this age gain much of their understanding of church and faith through what they see modeled by their parents and others with whom they interact. Their environment and the people within it form a context whereby they experience God intuitively.

Practically speaking, the involvement of parents and others at this age plays an important role in this first faith development stage. Loving and caring individuals in the nursery and toddler classrooms help children form the basis to relate to God and their view of church. The child's view of spirituality is affected by their families, relationships, and community.[38] In addition to adults who play significant roles in their lives, the environment in which children are taught also becomes important. Although in early childhood children might not delineate between a beautifully decorated classroom and a room that has been set up temporarily as an age-appropriate classroom, a child's perceptions and feelings toward their learning facility will influence their perceptions and feelings toward God. Also at this stage children in early childhood enjoy playing make-believe, and their faith is influenced by stories. Therefore, the use of stories or puppets in relaying biblical truths helps children imagine themselves as characters in the Bible and helps them to attach positive feelings toward God and his concepts.

---

37. Perry G. Downs, *Teaching for Spiritual Growth* (Grand Rapids, Mich.: Zondervan, 1994), 115.

38. Wendy Haight, "A Sociocultural Perspective on Children's Spiritual Development," in Ratcliff, *Children's Spirituality,* 182.

During stage two, "mythic/literal faith," Fowler describes children who are able to think logically but are limited to concrete thinking. At this stage children begin to make sense of reality versus make-believe. Yet at the same time children are literal in their understanding of biblical truths and concepts. So when discussing concepts or symbolism in the Bible, explanation needs to be given to help children understand and respond to God's Word. For example, when discussing John 14:2 ("In my Father's house are many rooms"), children could literally create a picture in their minds of heaven that consists of a beautiful mansion in an exclusive neighborhood. Providing understanding of these metaphors is an important role in the child's spiritual development.[39]

Understanding the faith development of a child helps a ministry determine which biblical truths will be taught and how they will be taught. Those that practice the Pragmatic-Participatory Model tend to rely heavily on age appropriateness and relevancy for children in order that children will be able to make sense of what they are learning and how children of different stages experience faith within the context of their own worlds.

Overall, children have a rich capacity for spirituality. According to Jesus' words in Matthew 18:2–5, children have a unique ability to enter into the kingdom of heaven. In Charles Spurgeon's words, "A child of five, if properly instructed, can as truly believe and be regenerated as any adult."[40]

The Teacher-Learner Process

Active learning helps form the basis of the Pragmatic-Participatory Model, and it defines the role of the teacher. Since knowledge is often gained during those interactive moments, the role the teacher plays is instrumental to the success of this model. The teacher's role is not simply to relay information and

39. Downs, *Teaching for Spiritual Growth,* 115.

40. Zuck, *Precious in His Sight,* 18, referencing Frank G. Coleman, *The Romance of Winning Children* (Cleveland: Union Gospel Press, 1967), 9–10.

knowledge but to provide shared experiences of learning where the child takes part in his or her own learning. [41]

In the Pragmatic-Participatory Model, many different people may help facilitate the learning process. In some ministries that adhere to this philosophy of ministry, the actual title of "teacher" might not be used although several individuals are responsible for helping to facilitate learning. In a more traditional method, a Sunday school teacher might be responsible for all elements of the children's classroom learning experience. The traditional Sunday school teacher might be asked to be responsible for attendance of children, teaching, and preparation of crafts; and sometimes the teacher role may even include leading a time of worship. Because of the varied activities that occur when using the Pragmatic-Participatory Model, there are more specialized roles for volunteers to play.

The volunteer roles may be broken down into different responsibilities according to the volunteer's spiritual giftedness and talents. Therefore, the teaching role is shared between the different volunteers in the room. Although many adults or volunteers will be involved, one teacher might share the Bible truths with the children from the front of the classroom or up on stage. Another teacher might lead a smaller group of children during a discussion time or small-group time that follows the children's church or Bible lesson. During a discussion time children are broken into smaller groups to talk about the lesson they just saw. These discussion leaders or small-group leaders are the ones who share the role of teacher since they engage children in discussions of the Bible story and facilitate activities that help the children apply the Bible truths to their own lives. The small-group leader or teacher is also the one responsible for getting to know the children and creating community and promoting friendships within the group. In addition, there may be other volunteers whose sole responsibility is to teach the lesson from stage and provide an interplay with a drama or video.

Examining how Jesus taught gives us examples of how we are to teach children and gives the teacher a model for effective

---

41. Gorman, "Children and Developmentalism," 153.

teaching. The methods Jesus used when he was on earth are transferable and the goal of teachers within the Pragmatic-Participatory Model. First and foremost, more than the words that Jesus spoke, he modeled his character to the disciples and to those he encountered. He surprised his disciples and the crowds by associating with people such as the woman at the well (John 4:26) or Zacchaeus the tax collector (Luke 19:2). The disciples learned important lessons about the type of person Jesus was and how they should treat others by watching him and interacting with him. In the Pragmatic-Participatory Model the teacher or leaders play an important role in modeling Christ as they interact on a consistent basis with the children and teach the biblical concepts. Often adult or teen leaders share significant personal experiences from their own lives in order to bring relevancy to the topic being discussed.

Jesus also shows us it is important to understand and know the details of the lives of those we are trying to teach. In the case of the woman at the well (John 4), Jesus basically tells her, "I know everything about you." Jesus establishes the relationship with this Samaritan woman and shows compassion to her that causes her to want to listen to what Jesus has to say. In the model of pragmatic-participatory children's ministry, the leaders are often getting to know the children through different activities that give glimpses into the child's personality, interests, and thoughts. Life change happens best when volunteers are able to build relationships with the children and provide personalized shepherding and spiritual direction for children.

Jesus taught so the learner would be changed. He used methods that would appeal to the different emotional and intellectual characteristics of an individual. The idea of communicating with someone in a way that meets their needs and challenges them in their thinking is the method that the Pragmatic-Participatory Model seeks to exemplify. Just as Jesus used parables to appeal to people's ability to think and reason, the children's ministries of this model tend to give children age-appropriate opportunities for them to think and reason on their own.

Jesus also taught appealing to an individual's different senses. Proponents who follow the Pragmatic-Participatory Model engage as many of the different senses as they can in any one given lesson. This may be seen through hands-on activities where children don't just hear the story but engage in it through multisensory experiences.

Overall the belief that children are capable of being transformed by God's Word in their lives is the basis from which these children's ministries operate. Children are capable of transforming spiritually because the Holy Spirit is alive and living in them if they are followers of Christ. In this particular model the learner is seen as someone who is able to engage actively in the learning process. By involving the child in the process of understanding and application, children are encouraged to think for themselves, which proves to be beneficial as they grow and mature in their faith and are faced with other real-life circumstances. Different methods of teaching are used to capture the attention and interest of the learners. Learners might be encouraged to put what they are learning into practice through role plays, artwork, or in questions presented in an application-oriented game. When a teacher is reading or speaking, children are given something to actively listen for, or they might be given a particular prop to hold during the presentation. In this model learners are also encouraged to express concepts or explain reasons for their answers because it allows them an opportunity to speculate and express the concepts they are learning.

Because there are different types of learners (visual, kinesthetic, and auditory), a model for spiritual development must be able to meet the different learning styles of children. Young children especially use all of their senses to learn about their world, and therefore lessons must be taught in a manner that engages all of the senses. Within the Pragmatic-Participatory Model, each type of learning method is considered and used when at all possible to convey the messages being taught.

The learning environment in which this model functions helps to achieve the overall values of creativity, and child appropriateness, and places a high value on learning styles. Some churches that use this model create extensive productions that involve lighting, audiovisuals, costumes, and set design. For other churches less extensive though highly intentional programs meet the same goals. An inviting environment is an important characteristic and element of this particular model. The environment needs to be conducive to learning and a child's age-appropriate needs. The environment also helps the child to develop positive feelings toward church and their own faith development. Having a positive attitude about church attendance helps children value the spiritual dimension of their lives.

Programatic Design of the Pragmatic-Participatory Model

Historical Development of the Model

As our culture has changed, the approach of Christian spiritual formation in children has changed in order to meet the changing needs of today's children. In recent decades the world's values are placing tremendous pressure on families and children, and weekly church attendance competes with Sunday child sporting events and a plethora of other social activities.

Program Elements

How the Pragmatic-Participatory Model is actually implemented within children's ministries may vary greatly depending on a church's denomination, size, and environmental constraints. Some common program elements guide the overall design of a ministry that functions under the Pragmatic-Participatory Model. As Lawrence Richards so aptly phrases it: "Teaching the Bible calls for the design of a variety of learning experiences in the teaching setting through which children will directly or vicariously experience, on their own level, the reality to be communicated. The entire classroom process needs to be designed to translate what is being taught into experienceable reality, which can then be linked with or interpreted by biblical terms."[42]

---

42. Richards, *A Theology of Children's Ministry*, 404.

Using a variety of different resources and activities is a common premise within ministry programs that function under the Pragmatic-Participatory Model. This particular model differs from others in that there is not a reliance on one particular method. Rather various methods in conjunction are to meet the end goal of spiritual formation. When the various activities are implemented within a children's ministry program, it results in a multilayered, thought-provoking, and life-transforming lesson.

Dramatic Presentations of the Bible. The foundation for a lesson of this particular model is always a biblical story or Bible concept. Dramatic presentations are often used as a method within the Pragmatic-Participatory Model because it allows the child to see God's Word brought to life through story. Drama can be a powerful medium for children because it allows them a visual, live action reenactment of the Bible story being taught.

As concrete thinkers, children often have difficulty understanding things that they cannot see. Powerful dramas, storytelling, puppet shows, and child reenactments provide a worthwhile tool for Bible teaching. Using drama within a lesson format helps the children to think of other additional insights within the context of the Bible story that they might otherwise miss. Variations of drama or even an expressive storyteller help to relay the human element of God's Word and bring the audience into the thoughts and feelings of the people involved. The use of props and costumes in addition to a dramatic presentation can also give insights into historical background, customs of the time, and biblical settings.

The other reason those within the Pragmatic-Participatory Model use drama is that it appeals to the learning styles of both visual and auditory learners. Creative drama presentations leave a visual and audible imprint on a child's mind that can help them apply the biblical truth to their lives and recount God's Word easily when faced with a similar situation in the future. Take, for example, a lesson that is a reenactment of Peter walking on water (Matt. 14:28–32). The reassuring and yet powerful voice of Jesus is heard as he tells the disciples to "take courage! It is I. Don't be afraid" (Matt. 14:27). In Peter's life, hearing Jesus speak those words as he stood in the middle of the sea must have been an astounding auditory experience. Children who hear God's Word spoken audibly are better able to identify with the story. Children who hear the words spoken by Jesus can have a powerful and transforming spiritual experience. When an actor portrays Peter's look of trepidation and trembling legs as Jesus calls him out of the boat, the passage takes on new meaning for a child as to the incredible amount of fear and panic Peter must have felt.

Drama is also used to illustrate concepts whose implications in everyday life are more difficult for a child to understand. Showing a drama of a real-life situation that a child may currently be facing allows children to put themselves into the story and think how they might respond when faced with a similar situation. Incorporating a reference to something or someone from modern-day culture helps to draw children in and equate an association with something familiar that they can understand. Biblical concepts then can be taught in a manner that gives the child a framework for the lesson aim.

Children's ministries that rely on the Pragmatic-Participatory Model for their programming see the benefits that drama and creativity bring to the learning process and the unique needs of children. Drama is more than one-dimensional learning. It allows the audience of learners an expanded view and experience that cannot be gained elsewhere.

Worship Arts. Just as the Old and New Testaments include numerous instructions regarding song, music provides a powerful way for children to express and communicate with a living God. Not losing sight that as believers we are to live a lifestyle of worship (Rom. 12:1), we are also called to worship in fellowship with one another as the body of Christ. Pragmatic-participatory ministry believes worship used in conjunction with Bible teaching provides another means that the Holy Spirit can use to guide children into a spiritual experience of loving communion with the heavenly Father.

Within this model practitioners would agree that worship with children can express a variety of thoughts and emotions. While children are capable internally of feeling some of these emotions, they often might not know how to communicate those in spoken form and understand how to respond to God with those emotions.[43] Worship provides a link for children to respond in a relational way and engage with a personal God. A children's ministry may rely on a variety of different types of worship songs and worship arts to add to the spiritual experience.

Planning for worship arts depends on the biblical content of the lesson at hand, the mood of the service, and the allowance to the Holy Spirit's leading. How worship is led within a programming segment may vary from church to church. Some children's ministries may use live worship teams of adults and/or children, sound tracks, or even live bands during their worship programming. However, a common denominator of worship leading within this model is that a live person is always present who interacts with the children and helps by directing their worship experience. Worship music combined with choreographed hand motions appeals to the child's active use of large motor skills. Choreographed worship songs are used to reinforce the lyrics of the songs and to engage the children actively in worship.

While Scripture teaches that true worship requires inward reverence, in the lives of the first-century worshippers, it also often included outward prostration (Matt. 2:2, 8; 28:9). When children are given opportunities through hand motions or choreography to respond with their whole body, they often experience worship as a physical response to their internal thoughts and feelings.

Within this model, songs are chosen that include meaningful and understandable lyrics for children. Lyrics that include symbolism are given an explanation or a context for understanding when being led in worship or sometimes not used at all depending on the age of the participants. Because of the important value on age-appropriateness within the Pragmatic-Participatory Model, selected songs may differ according to the different age groupings of children. All songs must be doctrinally and scripturally correct while including a selection of songs that are engaging and fun for children to sing. Catchy worship songs that

---

43. Ibid., 404.

are current in their sound and rhythm can appeal to children and often help to relay powerful and memorable biblical truths. Worship songs can also help children remember important biblical truths as they hum the tunes and words to songs throughout the week.

Application-Oriented Games and Activities. As children have unique physical development needs, active games also give another means and resource to learn the biblical objectives outlined in a lesson. Group Publishing's Hands-On Bible Curriculum is known for using many hands-on experiential learning activities to help children understand concepts and be transformed by God's Word. "While information (facts and concepts) can be efficiently transmitted from teacher to student through direct instruction, knowledge is best created by each student through the mental and physical manipulation of information."[44] Hands-on games and activities allow for children to add to their knowledge and understanding of particular concepts. Active games often include small props or game pieces that children can interact with kinesthetically. These learning activities also appeal to the kinesthetic development of children and help to create a fun atmosphere of learning that meets the needs of a growing child.

Many churches within the Pragmatic-Participatory Model use small groups or smaller group settings to help children learn the lesson aims presented previously in a larger group context. Not only do these smaller groups provide for personal interaction between children and between children and leaders, but they also provide a time for students to apply the biblical principles being taught. Since the Pragmatic-Participatory Model is based on active participation versus observation, this program element allows children to interact and apply what they are learning in an emotionally safe environment. The most effective small-group times are those that touch on the basic learning styles to allow children an experience whereby they are guided to answer the underlying question; given what I know of this biblical concept, what does that mean to me? Ministries who use a Pragmatic-Participatory Model hold firmly that Bible learning should encour-

---

44. Biehler and Snowman, *Psychology Applied to Teaching*, 59.

age a response and a change in thought that draws one closer to God (Rom. 12:2).

As stated previously, the teacher-learner process is more than just imparting knowledge and information. In order to maximize learning, a ministry must have maximum involvement on behalf of the learner.[45] Psychologists have proved that when we hear something we have only up to a 10 percent chance of remembering what we hear. If we add seeing and hearing to the learning process, the potential to remember goes up to 50 percent. Yet the combination of doing, seeing, and hearing brings the potential to remember up to 90 percent.[46] Proponents of the Pragmatic-Participatory Model believe that this particular model of spiritual formation helps to influence the way a child thinks, which then results in spiritual transformation.

By involving learners in what is being taught, children are able to participate in activities that help them to see their faith in action. Take for instance children who are taught about the Great Commission in Matthew 28:16–20 and then are given the opportunity to practice what it would be like to share their faith with an unbelieving friend or to participate in leading a gospel message drama on a short-term missions project. Because of the child's experience in a meaningful activity, those children are impacted in a way that causes them to think and act differently about God. Jesus himself focuses on responding to God's Word by doing something when he says in Matthew 7:24, "Therefore everyone who hears these words of mine and puts them into practice is like a wise man who built his house on the rock."

For those who believe in the Pragmatic-Participatory Model, Jesus himself proves that it is not enough just to hear something or see it, but we must guide children to put God's Word into practice. By actively engaging their minds, children are encouraged to think critically and internalize the biblical truths being taught. Active games and activities meet the needs of

---

45. Howard Hendricks, *Teaching to Change Lives* (Portland, Oreg.: Multnomah Press, 1987), 81–82.
46. Ibid.

"postmodern kids [who] expect learning experiences in which they are active participants, not passive witnesses."[47]

Instructional Technology. Postmodern generation children have grown up being exposed to technology. "More than 4 out of 5 children under 13 years of age use a computer at school on a regular basis."[48] To effectively reach and teach this media-driven generation, children's ministry models should include modern technology as a method to help reinforce the lessons being taught from the Bible. While this particular model balances the use of technology with other methods, media and technology are used creatively to enhance the biblical content.

Media and technology help to capture the attention and the minds of children. Computer media presentations and video components are often one of the different program elements of the Pragmatic-Participatory Model. Projecting song words on video screens can help to engage visual learners and focus attention on the words children are singing. Photos on PowerPoint can help to provide visual aids for map locations, cultural references, and verse references.

Videos are also used as a way to help illustrate stories or concepts. A memorable and powerful video developed by one church illustrates the concept of "Jesus as the Good Shepherd" (John 10:1–18). Children see a live person on the screen interacting with a large flock of sheep. As the leader on the screen teaches the passage, he references the characteristics and habits of sheep; he shows the gate on the sheep's pen and brings a realistic understanding of the passage to the children. Video captures children's attention in a unique way; however, when spiritual formation is a goal, it should be used to draw the children's attention to spiritual matters and enhance their learning.

Reliance on video as the sole method of ministry programming is viewed by the Pragmatic-Participatory Model as lacking necessary interpersonal relationships and inactivity that runs contrary to children's developing attention spans. From this viewpoint, video is often used in conjunction with a live teacher and

47. Miller and Staal, *Making Your Children's Ministry the Best*, 76.
48. Barna, *Transforming Children*, 19.

a subsequent guided discussion time that draws out the child's perceived thoughts and encourages personal introspection.

Featured Distinctives and Highlights

The Role of Volunteers

Volunteers are often the cornerstone on which effective ministry in a local church rests. For professional children's Christian educators, the recruiting, ongoing development, and retention of volunteers seem to be never-ending issues that must be addressed. While it's evident that there are a variety of different means by which spiritual formation goals are met within this model, at first glance this variety seems to exacerbate the issue of volunteerism. Yes, when a ministry offers a variety of different methods within its program, it may require additional personnel support. However, in many cases a variety of activities or roles within a children's ministry attracts volunteers that have a diversity of gifts and talents.

In more traditional methods of Sunday school, one or two teachers are responsible for most of the Bible teaching and other elements of a weekend children's program. When this particular model is implemented, different individuals are responsible for different areas of the ministry program. Gifted worship leaders and communicators are called upon to lead and communicate God's truth in the main teaching component. Discussion leaders or small-group leaders get to use their gift of shepherding to ensure that children are known and guided during application-oriented activities. Those with the talents of acting can serve in the drama presentations. Even people who prefer to serve "behind the scenes" have the opportunity to work as an audiovisual technician, classroom administrator, or designing props or costumes. As one church transitioned its ministry to one that fit the framework of the Pragmatic-Participatory Model, they saw an immediate jump in the number of volunteers. In just one year they went from 19 committed volunteers to 187. The different gifts that are required for a ministry of this type attracted new volunteers who were eager to find a way to use their gifts within the children's ministry as a way to serve God.

Jesus linked modeling when he said that a fully trained disciple "will be like his teacher" (Luke 6:40). An effective teacher isn't necessarily a professional Christian educator. The volunteer or teacher is one who helps relay information, facilitate growth and Bible application, and model a faith in Christ. The goal is that volunteers and children would be growing more and more like Jesus.

Providing consistent volunteer staff that are able to develop relationships with children is extremely important. While the Old Testament clearly shows that parents have the primary role of instructing their children in faith (Deut. 6; 11; Exod. 12:25–27), research has also shown that children need to have people other than their parents who can model and help to influence a child's faith development.

Relationships

Although this model may vary in how it is actually applied among different churches, relationships carry a high value. An adult or student volunteer is more than just someone who performs a task or relays information. Those who directly work with children provide godly shepherding and love. When leading a discussion or an activity, these volunteers are the people who get to know the children personally and are able to build an ongoing relationship with the children. A consistent volunteer who works directly with children is someone children interact with who models a life committed to Jesus. These volunteers are also able to foster learning and friendships among the group of children. In the Scriptures we are reminded time and time again of the important value of the fellowship within the community of believers. When teams of people are serving in the children's ministry classroom, these volunteers become living examples of the body of Christ and role models of Christ's servanthood for children.

Many churches these days that practice the Pragmatic-Participatory Model use small groups or breakout discussion groups that follow the larger group time of presentation and worship arts. These smaller groups are led by student or adult volunteers. As mentioned earlier, often within this smaller group time hands-on activities and application-oriented discussions pertaining to the Bible lesson will occur. When an ongoing volunteer and child shepherding relationship exists, volunteers are able to see and witness a child's spiritual growth firsthand. This small group time also provides a great avenue for Bible memorization work as well as time to pray for a child's prayer requests.

Biblical Curriculum with Life Application

An effective curriculum must be grounded in the truth of Scripture. The lesson aims of a Pragmatic-Participatory Model of curriculum are based on the fact that God's Word can and will transform lives. In curriculum of this genre, special consideration is given to meet the cognitive and emotional levels discussed previously in order to be most effective for a particular age level. While the emphasis tends to be more on topical lessons, passages of Scripture from both the Old Testament and New Testament are usually covered throughout the year. A scope and sequence of curriculum builds upon children's knowledge as they mature in their faith and grow throughout their childhood.

Although sometimes the curriculum may build upon the lessons children have learned in the past, lessons are also crafted not to exclude those who have not previously attended the children's service. Teachers will frequently reexplain concepts that were introduced during the weeks; or before a lesson starts, children might discuss in their small groups concepts that were taught previously. This practice of giving the lesson a biblical context or a slight review each week meets the population of many churches who have both first-time visitors and committed believers who attend each weekend. When children come who are unfamiliar with church or are seeking to know more about who God is, they don't feel excluded when it comes to the Bible teaching component. This model also allows for a comprehensive spiritual formation process that addresses nurturing a child's faith beginning in the early childhood stage and throughout the elementary childhood years.

An example of a lesson plan might start with some type of attention grabber or opening context that captures the child's interest. Next children are taught the Bible story or concept through some type of creative program element. Lessons are usually concluded with implications that cause the child to think of how life might be different by applying this concept. When small groups are included as part of a program, the lesson concludes with leaders helping to guide the children in their response to what was taught and relational time between leaders and adults. Additional relationship-building time is usually built in as children arrive to class and are waiting to be picked up.

The rationale in teaching the Bible to children is not just to instill ideas they will need to know someday. The Bible holds truths children can hold on to today to develop a vital relationship with God.[49] It is important in leading children to understand the crucial issues in their own lives and how the Bible relates to those issues. In order to do this, children must be given opportunities to respond to God and to think about ways his Word can be applied to real-life situations they are currently facing. "If you hold to my teaching," Jesus taught, "you are really my disciples. Then you will know the truth, and the truth will set you free" (John 8:31–32). Jesus' teachings were not to be processed as information; instead the words of Jesus were to be lived.[50] The philosophy of this model is not merely to impart knowledge but to allow children to discover and experience for themselves how they might respond differently by living according to what God's Word says to them.

The Fun Factor

When speaking of featured distinctives of this model, it is important to note the value that is placed on fun. In the past fun has not been emphasized in children's ministry models. The Pragmatic-Participatory Model seeks to influence a child's spiritual

---

49. Lawrence O. Richards, *Creative Bible Teaching* (Chicago, Ill.: Moody Press, 1970), 185.

50. Richards, *A Theology of Children's Ministry*, 65.

development by creating a fun and inviting environment where children are challenged to grow more and more like Christ.

Fun appeals to children, and it doesn't have to compromise the Bible or the learning that is to take place. Churches of this model place a high priority on fun, and it is usually evident in everything they do. Children respond to God when they feel comfortable and safe. A fun environment helps children to feel welcome and helps them to be motivated to learn. If children are growing spiritually and having fun in a ministry program, they will want to come back because *the* church soon will become *my* church.

Children who enjoy coming to their church will invite their friends to do the same. It also should not be overlooked that fun can also go a long way when recruiting and retaining volunteers. People who volunteer their time and talents to serve God play a large role in a successful ministry program for children. Being able to serve on a ministry team that witnesses spiritual life change and has fun at the same time can help lead to a fulfilling ministry experience.

Why It Works

The Pragmatic-Participatory Model is the basis that many successful children's ministries use for spiritual formation in children. Its multifaceted approach powerfully meets the needs of all learning styles and cognitive growth levels of children. While providing a structure and various methods to enhance spiritual growth, it also allows for flexibility to meet the needs of different church demographics and children's ministries.

As seen in many churches, the Pragmatic-Participatory Model is not just effective with a certain age group; it can be applied in various age spans because of its focus on developmental learning and age-appropriate biblical relevancy. A key benefit to this model is that it is versatile enough to be implemented for special events, weekday club programs, and camps as well. In some cases the Pragmatic-Participatory Model has been applied to launch successful family and intergenerational ministries within a church. These family and intergenerational ministries are successful because of the concepts that are carried through to make it effective for children instead of just adding children into a regular adult service.

The overarching principle in any model is a reliance on God's grace and his power that allows ministries and God's people to be used to transform the lives of children. "Now to him who is able to do immeasurably more than all we ask or imagine, according to his power that is at work within us, to him be glory in the church and in Christ Jesus throughout all generations, for ever and ever!" (Eph. 3:20).

Responses to Pragmatic-Participatory Model

Response by Scottie May

I affirm much of what is in this chapter regarding this model. Ms. Graves cites several significant voices for Christian education in recent decades, voices such as Howard Hendricks, Lawrence Richards, James Plueddemann, and Julie Gorman. As it is described here, the Pragmatic-Participatory Model might possibly be the most common approach used for the church education that takes place on Sunday mornings. In fact, the Richards quote, cited later in her chapter, speaks to the well-established history of the model since his statement was written about twenty-five years ago. This model is time-tested.

Beginning with Lawrenz's definition of *spiritual formation* that describes the "progressive patterning" of the journey toward the image of Christ, the chapter emphasizes core Christian values. I note that the Pragmatic-Participatory Model "helps to engage children's minds" and seems to take the Instructional-Analytic Model to the next level by encouraging users "to think and apply the practical and biblical concepts being taught." The Pragmatic-Participatory Model focuses on assisting children to realize that biblical truths must be applied to their daily lives rather than assuming that application will happen if children simply learn the Scriptures.

I support Ms. Graves's description of the role that Scripture plays in this model. The model attempts to use age-appropriate texts even for young children. Graves not only identifies prayer as vital to support the ministry and its volunteers, but prayer also must be modeled intentionally before the children. She also notes the importance of being alert to the promptings and work of the Holy Spirit within a child so that a godly adult can come alongside with guidance and support. The children are to experience God and who he is and are able to be transformed through such experiences.

Graves describes the role of ongoing interaction between adults and children, resulting in personal relationships. Activity stations prior to the service and small-group interaction enhance the relationship between child and adult. She cites Plueddemann who writes that good education in the church requires people involved and interacted with the body of believers, the church.

I appreciate the balanced view of the use of instructional technology in her description of the Pragmatic-Participatory Model. As she describes it, media should be used to enhance and reinforce the Bible lesson, not as the focal point of the experience.

Graves uses findings in the social sciences to support the Pragmatic-Participatory Model, including the works of Erikson, Piaget, and Fowler. She notes that the model easily accommodates the differing ways children learn through its use of various methods and experiences. Examination of the model reveals several types of cognitive learning experiences for children: there is opportunity for *assimilating* new information from the Bible presentation; activity stations may allow for creative expression, a *divergent* activity; applying the biblical content to one's life requires a *convergent* activity—bringing together the truths of the story with the child's own story; lastly, the application of these truths must be lived out, which leads to an *accommodating* activity—changing one's behavior. So the Pragmatic-Participatory Model employs Kolb's learning cycle as described in *Experiential Learning*. Interestingly, these same four types of activities are present in the Bible time museum approach I describe in the chapter on the Contemplative-Reflective Model. Added some years ago to that approach, which we still use, are the activities of contemplation and reflection.

Graves describes the model as valuing volunteers and enabling them to use their gifts and abilities rather than all of them being teachers, doing the same thing each week in different classrooms. This is commendable in that it is fulfilling for the volunteers and enables them to take ownership of their contribution in the ministry without the onerous feeling that sometimes accompanies the need to keep children engaged for the entire Sunday school hour.

Graves rightly identifies the overarching principle for any children's ministry: reliance on God's grace and power to transform the lives of children. To that I say a hearty "amen."

Having identified the areas that I confirm in Graves's discussion of the Pragmatic-Participatory Model, I will now identify questions or areas of concern that arose while reading about the model. The first issue I want to raise is in regard to what appears to be defense of a distinct theological position, namely the baptistic tradition. About ten pages are devoted to an explanation of that theology. For example, she writes that many churches believe that the number of children making decisions for Christ is one of the measures used by an evaluator of effective children's ministry. In stating this, is Graves inferring that baptistic theology is inherent in the Pragmatic-Participatory Model or possibly that baptistic churches use the Pragmatic-Participatory Models more than any other tradition? From my experience, neither is the case. I traveled for several years as a Christian education consultant and had the privilege of being in about one hundred churches a year. I have observed the Pragmatic-Participatory Model being implemented in a wide theological range of churches—from Baptist to Methodist to Presbyterian to Anglican.

That being said, I was surprised by a couple of other related factors that Graves associates with this model: first, that the curriculum developed by one large church "strategically" schedules the presentation of the gospel once a year for preschoolers and three times for elementary children; second, that the gospel message can be done "correctly." I wonder what is meant by the "gospel" in this context. I leave the reader to ponder the implications of Graves's use of the term *gospel* and now move on to more explicit discussion of the model itself.

Graves rightly points out the Old Testament's emphasis on the significance of family. (In the case of the Israelites, this usually referred to the extended family, multiple generations, and even to the tribe more than to the nuclear family.) Given the stated importance of the family, Graves should have included explicit ways to involve multiple generations of families while using the Pragmatic-Participatory Model. How can this model help bridge the gulf between the church and the home that is present in so many congregations?

Although not excessively emphasized by Graves, there are a couple of references to the need for fun within the model. Since about 1990, the value of fun has become an intentional goal for many ministries with children. Certainly fun has a place in the lives of children; but when most children are in church for only an hour a week, what if we replace "fun" with "meaningful"? I wonder what might change. Children are eager to be involved in things that are meaningful to them, things that may not always be categorized as fun.

I appreciate the articulation of values ascribed to this model—the use and application of Scripture and prayer in particular. However, in my years of visiting various churches, I have not seen Scripture read directly to children in the way Graves suggests is "one of the most basic methods to assist in the spiritual formation of children." Nor have I seen prayer evident more in the Pragmatic-Participatory Model than in any other model. If these values are so significant, I wonder why they are not incorporated more directly into the model rather than having their implementation vary from church to church. She also wants teachers to make the application of the text for the children. The teacher must know a lot about each child for that application to occur. What if the teacher guided the child through questions to make her or his own application?

Although I value the use of activity stations, from my observation many churches using Pragmatic-Participatory Models have activities with no relevance to the aim of the lesson or Bible story. In presession activities I've seen children play ring toss, make domino structures, do glitter crafts, and so forth. What if in the Pragmatic-Participatory Model everything the child does, hears, and discusses during that session relates to the point of the session? It might take more thought on the part of the leaders to develop germane activities for each lesson series, but it seems that learning would be enhanced considerably and made to be for more "meaningful" for the learner.

Graves's description of the scope and sequence of curriculum or materials is helpful in that it spirals, revisiting familiar themes at later stages of a child's development. This approach often results in new insights as the child matures. I agree with that approach but with caution. Interestingly, researchers in children's spirituality are rethinking some of the implications of the stage theory of development as presented by scholars such as Piaget and Fowler. Practitioners often take stage theories and make them prescriptive rather than descriptive of what most children are like. For example, a prescriptive approach says that school-age children are concrete thinkers; and therefore they need to hear Bible stories about people, places, and things, while preschoolers are sensorimotor and learn through those means. A descriptive approach would say that many school-age children are concrete thinkers, but they are also capable of age-appropriate conceptual thinking.

A similar point can be made about preschoolers. Current work with the spiritual formation of young children demonstrates that many of them are able to attend and reflect for extended periods of time on parables, often resulting in remarkable depth of meaning and insights. These findings have been replicated often enough that it behooves us to suspend prescriptive applications of stage theory. The chapter suggests that, when using biblical metaphors, meaning should be made for the children. Here again, current research would suggest otherwise. Studies show that even young children are able to draw meaning from parables and metaphors on their own—making that meaning deeply personal.

Children are comfortable with the mystery of the Christian faith and of our God. It's easy, and often counterproductive, to overexplain a story or parable. That can diminish a child's sense of wonder and awe over these mysteries and even God himself. I would like to suggest that, in a context prayed for and prepared by godly leaders, the Holy Spirit initiates the insights that come to even young children. I also have found that a well-told biblical story is able to stand on its own with children—that it does not need sound effects, gimmicks, or other devices—to hold their attention. Those extra trappings often get in the way of the power of the story that should be centered on God's actions and character. Many times the embellishments are remembered more clearly than what the story said about God.

Here is another observation about the description Graves provides of the curriculum in the Pragmatic-Participatory Model. She notes that "the emphasis tends to be more on topical lessons" drawn from both Testaments. My concern with this is that too often children, and volunteers as well, lose the meta-narrative—the overarching story beginning with creation and carrying through the eschaton as described in Revelation. The topical approach can turn redemption history into little more than exciting vignettes about fascinating people who lived long ago that have moral application for today. Even though young children often do not grasp chronology, the themes of the church year allow a more cohesive flow to the sequence of lessons than does a topical approach.

When writing about the design of the Pragmatic-Participatory Model, Graves makes a statement that seems presumptuous: "When the various activities are implemented within a children's ministry program, it results in a multilayered, thought-provoking, and life-transforming lesson." It seems more appropriate to use the word *engaging* rather than *life-transforming*. The Holy Spirit is the only person who transforms lives. We humans do the best we can to provide ministry contexts that enable the Spirit to transform the life of a child. Praise God that it can happen in various forms of ministry!

Although I seem to have found many points to critique in the description of the Pragmatic-Participatory Model, it is one I have used for many years. I appreciate, among other things, the way a variety of learning activities may be present and how an environment can be created that enables children to enter into the biblical story. The additions I like to make to this model are contemplative-reflective activities.

Response by Greg Carlson and John Crupper

There is much to commend in this model. Many areas of congruence between this approach to children's spiritual formation and the one we espouse should be obvious to the reader. We will reference a few. There are also several areas where we would differ in our perspectives. Such critique is offered with a spirit of mutual respect as we realize that no method is perfect and that elements of both approaches may be of benefit.

The Instructional-Analytic Model and the Pragmatic-Participatory Model share the same hermeneutic. For example, both models view the nature of the child as sinful and savable. That is, there is not a disregard for the clear teaching of Scripture that the child is in need of salvation. The idea that children should grow up thinking they are Christians may indeed prevent them from ever becoming Christians through the regenerative work of the Holy Spirit. The Pragmatic-Participatory Model outlines what we would view as a proper interpretation of this important concept. This model is also careful to interpret Scripture in a responsible manner, not in a casual approach with questionable applications.

The Pragmatic-Participatory Model also shares a common base of adherence to the Scriptures. The Bible is the basis of the curriculum. While the insights taken from the social sciences inform our development of lessons and selection of methods, we are not driven by the latest survey on technology. We are not looking to a psychological understanding of the child's nature to guide our ministry, but we are relying on what the Bible says for our foundation. You can see this when you observe who the author appeals to as the final authority in areas of disagreement.

While some would appeal to sociological, psychological, or even philosophical underpinnings, I appreciate Trisha Graves's appeal to the Bible in establishing this model.

There also seems to be a shared perspective on the important aspects of a philosophy of education. On the opening pages of the chapter, reference is made to goals, setting, and instructional methodology. Later we will mention the congruence regarding the perspective on the nature of children. The role of the teacher also has much that is commendable. Philosophically, we find more congruence with this model than with the other two although each of them is perhaps a "sibling."

In areas where we share agreement, certainly the evangelism of children is of utmost importance. This chapter outlines well the reasons this seems to be true both biblically and practically. We particularly like, "Presenting the gospel and allowing children to respond to the prompting of the Holy Spirit is one of the most significant roles a children's ministry may have in impacting the future of Christ followers." The Instructional-Analytic, Pragmatic-Participatory, and Media-Driven Active-Engagement models all seem strongly to agree on this issue. The creative methods and the sound push toward volunteer involvement do not crowd out the high priority of evangelism. An appeal to Scripture demands no less than a high emphasis on children's evangelism. In relation to the nurturing needs of children as they apply to evangelism, Larry Fowler states: "Nurturing is appropriate and necessary. It is comparable to the watering, fertilizing and weeding of a garden—critical to healthy vegetables! The importance of shepherding and nurturing cannot be diminished. *But we musn't let it crowd out evangelism of children.* We must accomplish them both."[51]

The presentation/invitation of the gospel to children demonstrates sound technique. We would caution, however, that evangelism should not only become a programmatic function but one where parents and ministry leaders are also trained in leading a child to Christ.

---

51. Larry Fowler, *Rock Solid Kids* (Ventura, Calif.: Gospel Light, 2004), 123.

The description of the key teachings on the age of account-ability and the evangelism of children are well thought through, clearly articulated, and well received by us. The Scriptures do not speak to the specific age that a person is responsible to respond to the Lord, but this teaching is stated and demonstrated. When Graves quotes Scripture on the high value that the Lord places on children, we most heartily agree. When there is practical im-petus and persuasion to engage in children's evangelism because of these understandings, we most assuredly agree.

We are in agreement regarding the key time the age of child-hood becomes for receiving Christ. A nice balance is struck when Graves says, "Because of the value God has placed on children, he clearly desires that they be raised with a full knowledge of him." Later Graves asserts: "Children have the potential to become fol-lowers of Christ, and the church plays a significant role in intro-ducing children to Jesus and then helping them grow more and more like him." We affirm these statements. Researchers, like George Barna (as quoted in this chapter), are highlighting the importance of early spiritual formation. Christian Smith speaks of a "moralistic therapeutic deism" and the way teenagers view their religious lives: "The religious and spiritual lives of most U.S. teenagers are significantly shaped by what are to them largely in-visible cultural scripts about how people of various ages are sup-posed to engage religion. Most American youth, in other words, bring strong life course assumptions and expectations to their experiences of religion, often tacitly viewing faith's relevance and importance in terms of 'age-appropriate' stages."[52]

I believe these scripts are developed first in childhood and only later demonstrated in the teen and adult years. That's why children's ministries must be aware of the importance of early spiritual formation.

The use of the Bible (especially the exposition of Old Testa-ment passages) to give foundation to the model is admirable. Look at the areas where the Bible is highlighted:

---

52. Christian Smith, *Soul Searching* (New York: Oxford University Press 2005), 158.

- Affirmation of the Scriptures as the source of spiritual truth.

- The public reading of the Bible.

- The practical teaching of the Word of God in small and large groups.

- The prompting of Scripture toward worship. (Note especially the use of events to create children's questions and the opportunity to respond with parental testimony of the works and words of God.)

- The importance of prayer in response to hearing the Word of God.

- The significance of the modeling of biblical values.

- The meaning of baptism.

- The emphasis on service.

- The fun factor.

- Methods serve the message, not the methods, as overly important.

Parental opportunity and responsibility cannot be over-emphasized. The fine outlining of the role of the parent in the spiritual formation of children is a major point in Scripture. It's lightly addressed in the Contemplative-Reflective and Media-Driven Active-Engagement models. The detailed list of Old Testament passages in this chapter highlights how the Bible views the parent in the spiritual formation of children.

Parent education is the great frustration of many children's ministry programs. Any gathering of children's workers will have discussion regarding the importance of the parent dimension. The Pragmatic-Participatory Model seeks to implement a practical merging of this discussion. There remains a program-driven model of parent involvement from all of the models described in this book, and certainly much creative work will need to be done in the future to ensure parents as the lead disciplers of their children.

This is not to say, however, that we are in complete agreement in all regards. One particular difference would be in relation to the frequency of opportunities that a child should have to believe the gospel. The Promiseland curriculum presents the gospel three times a year, only once in the spring of the year when children are younger. I believe this may be too little. Parents may find that their children are ready to respond in faith at opportune times. The caution of pushing children to a decision is well noted, and we agree that children younger than kindergarten "need time to develop a deeper understanding of who God is before they are able to respond in faith."

Early in the chapter Graves declares that "children's ministries typically have approximately one to one-and-one-half hours a week." I do not concede this to be typical for two reasons. While many are saying that the Sunday school and midweek club programs for children are dying, millions of kids still attend every week. The other reason is one of priority. Some parents spend considerable hours in recreational and educational pursuits. One family shared with me that they could not attend the family training event on Sunday morning after worship because they had to get ready for an extra practice for their son's soccer team—not related to anything other than the coach's desire to "brush up a few skills at mid-season." Give me a break! Is spiritual development of children so low a priority? I wholeheartedly agree that we need to maximize the time that children are involved in church education programs as Graves describes.

While we agree with the description of the age of accountability contained in this chapter, we believe that each person will stand accountable to God for the light they have. Graves quotes Romans 14:12 in relation to each person (including children of accountable age) in relation to the gospel. In Romans 1, the person is said to be without excuse (verse 20) "because that which is known about God is evident within them; for God made it evident to them" (Rom. 1:19 NASB). Later in this same book Paul declares:

For there is no partiality with God. For all who have sinned without the Law will also perish without the Law, and all who have sinned under the Law will be judged by the Law; for it is not the hearers of the Law who are just before God, but the doers of the Law will be justified. For when Gentiles who do not have the Law do instinctively the things of the Law, these, not having the Law, are a law to themselves, in that they show the work of the Law written in their hearts, their conscience bearing witness and their thoughts alternately accusing or else defending them, on the day when, according to my gospel, God will judge the secrets of men through Christ Jesus (Rom. 2:11–16 NASB).

It would seem that each person stands accountable before God because of what he or she has done in suppressing the truth in unrighteousness (Rom. 1:18), and not because they have missed the news of Jesus' death, burial, and resurrection. We must tell them the gospel because they have no hope in their depravity.

Perhaps the most serious contention we have with the Pragmatic-Participatory Model as described is that it's oriented toward a larger church staff and context. Most churches have fewer children, limited resources, and broadly used staff. We will then need to adapt the descriptions given to more of a team-teaching approach. Rather than many specialists with a few generalized roles, we will need many generalists with specialized roles. This will enable teachers in smaller settings to still enjoy the benefits of this model.

In conclusion, we see many valuable additions to the discussion of children's spiritual formation from the description of this model. The strengths are in the balanced approach and varied instructional methods. The values of creativity, age-level appropriateness, and attention to learning styles are well received. Few weaknesses are obvious. Of course, the caution to depend on God's grace is appropriate for each of these models.

Response by the KIDMO Team

"If one is to help a child grow to be more like Christ, how is this best achieved?" This is the question raised by the author advocating the Pragmatic-Participatory Model of children's ministry. It's also a question that demands we do our due diligence in arriving at an adequate answer.

The purpose of this essay is to critique the arguments advanced by the author in favor of the Pragmatic-Participatory Model of children's ministry while actively arguing for the adoption of the Media-Driven Active-Engagement Model. First, we will expose specific logical fallacies, both theological and philosophical, offered in furtherance of the Pragmatic-Participatory Model. Second, we'll demonstrate that the Media-Driven Active-Engagement Model is the natural evolution of the Pragmatic-Participatory Model within the cultural context of children's ministry in twenty-first-century America; and as such, the Media-Driven Active-Engagement Model affords all of the acknowledged benefits of the Pragmatic-Participatory Model while offering additional benefits as well.

In promoting the Pragmatic-Participatory Model, considerable time and thought were given to the "significance of the family to God's people in the spiritual development of their children," and rightly so. A thorough treatment is given to Old Testament principles of family life as a covenant relationship wherein the parents have primary responsibility for raising their children to be faithful and obedient to their covenant God. There are, however, three issues with this appeal to Scripture to make a case for the Pragmatic-Participatory Model.

First, there seems to be an implied presupposition that consideration of the biblical principles that govern the parent-child relationship and the spiritual formation of children is particular to those churches that use the Pragmatic-Participatory Model of children's ministry. Parental responsibility for the spiritual formation of their children is a thoroughly biblical idea: what is taught in the Old Testament is reinforced in the New Testament. Shouldn't these biblical principles inform both the immediate and ultimate goals of all the models of children's ministry presented in this book?

Second, there is a failure to recognize that God's ideal for the parent-child relationship is just that, an ideal: the vast majority of parents today, even "good Christian" parents, are not fulfilling their responsibilities to their children in terms of spiritual formation. Today's parents have been infected with "radical individualism," a just-me-and-Jesus state of mind that causes them to see their personal relationship with Jesus and their relationship with other believers, including their responsibility for the spiritual formation of their own children, as separate and essentially unrelated issues.

As a result, today's kids are a generation of spiritual orphans: while these kids are provided for physically and maybe emotionally by their parents, they are neglected spiritually. We, the local church, must accept the responsibility of being their spiritual foster parents. Our ultimate goal is not to adopt these kids and assume the full responsibility of spiritual parenthood, but rather it is to have these kids reclaimed by the parents who abandoned them on the doorsteps of the local church. This is the two-pronged task of the local church in regard to children's ministry. Our immediate goal is to help facilitate spiritual formation in our kids through programs and relationships; and our ultimate goal is to assist parents in assuming their covenant responsibility of spiritually nurturing their own children.

Finally, there is no demonstrated nexus between the enumerated biblical principles, their almost universal violation, and the Pragmatic-Participatory Model per se. Only some individual program elements, which are almost universally practiced in other children's ministry models, are directly attributable to the methods of spiritual formation outlined in the referenced verses. The other models presented in this text also use the elements of teaching from Scripture, practical application of God's Word, worship, and prayer as methods of spiritual formation for kids. Advocating the Pragmatic-Participatory Model over other models on the basis of these programmatic elements, which are common to all ministry models, is a nonargument.

The nature of the parent-child relationship not only defines the parents' responsibilities to their children; it also affords parents a unique ability to influence positively the spiritual formation of their children. According to the studies of Barna and others, most Christian educators agree that the most effective way for children to begin to know and understand biblical principles is through a parent-child covenant relationship. But what alternative methods are most effective for facilitating this spiritual formation in kids where this biblical relationship between parent and child is lacking?

The nature of the church-child relationship likewise defines our responsibilities to our kids, but it affords us little ability to influence the spiritual formation of our kids relative to their parents. The abdication of parental responsibility to the local church for the spiritual formation of the vast majority of children coupled with our relative inability positively to influence kids in twenty-first-century America must be considered in determining which model of children's ministry is most effective in helping to facilitate spiritual formation in today's kids.

One sound argument offered for the adoption of the Pragmatic-Participatory Model for the one to one-and-a-half hour program typical of most children's ministries is the need to "maximize this time and obtain the greatest spiritual impact possible."

If we truly want the best for our kids in terms of spiritual formation, we must move the lesson outside of the church and into the home. The most powerful ministry is not confined to a brief session on Sunday morning in the children's ministry center, but it can happen anytime and anywhere. And children's ministry workers do not facilitate such ministry and the accompanying spiritual formation; instead, it is facilitated by parents.

Within this model, consideration is also given to numerous New Testament passages in making a case for the Pragmatic-Participatory Model. The scriptural appeals advocating the Pragmatic-Participatory Model on the grounds of the age of accountability, evangelism of children, and baptism are problematic, too. The arguments advanced are deficient because they are often speculative and contradictory at times.

The idea of the age of accountability as outlined under the Pragmatic-Participatory Model is speculative at best. While it is conceded that "the Bible itself does not point to a specific age" and there are "many different viewpoints" regarding a child's accountability for sin, a long discussion of the concept is offered in furtherance of the Pragmatic-Participatory Model of children's ministry. No real scriptural support can be cited for the age of accountability argument as it is articulated; and when Scripture is cited, the arguments are somewhat speculative. Propositions being offered in support of the Pragmatic-Participatory Model do not follow from the overall message of the passage while context is ignored. A more informed historical-grammatical hermeneutic would be beneficial here.

Finally, the conclusions reached are contradictory: "Infants and young children are not to be held accountable for their original sin, until they are mentally capable of making a decision of faith in Jesus Christ," and, "Until children are capable of making a conscious and understandable decision to accept Christ, we must assume they are not saved." Which is it? Do children become accountable when they knowingly sin or not until they understand the concept of salvation in Christ? Are we to assume that kids are accountable or not accountable for their sin?

While the lengthy discussion of the age of accountability in furtherance of the Pragmatic-Participatory Model is confusing and not exactly helpful in assessing the model per se, there is an appropriate focus on child evangelism. The "5–12 Window" (the time of opportunity with significantly higher probabilities of conversion between the ages of five and twelve years old) seems to be a key consideration in the approach to children's ministry that characterizes the Pragmatic-Participatory Model. Although it is stated that "presenting the gospel message is paramount" to the Pragmatic-Participatory Model of children's ministry, the standard approach seems to plan a lesson on salvation only once during the school year for younger children and three times during the same period for older children. Such strategic planning seems to be inadequate.

The Media-Driven Active-Engagement model has the benefit of greater flexibility in terms of when and how to deliver the truth of salvation by grace through faith in Christ. Because series in this model tend to be shorter (five weeks) than series in the Pragmatic-Participatory Model (thirteen weeks to a quarter, although some are shorter), the Media-Driven Active-Engagement Model can be more responsive to the evangelistic needs of the local children's ministry. A periodic, five-week series on salvation is a powerful way to lay a firm foundation for a clear understanding of the gospel message. And regardless of the lesson topic, the teaching video can always be supplemented with live, up-front teaching or small-group discussions that tie in the biblical idea of salvation. For example, during a series on the Ten Commandments, it might be emphasized to the kids that obeying these rules does not save them, but only Jesus and faith in him does that!

The Pragmatic-Participatory Model also emphasizes children "playing an integral part of the ministry implementation." However, it is possible for kids to employ their area(s) of giftedness in the other models of spiritual formation as well. The issue here is more a commitment to using children in ministry service rather than the model per se. Granted, some models might be structured to accommodate this more than others. For example, in the Pragmatic-Participatory and Media-Driven Active-Engagement models, the large-group creative program encourages kids actively to lead their peers in worship. It also affords kids the opportunity to take the microphone and help their children's pastor emcee the program, assist in administering review questions, and coach their teams during Scripture memory.

To be honest, we see the Pragmatic-Participatory Model as evolving out of the Media-Driven Active-Engagement Model of children's ministry. Even advocates of the Pragmatic-Participatory Model seem to recognize this when they begin making their case for their preferred model of children's ministry by describing it as "active" and "engaging." Both models use the same variety of methods to teach, reinforce, and apply the Bible lesson and appeal to the same broad spectrum of learning styles of children.

The basic goals of the Pragmatic-Participatory Model are for children to know God as their heavenly Father, believe in Jesus Christ as their personal Lord and Savior, and live faithfully in the power of the Holy Spirit. We believe the Media-Driven Active-Engagement Model is the best solution for the local church in accomplishing these goals of spiritual formation in today's kids. It offers all of the elements, methods, and benefits of its predecessor, but this new upgrade in children's ministry programming also incorporates the influential power of media into its efforts at facilitating spiritual formation in kids.

Other values of the Pragmatic-Participatory Model are for children to establish positive relationships with other kids, volunteer leaders, and children's ministry staff; and to create a fun learning environment so kids will be motivated to attend themselves and invite friends, too. Again, the Media-Driven Active-Engagement Model achieves these desired outcomes by its nature and structure. There is less programmatic pressure because the worship and teaching are driven by the media, so the volunteers that are recruited, trained, and deployed for ministry to children are freed up to focus on relationship through shared, positive experiences and personal sharing. And the Media-Driven Active-Engagement Model is a veritable kid magnet that fuses faith and fun to create a learning environment that is extremely attractive to kids and simultaneously conducive to spiritual formation.

Evaluating the various models of children's ministry is like playing the TV game show *Jeopardy:* it's not enough to answer the question; we must also question the answer! There is so much at stake! While the purpose of this essay has been to critique the arguments advanced in favor of the Pragmatic-Participatory Model, it must be acknowledged that the other models are *good* models of children's ministry too. But which is the *best* model of children's ministry? While God certainly can and often does use less than our absolute best in accomplishing his purposes, only our best will do! The sovereignty and grace of God are not excuses for us to think that anything less than our best is an acceptable offering to him.

CHAPTER 4

Media-Driven Active-Engagement Model

TIM ELLIS, BILL BAUMGART, AND GREG CARPER

The Media-Driven Active-Engagement Model uses technology and interactive media to emphasize discovery-based and cooperative learning. Based on the assumptions of educational psychologists Jean Piaget, Jerome Bruner, and David Ausubel, this instructional design takes into consideration the unique learning styles of all learners. Rather than relying solely on lecture, which appeals to only the analytic learner, the Media-Driven Active-Engagement Model employs a variety of methods in its instructional design to facilitate and maximize learning for all learners.

The four major desired outcomes of this new pedagogy are:

1. Conceptual understanding of the lesson

2. An introduction to teamwork and collaborative learning

3. Deeper retention and integration of a biblical worldview into daily living

4. Ability to engage in independent learning on a daily basis

Brady's Story

Brady came to our church in early June. We had just started "I Can Be Brave," the latest of KIDMO's new media-driven preschool series Lil' K. Every week when the countdown begins, the kids scramble to clear toys and then run to the screen. That week Brady came in and was quiet for the most part but totally engaged. Another child asked him why he did not have any hair, but a teacher intervened. Brady, at age four, is undergoing chemotherapy for a brain tumor. His family is visiting at the invitation of another family. They do not consider themselves to be churched people.

The video screens lit up with lots of interaction and lots of happy, engaged children. Small-group time and a large-group play activity ended the hour. Brady went home with his mother. We were glad to see him. The following afternoon this e-mail started spreading through our church sent from Brady's mother:

> It's Monday morning, and Brady is back in an Atlanta children's hospital for another round of chemo. Previous treatments required four medical personnel to hold him down. Today Brady lay still and quiet requiring no assistance and did not struggle during any of the procedure. When the procedure was over, the doctors were praising Brady and asked him what made the difference in how he did during his treatment. He told them, "I learned in Sunday school yesterday that God is with me and he helps me to be brave."

This e-mail about little Brady has been a lift to our entire church, and he along with Lil' K, was the subject of the sermon a few Sundays ago. His story received a standing ovation from our seventy-five-hundred-member congregation, many of whom were moved to tears.

In children's ministry you don't often have the benefit of witnessing the transforming impact that our work can bring about. At least we know this time. Thanks for making such a life-altering program for Brady and all of our little ones here at Roswell United Methodist.

> Sharon Yancey, Director of Children's Ministries
> Roswell United Methodist Church
> Roswell, Georgia

Since the launch of KIDMO, we've received lots of letters and e-mails filled with powerful testimonies but none with as much sobering reality as young Brady's story.

Two years earlier we set out with an ambitious and utopian vision to "inspire world changers" of the youngest variety. Word of Brady's story seemed to bring us full circle. Our mission was actually happening. And this from a child at the youngest end of our target market who had seldom visited a church.

KIDMO is an innovative, multimedia-driven program for children's ministry. It is being lauded in some parts of the church as "The Reinvention of Sunday School." While KIDMO is one of the most popular and comprehensive applications of multimedia for children's ministry, it is by no means the only offering in this model. However, it is a successful example of how the Media-Driven Active-Engagement Model is transforming ministries.

In the following pages we'll share our story and our conviction that technology and media are effective tools to reach the children of today. We'll explore being relevant to an ever-changing culture with an unchanging gospel, and we'll unpack this new media-driven model in light of Scripture, education, and broadcast truths. We'll also shed some practical light on how these tools can best find their way into your children's ministry.

Defining Generation M

Our kids' culture can be defined by a single word: *media.* Indeed, media is such a defining element of today's culture that kids between the ages of eight and eighteen have been dubbed Generation M, or the Media Generation. Advertisers, educators, librarians, and even pediatric medical personnel embrace using technology to teach and influence kids. Within churches, though, controversies abound regarding the appropriate use of media.

So what is media, and what does it represent? Most importantly, *media* means different things to different generations. For our grandparents it was the advent of radio. Their imaginations soared as they eagerly huddled around this marvel of innovation and technology, embracing each nightly story or adventure.

For boomers it represents one central invention: television. We were inundated with TV from early childhood, and it continues to represent a significant hold on time and mind for boomers everywhere. *Nick at Nite* is like an old friend rich with childhood memories. This medium certainly brought about a new age of news delivery and information dissemination, but other than an occasional exuberant outburst during *Monday Night Football,* or throwing nearby objects at Dan Rather, this form of broadcast is largely a spectator sport for our generation.

We are here to talk about our kids and, consequently, their generation. To Generation M, media is far more than merely TV. In fact, the average elementary-age child rates TV significantly down the list of preferred media pastimes. For every one hour of television watched, kids today spend four hours using other media. Online gaming, music, instant messaging, blogs, Xbox, PlayStation, portable handheld games, and computer-based interactive games make up the collective television for this generation. However, the significant distinction of their media is that at its core it is participatory, engaging kids in a customized journey based on their skills and interests.

So a new model of children's ministry was formed to reach Generation M kids. It is the Media-Driven Active-Engagement Model. This model is based on the assumption that ministry, regardless of audience or culture, must take into consideration the unique distinctives of those it seeks to bring into God's kingdom. It uses technology and interactive media to emphasize discovery-based learning. Technology and media are effective tools in reaching the children of today. They enable leaders to communicate the gospel message in ways that engage kids to Bible action, inspire children's workers into deeper relationship with their students, and transform both children and their leaders into the spiritual champions God intends them to be.

Church analyst and futurist Leonard Sweet addresses this new paradigm and illustrates the need to become more fluid in ministering to a postmodern culture. Sweet argues that this particular turning is actually a return to the past, to medieval forms of worship. Multimedia is a throwback to a preliterate culture, before the Protestant Reformation, before the invention of the printing press, when churchgoers read images—church paintings, stained-glass windows, tapestries—instead of words. "Images and metaphors are so much deeper and more complex than words," says Sweet. "It's the most primary language—when you dream, do you dream in words? The natural language of your mind is metaphors and images."

Consider these key findings from *Generation M: Media in the Lives of 8–18 Year-olds,* a Kaiser Family Foundation study from March 2005:

- Kids spend an average of nearly 6½ hours a day, well over a third of their waking hours, with media.

- Kids spend more time with media (44½ hours a week) than dad or mom spend at their full-time job (40 hours a week).

- Kids spend more time with media (6½ hours a day) than they do with their parents (2¼ hours a day).

- Kids spend more time with media (44½ hours a week) than they do in the classroom at school (30–35 hours a week).

- Kids are natural media multitaskers who absorb 8½ hours of media content a day in only 6½ hours. By using more than one medium simultaneously about a quarter of the time, kids are exposed to 59½ hours of media content a week. About one out of three kids talk on the phone, use the Internet or instant messaging, watch TV, or listen to music while doing their homework.[1]

Media is everywhere. Our kids literally have access to media almost on demand. They can get wired, plug in, tune in, or turn on whenever and wherever they want. According to the Kaiser study, the typical Generation M kid lives in a home with an average of 3.6 CD or tape players, 3.5 TVs, 3.3 radios, 2.9 VCRs/DVD players, 2.1 video game consoles, and 1.5 computers. Many kids' rooms have "evolved into multimedia centers." Two-thirds have a TV in their bedrooms; half have a VCR/DVD player and a video game player, and one-third have a computer in their rooms. And when they leave home, portable media devices go with them: two-thirds have a portable CD, tape, or MP3 player, over half have a handheld video game player, and over one-third carry a cell phone. Generation M kids have media in their homes, in their bedrooms, in their classrooms, in their minivans, in their backpacks and in their pockets.[2] Why not at church?

Active Engagement and Biblical Truth

Although it's evident that the Media-Driven Active-Engagement Model is culturally relevant, it must be analyzed in the light of Scripture. We must answer the question: Is this model and approach consistent with what God has revealed through his Word and through the life and person of Jesus Christ?

God made no express statements in Scripture either commanding or forbidding the use of multimedia in ministry. Nowhere in the Bible will you read, "Thou shalt build me a multimedia empire." Likewise, you will not read, "Thou shalt not suspend disco balls from the sanctuary ceiling." There simply are no concrete rules governing the use of technology in communicating the gospel to kids or anyone else. For this reason we have seen a dramatic increase in the number of Christian radio stations, television broadcasts, Internet sites, etc. All are committed to fulfilling the Great Commission with whatever resources they

1. Victoria Rideout, et al., "Generation M: Media in the Lives of 8–18 Year-olds, Executive Summary," Kaiser Family Foundation (March 2005), 6–7, 23.
2. Ibid., 9–11.

have at their disposal. It's obvious, given the fruit of such labors, that God is richly blessing this integration of timeless message with contemporary methodology.

The absence of specific, concrete rules, however, does not mean that we are free to do whatever we want, whatever is popular, or whatever seems to work. Rather, God has revealed some dynamic principles in his Word that guide us, the church, in our efforts to fulfill the Great Commission. A careful consideration of these God-given principles must inform every conviction we hold about what constitutes true biblical ministry.

Principle 1: Ministry Is Culturally Conditioned

In his first letter to the church at Corinth, the apostle Paul wrote, "To the kids I became as a kid, in order to win kids." Well, sort of. OK, Paul didn't *actually* write that. Or did he? Let's take a look at 1 Corinthians 9:19–23:

> For though I am free from all, I have made myself a servant to all, that I might win more of them. To the Jews I became as a Jew, in order to win Jews. To those under the law I became as one under the law (though not being myself under the law) that I might win those under the law. To those outside the law I became as one outside the law (not being outside the law of God but under the law of Christ) that I might win those outside the law. To the weak I became weak, that I might win the weak. I have become all things to all people, that by all means I might save some. I do it all for the sake of the gospel, that I may share with them in its blessings (ESV).

Writing under the inspiration of the Holy Spirit, Paul articulates this general principle: ministry is culturally conditioned. In humble submission to God who called him and to those whom God called him to serve, the apostle was willing to "become all things to all people, that by all means [he] might save some." Paul was willing to accommodate the culture of his hearers in presenting the gospel of Christ, whether they were Jews or Gentiles, proselytes or pagans. He was willing to adopt a different approach for different people to bring as many as possible to faith and devotion to Jesus as Lord and Savior. Paul understood that his ministry was not about him but about Christ and his kingdom. Paul realized that he served God best when he helped those God called him to serve.

If we are going to be faithful to the Word of God, we must take this biblical principle seriously and apply it to our ministry to kids. We have been given the amazing privilege and the awesome task of reaching children with the gospel and bringing them into the kingdom of God. To us, brothers and sisters in Christ, "To the kids, become as a kid, that you might win kids!" But what is the consistent language of faith? How does the speaking and acting out of that language not only reinforce but actually form children?

Kids need the gospel in their own language. Our kids, like everyone else, have a language complete with vocabulary and idioms, a mind-set, and an ability to understand certain concepts that are particular to their culture. These peculiarities can negatively impact their ability to accept the gospel message if it is not translated into their native language. In response to this, God poured out his Holy Spirit on the first Christians in the day of Pentecost almost two thousand years ago in Jerusalem. People from different nations and cultures could gain entry into the kingdom of God.

Contemporary multicultural settings are scary and overwhelming. How can we raise children who can engage and transform the realm of media and culture for the kingdom? This biblical learning model helps navigate the journey by giving children critical facilities to analyze, deconstruct, and assess what is dangerous, evil, or false. Churches all over the world spend countless millions of dollars every year on mission endeavors. Many of these initiatives are designed to translate the Scriptures into languages that other cultures and people groups can understand. In addition to this noble investment, we should also ask, "What are we willing to do so that our kids can have the gospel in their own language?"

Given the influence of electronic media in the last century, it is clear and generally unquestioned that something must be offered to speak into the lives of all who live in the media-created worlds. Often the home is not a refuge, so community becomes the source. In community all are educators. All behavior is teaching. All must be trained to use the evolution of tools to the greatest benefit.

For Paul, the word *gospel* had a definite meaning as used in 1 Corinthians 9:23. The apostle insisted in Galatians 1:6–8 that there was only one gospel, "the gospel of Christ." Another "gospel," a different "gospel," a distorted "gospel," or a "gospel" contrary to the one he and the other apostles preached was not to be accepted. Regarding Christ, the gospel asserted: his full divinity as the Word of God incarnate, his perfect life, his sacrificial death, his resurrection, his ascension into heaven, and his unique role as Lord and Savior. When this gospel is ministered to kids in a way that is conditioned by their culture, the gospel is validated and God's universal Word to man transcends human culture.

Principle 2: God Reveals Himself in Multimedia

The inspired author of the letter to the Hebrews begins his message this way: "Long ago, at many times and in many ways, God spoke to our fathers by the prophets, but in these last days he has spoken to us by his Son" (Heb. 1:1–2 ESV). The Greek word translated "many ways" is *polutropos,* which carries the meaning of "variously as to method or form."[3] From the beginning of history, God has revealed himself to his people in many ways, and ultimately in the person of his Son, Jesus Christ.

Page after page the Scriptures confirm this principle: God reveals himself in multimedia. God communicates his truth through the written and spoken words of the prophets, through visual signs and wonders, through fragrant smells, through sweet tastes, and through the power of touch and movement. God uses the pen of Moses and the mouth of Elijah. God uses

---

3. James Strong, *The New Strong's Complete Dictionary of Bible Words* (Nashville: Thomas Nelson Publishers, 1998), 684, #4187.

the thunder, lightning, and the thick clouds on Mount Sinai and the fire on Mount Carmel. God uses the fragrance of the incense in the tabernacle and the temple. God uses the sweetness of the manna in the wilderness and the taste of the bread and meat delivered by the ravens. God uses the act of applying the blood of the Passover lamb to the lintel and the doorposts. God speaks in many ways and through multiple media, especially in the person of his Son.

Jesus was truly phenomenal in every sense of the word! His coming as God in the flesh can only be described as the rarest of occurrences. As a man, he was superlative in that he was the holy and righteous one, perfect and without sin! Everyone marveled at the miracles and teachings of Christ. But Jesus was phenomenal in a more mundane sense, too, in that he could be perceived and observed. In the person of Jesus Christ, God personally revealed himself to us in a way that we could see, hear, and touch. Jesus was phenomenal!

The apostle John records the significance of the Jesus phenomenon in his first letter. First John 1:1–4 reads:

> That which was from the beginning, which we have heard, which we have seen with our eyes, which we looked upon and have touched with our hands, concerning the word of life—the life was made manifest, and we have seen it, and testify to it and proclaim to you the eternal life, which was with the Father and was made manifest to us—that which we have seen and heard we proclaim also to you, so that you too may have fellowship with us; and indeed our fellowship is with the Father and with his Son Jesus Christ. And we are writing these things so that our joy may be complete (ESV).

Here, the beloved apostle gives a concise summary of the gospel. Jesus Christ is the eternal Word, the Son of God. He came in the flesh to reveal the divine gifts of eternal life and fellowship with God. We receive these blessings by believing that Jesus is the Christ. Our present discussion, however, demands that we not only consider the content of John's gospel message but also the manner in which that message was received and subsequently passed on by John and the other apostles.

John emphasizes the apostles' multisensory experience of the incarnation of Christ. Not only did they hear Jesus with their ears, but they also saw him with their own eyes, and they touched him with their own hands. The Twelve spent three and a half years experiencing Jesus. Jesus spoke the words of eternal life; employed occasional dramatic flair; performed signs and wonders, mind-bending feats of faith; and in the most dramatic display of all, he rose from the dead. Life with Christ was an audiovisual-kinesthetic learning adventure.

In turn the apostles made Christ known by testifying to what they had experienced, proclaiming the gospel and writing the Holy Scriptures. They too performed signs and wonders as a visual confirmation of the truth of their message. Hearing, reading, and seeing were all ways the early Christians received the gospel message. From its foundation, the church has used multimedia to make Christ known!

Indeed Jesus was a true multimedia teacher. While there is really only one word in Greek for *hear,* there are seven different and distinct words for *see.* These words range in meaning from a wide-eyed gaze at something remarkable to mechanical or passive vision, from a close and continued inspection to watching from a distance. And Jesus used these words in his teaching.

In Luke 12:24, 27, Jesus tells his disciples to "consider" (literally "see") the lilies and the ravens. In Matthew 12:41–42 Jesus says that in him, the disciples "behold" (literally "see") something greater than Jonah and Solomon. The examples could be greatly multiplied, but the point is this: seeing played an important part in Jesus' teaching and subsequent New Testament proclamation. Romans 10:17 stresses that "faith comes from hearing, and hearing through the word of Christ." But seeing is also an important aspect of strengthening and confirming that by faith, working through the Word, we receive from the Holy Spirit. When seeing and hearing are coupled together, they denote not only intellectual but also spiritual perception.

Principle 3: Whatever Is Helpful Is Biblical

In his first letter to the Corinthians, the apostle Paul wrote against false teachers who were spreading the destructive doctrine of antinomianism. Antinomians believed and taught that because of the grace of God, they were free to do whatever they wanted. This "anything goes" approach to faith was destructive not only to the antinomians but also to those around them. Their abuse of freedom led others into slavery to sin.

Paul rejects the antinomian belief, "All things are lawful for me," as a thoroughly unbiblical idea. In response to this error, the apostle lays down this general principle: whatever is helpful is biblical. First Corinthians 6:12 and 10:23, 33 read: "'All things are lawful for me,' but not all things are helpful. 'All things are lawful for me,' but I will not be enslaved by anything. . . . 'All things are lawful,' but not all things are helpful. 'All things are lawful,' but not all things build up. . . . I try to please everyone in everything I do, not seeking my own advantage, but that of many, that they may be saved" (ESV).

We are not free to do whatever we want. Such freedom is nothing more than self-centeredness at best—or worse, slavery to sin. In children's ministry we are free to do whatever is helpful. We are free to do whatever builds kids up in their faith in Christ. Whatever is helpful is biblical.

The question must be asked, "Is multimedia helpful to the cause of ministry or hurtful?" In ministry, helpfulness is never measured in reference to the minister but always in reference to the people who are being served. The Greek word translated *helpful* in 1 Corinthians 6:12 and 10:23 above is *sumphero*. The same Greek word is translated *"advantage"* in 1 Corinthians 10:33. And we are not to seek our own advantage but the advantage of others. *Helpful* is a relative term—relative to everyone else! It's not about you! It's about the kids! If we ask the question, "Do I want or need multimedia or technology to be helped along in my Christian faith?" we have missed the point entirely. Rather, we must ask the question, "Do the kids want or need multimedia to be built up in their faith?"

"To please everyone in everything we do" does not mean giving kids what they want regardless of its effects. Rather, we do it with a view of giving them what they need, what is helpful, and what will build them up, in a way that makes them want it, "so that they may be saved." We must answer the question, is multimedia helpful or hurtful? Can it bring kids closer to a relationship with Jesus? Can it contribute to kids' growing in the Christian faith? Can it be conducive to spiritual formation?

Practical theology demands that we seek to be as influential as possible in sharing the gospel with kids. In a world shaped by pluralism, democracy, religious freedom, consumerism, mobility, and increasing access to entertainment, how does the church engage children and communicate the Word of God? Through multimedia! If we are willing to tap into the potential benefits of multimedia as it relates to the spiritual development of our kids, we can begin to assert greater influence in bringing them to faith and growing them in their relationship with Christ. We must reject the audiovisual asceticism in some quarters of the church, where "do not watch, do not listen" has replaced "do not handle, do not taste, do not touch" as the new self-made religion that is according to human traditions and precepts (Col. 2:20–23).

We can create a story and a personal history that ultimately finds its place and home in the community of believers. Recent forays into media and child development studies have come to see narratives as powerfully formative in the lives of children. The Bible is a story, and its truths speak a language. How can that dialect become the main articulation of each child? The goal of the Media-Driven Active-Engagement Model is to cultivate a love of the kingdom by equipping kids with more than resolution. It seeks to create concrete activities that confirm truth.

Theology plays a powerful role in the creation and ongoing formation of the Media-Driven Active-Engagement Model of children's ministry. The importance of narratives and the symbols that accompany them are being championed across all learning disciplines in our current educational landscape. Learning through sharing stories is now understood to be a primary force from which human identity is formed. Because so much of our sharing now happens via computers, mobile phones, and other media devices, the active engagement model seeks to assimilate direct social encounters with the virtual or media-driven ones. There is an emerging awareness of the importance of the communal family and that the Christian experience is a drama lived out together encouraging interaction of all types from e-mail to the dinner table.

Our program was formed through extensive and consistent exploration. We seek a properly ordered hierarchy of values, virtues, and behaviors based on Scripture. Although art and media provide highly visible expressions of our values and virtues, ultimately the ongoing, daily role of the community of like-minded people models and forms these values and virtues into lifestyle expressions, or behaviors, of individuals. This is precisely why relationship is the cornerstone of the media-driven model.

In the light of Scripture, the Media-Driven Active-Engagement Model is faithful to the Word of God in reaching kids with the gospel. The concept rests on a solid foundation of biblical principles. While this model certainly is not the *only* way to make Christ known to young kids, it must be acknowledged as a viable and powerful method to communicate to this audience. This media-driven approach is highly effective because it is culturally conditioned. It gives the gospel message to kids in their own language and allows God to speak and reveal himself through creativity and imagination. Active engagement effectively leverages the influential power of multimedia and applies it to communicating biblical truth aimed at the spiritual transformation of kids.

Active Engagement Methodology in Practice

OK, set down this book. Go pick up the phone and call your mom, sister, brother, or significant other family member, and say, "Reading makes my brain fizzle, but you dear, make my heart sizzle!" Did you do it? We are completely serious! Who knows the last time you made that relational connect. If you followed these precise instructions, then congratulations! You have just been actively engaged. (And you made Mom feel good also.)

Grant's Story

Hey Team KIDMO, I just wanted to share this e-mail with you from my niece. Her son, Grant, is a five-year-old autistic little guy. I had wondered how he would accept Lil' K. Thanks for doing a fantastic job! —Rachel Bess

> I have to say a great big thank-you for bringing Lil' K to Central. The kids seem to respond well to it. Mostly, though, it has been a blessing for us! Grant has never really tuned in to Bible lessons, much less remembered them. He also has not had any interest in letting us read Bible stories to him at home. Since Lil' K began, he has been so excited about coming to church and seeing each and every new story! He talks about it all week trying to figure out what story will be told next! He keeps every MAP Book. He asks me to read them to him over and over again. (He has them memorized and informs me when I miss a word.) He lines them up and taps each one mumbling about what that story was about. He talks about the Bible verse and the Doodad for the week! He carries the MAP Books all over the house and in the car! He has even asked to have Bible storybooks read to him at home. Wow! What an impact this program is making on my child. This very visual child is being given the opportunity to hide God's Word in his heart because of Lil' K. Up to now, I wondered if Grant would ever really understand biblical truth. I don't know what the future holds, but for now he is taking the first steps in learning about our wonderful Creator. Thank you doesn't seem enough to say, but it is the only way I know to express my appreciation for making such a difference in Grant's spiritual life!
>
> Michelle Adams, Tulsa Central Church of the Nazarene
> Tulsa, Oklahoma

Philosophy of Active Engagement

The Media-Driven Active-Engagement Model of children's spiritual formation is based on clearly defined biblical principles. Likewise, it has a thoroughly reasoned philosophy of ministry as well. This philosophy is based on the assumption that ministry, regardless of audience or culture, must take into consideration the unique distinctives of those it seeks to bring into God's kingdom.

During the technology boom of the 1990s, many people feared that the Internet would drive people into the isolation of their online cocoons, forever hibernating in their back bedroom, leaving the world of face-to-face relationships, comforted by their chat-room friends and virtual communities. With the advantage of hindsight, we can see that this fear has not come to pass.

While the Internet and its World Wide Web has amplified and, in a number of cases, exacerbated some social and relational problems, it has not become a substitute for seeking out real and authentic relationships where people meet together to agree for social interaction. In fact, as Leonard Sweet points out, the Internet is actually making it easier for people to find one another.[4]

For the person in your neighborhood who's looking for some direction and purpose in life, your church and your children's ministry are just a Google and a click away. And if your church isn't, then the church down the street from yours is.

It is important to understand the role of technology in bringing people together in an actively engaged children's ministry. Kids understand this inherently. It is no secret that computers, video games, mobile phones, and the television are communal gathering points for kids. It is not uncommon for a group of friends to be huddled around any one of these appliances sharing a story of some conquest or defeat, or the latest happening at school. Even television has evolved into an interactive device. Kid's programming on television often expects and even requires one to chime in and play or learn along.

Blue's Clues pioneered the concept of "talking back" to the TV. Now a whole roster of shows requires feedback to help solve

---

4. Leonard Sweet, INCM Leadership Challenge Cruise, November 3–6, 2003.

puzzles, determine the correct road to take on an adventure, or yell out loud for a team. Many shows even provide the means for live participation by offering feedback through your computer's Internet connection. This phenomenon is not new of course; fans of sports events, reality shows, game shows, and in some cases news watchers have been yelling at their televisions for years.

Television, especially too much of it, is commonly criticized as having a negative impact on children. Generation M kids, especially the younger ones, spend a lot of time with television. Kids between the ages of eight and ten spend an average of just over four hours a day watching TV, if you include DVDs and videos. The parental fear is that splitting kids' attentions into short and numerous video segments and sound bites is not good for them.

Science Daily reports that studies are actually finding that "some types of television viewing may actually enhance children's intellectual development."[5] Lee Rainey, the director of the Pew Internet & American Life Project, argues that a positive effect of our kids' immersion in multimedia is that they are "more efficient" thinkers who can process information more quickly.[6] There are other developmental benefits, too; according to the Kaiser study, kids who spend the most time with media also spend "more time with their parents, being physically active, and pursuing other hobbies."[7] Intellectual, family-social, physical, and personal developmental benefits seem to follow higher multimedia use.

What are the potential spiritual benefits of multimedia? Can it be helpful? Can it build up? The simple answer may lie in media's ability to influence kids.

According to George Barna, author of the groundbreaking book *Transforming Children into Spiritual Champions,* media is one of the greatest agents of influence in the lives of kids. Barna outlines a three-tiered system of influence as it relates to kids, with the most influential factors being in the first tier and the

---

5. http://www.sciencedaily.com/releases/2001/09/010924061623.htm.

6. Deborah Fallows, "The Internet and Daily Life," Pew Internet and American Life Project (August 11, 2004), 22.

7. Rideout, et al., "Generation M," 14.

least influential factors being in the third tier. Parents are in the first or most influential tier, as are most forms of media, including TV, contemporary music, the Internet, books, and publications. The second or middle tier includes school and friends. The third or least influential tier includes church groups and extended family, among others.[8]

TIERS OF INFLUENCE

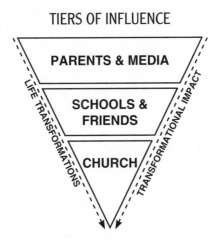

When coupled with other findings in Barna's studies, these tiers of influence give great insight into what is helpful when it comes to children's ministry. Consider the following:

> Our national surveys have shown that while more than 4 out of 5 parents (85 percent) believe they have the primary responsibility for the moral and spiritual development of their children, more than two out of three of them abdicate that responsibility to their church. . . . In a typical week, fewer than 10 percent of parents who regularly attend church with their kids read the Bible together or pray together (other than at meal times). . . . Even fewer families— 1 out of 20—have any type of worship experience together with their kids, other than while they are at church during a typical month.[9]

---

8. George Barna, *Transforming Children into Spiritual Champions* (Ventura, Calif.: Regal Books, 2003), 57–58.

9. Ibid., 77–78.

Mom and Dad have abandoned their roles as the spiritual leaders of their children and given them over to their churches, with about as much influence as Cousin Joe from Idaho who visits every other year at Christmas!

Looking to the first tier of influence, it seems only wise that churches would harness the power of media to be used as a positive influence in the lives of children. Media is often lambasted as the distraction that distances families and dims social interaction. Used in positive and educational ways, however, media-driven properties have the potential to revolutionize entire generations.

The Next Generation: The Coming Media Revolution

The church has strong opinions regarding media, and for good reason. Whether we the church like it or not, the prevalence of media in the lives of our kids and its influence on their development isn't going to diminish in the years ahead. If anything, the influence of media will be even more prevalent and influential in the generations to come. Studies conducted by the Kaiser Family Foundation measuring media use by children ages six months to six years document the unprecedented immersion of these younger kids in multiple electronic media: television, DVDs and videos, computers and video games, CDs and radio. The report identified this trend of growing multimedia use by younger kids as "a potentially revolutionary phenomenon" in American society.[10]

The media revolution is already here! Rejecting the power of the medium because of association would be like a medieval knight not using a sword because it's sharp and someone might get hurt. We can run into the battle of counterculture unarmed, or we can suit up and wield one of the most adaptable, transferable, culturally relevant tools ever offered to the church. As biblical knights, the church must be ready, willing, and able to engage Generation M on its terms. We must leverage the prevalence and influence of media so that we may capitalize on the

---

10. Victoria J. Rideout, et al., "Zero to Six: Electronic Media in the Lives of Infants, Toddlers, and Preschoolers," Kaiser Family Foundation (Fall 2003), 12.

244 — PERSPECTIVES ON CHILDREN'S SPIRITUAL FORMATION

unprecedented opportunity we have to reach kids with the gospel of Christ "so that by all means we might save some."

The stakes are high. Creating a biblical worldview in children is a big assignment. There are steep requirements for abstract learning. To understand fully an abstract thought challenges the limitations of both our ability to process information and to remember it. This is why the most effective way to bring Generation M to understand and integrate the abstract ideas embodied in a biblical worldview is to use a variety of teaching styles and approaches to learning. Participating in learning activities as a group offers many different dynamics and experiences which can present and model abstract concepts such as virtue, love, and compassion. In a culture such as ours, which espouses privacy and personal choice with high value, the active-engagement model can break through this potential cultural barrier by demonstrating Christian faith as an identity that is shared in the group experience. This helps the student understand that abstract ideas influence behavior, speech, and thinking. Truth is not just talked about, leaving it as an abstract concept, but rather is made visible through the shared group experience. One of the most distinctive qualities of the Media-Driven Active-Engagement Model is its exceptional ability to enhance creative communication, improve biblical application, and demonstrate mnemonic techniques.

This is not a treatise for TV and technology but rather a call to reach out and inspire world changers. In fact, at KIDMO, we believe our purpose is to *inspire world changers:* to be in the world, understanding and using all the tools God has given through his innovative creation, to transform people into spiritual champions. We believe in liberating children from the idea that they cannot or should not be world changers at their young age.

In the Media-Driven Active-Engagement Model of children's ministry, media-driven content should not be passive but active. In fact, it should be interactive. One of the most common misconceptions about this model is that kids sit passively in front of a large screen for long periods of time being entertained with mind-numbing frivolity. The reason for this misconception is that too many people have stuck a well-produced video of a funny purple reptile into the cathode-ray box and used it as a video babysitter. This is not what we have in mind as media-driven content that promotes the Media-Driven Active-Engagement Model.

How High Tech Can Bring about High Touch

Relationship permeates the Media-Driven Active-Engagement Model. This is true at every level and at each point of contact with the participating children. The core components of this model are the media character, the media content, the leaders involved, and the interaction that the leaders enjoy with the students.

Media-driven curriculum in the Media-Driven Active-Engagement Model features characters who feel like people kids want to know. They are interesting, likable, and attract kids to participate in conversation. Without conversation, there is no relationship. If there is no conversation, there is no media-driven active engagement, there is just an audience watching. Conversation means just that. The kids talk back to the characters; they are prompted by their on-screen friends to talk to one another and to participate. They participate with their voices, with their gestures (such as hand motions), and with their entire bodies (such as moving around the room or running in place). There is no end to how interaction can be prompted in this way.

The content itself should be relationship based. For example, at KIDMO we say that we don't engage in Bible *study* but, rather, in Bible *action*. It's not enough to present information. In the Media-Driven Active-Engagement Model there must be credible linkage to the lives and the relationships in which we're involved. Our world is a world of relationships; and as we develop a biblical worldview, we're equipped to make a difference in the lives of the people around us, or the people we are in *relationship* with. A person may be a Bible scholar, but that doesn't mean he or she has developed a biblical worldview and the relational skills it requires. World changers understand the nuances of relationship and how God desires us to interact with those who bear his image.

What Is the Role of Teachers and Leaders?

Those migrating to the Media-Driven Active-Engagement Model often fear that teachers or ministry leaders play a diminished role in the children's ministry program. This is false and counterproductive to the mission of this model. This model does not promote a passive, noninteractive role of media whereby students sit in front of a screen and stare while teachers and leaders watch from the sidelines. Instead, this model raises the bar on relationship-building expectations of the children's ministry staff and leaders.

The Media-Driven Active-Engagement Model is a reaction to what limits teachers, volunteers, and ministry staff from connecting relationally with the children. One factor that limits a teacher's ability to connect relationally with children is the inordinate amount of time spent in preparation for class. A volunteer may invest hours studying the lesson plan, preparing activities, and getting supplies. Most leaders, when asked, felt preparation was a burden, not an asset, to their classroom time. What's more, because they invest so much time in preparation, when they arrive for their ministry time, they're more agenda minded than relationally minded. "We've got lots to do, so let's get busy doing it."

Using media lightens the preparation demand and allows teachers to be with kids, focusing more on each child's needs. As much as we would like leaders to invest their time and energy preparing lessons, praying for their kids, and keeping up on personal contact during the week, the reality is that most leaders have a limited amount of time each week, and they must choose where and how to invest that time. Often, because a presentation is needed, preparation becomes the priority, and the personal and relational touch is lost beneath a layer of perfunctory busyness. By redirecting the time previously required for preparation, leaders can focus on what is important to each child, what life issues they face, how they live out God's Word, and can specifically pray for each child.

The Media-Driven Active-Engagement Model expects leaders to turn their preparation time into relationship time. Since much of the teaching is presented through interactive media via video or DVD, the need for leaders to prepare and practice their presentation is minimal. They need only to acquaint themselves with the material that the media will present. Programs using the Media-Driven Active-Engagement Model provide not only the presentation material for the teaching and competitive games that challenge comprehension and Scripture memory but also the discussion material for small-group interaction. This assistance represents hours typically spent by staff and leaders in preparation for the weekly program. In the Media-Driven Active-Engagement Model, leaders are encouraged to convert some or all of this time into relationship time. During the program this includes leading small-group discussions and prayer time and interacting with kids during competition and media-driven sessions. During the week this includes prayer time, phone calling, note writing, e-mailing, and personal visits.

While not all children's ministry leaders and teachers are proficient in engaging through their personal presentation style and skills, by definition all should be intent on loving, relating, and caring for the children under their tutelage. Relationship development is at the core of disciple making, and those who desire to see kids develop into spiritually mature disciples of Jesus should have relationship development as a primary focus of their ministries.

The Fatigued Program

This paradigm shift in expectations and requirements for children's ministry leaders has breathed new life into many plateaued or dying programs. Two things commonly happen when a children's ministry program effectively adopts a Media-Driven Active-Engagement Model.

First, the program finds that it's easier to staff than with any of the other models of children's spiritual formation. The staffing requirements are often less. This is especially true during the large-group portion of the program. The small-group time should have a teacher-to-student ratio between one-to-four and one-to-eight.

Second, recruiting teachers is often much easier than with other spiritual formation models. The media-driven active-engagement program is dynamic and fun which translates to an exuberant and enjoyable time for everyone, students and teachers alike. Since teachers are not required to be dynamic presenters themselves, many more are qualified to participate as leaders with minimal training. The main requirement is that they are relational and love kids.

Enthusiasm

Another benefit to the children's ministry that uses the Media-Driven Active-Engagement Model is a renewed sense of purpose and well-being. Since each lesson and series is sharply focused and defined by scope and sequence, the entire audience is aware of what is being learned, practiced, and accomplished.

Enthusiasm is elevated due to the high-quality production value that a media-driven active-engagement programming brings to children's ministry. Even though leading voices of the church such as George Barna are trumpeting the high value that must be placed on children's ministry, many children's programs still suffer from lack of funds and attention. These programs are still a low priority on the church's budget. Media-driven active-engagement programs offer cost-effective solutions immediately to raise the quality of presentation on a weekly basis. A media-driven program can offer high production value for just a few dollars a week for an entire elementary program. For many churches the week they start KIDMO is the week they offer the best production value in the entire church, including what takes place in "big church" (the adult worship service).

We strive to teach God's truth in ways that impact a child's choices and actions. Creativity and imagination are precious resources for penetrating their language and culture. Kids must be needed, valued, and connected. Their church experience must be relevant to their daily lives. Kids have time, availability, and enthusiasm to accomplish great things for his kingdom. A kid's day-to-day existence is not sidetracked by many of the complications that distract their adult counterparts. By using their language to teach them to develop a biblical worldview, we can ignite an awakening that will impact generations to come.

Active-Engagement Methodology in Practice

Stop. Stand up. Pretend that your nose is a skateboard ramp. Using your finger as your board, see how many different stunts you can create while simultaneously reciting the entire lineage of temple servants from the book of Ezra. (Hint: They begin with Ziha and end with Hatipha. And don't forget Uzza!) It's best to keep your finger from entering the nasal passage. Did you do it? Congratulations once again! You have just engaged in simultaneity using visual, auditory, and tactile learning.

Ethan's Story

We have been so impressed with the Lil' K curriculum and the impact we've seen it have on our four-year-old son, Ethan. Ethan had been going through a phase where he wasn't very excited about going to church. This was a problem because we volunteer on the worship team during every service. Church is not an option for our family; it's a priority. Then Lil' K came to the rescue! I've never heard my son get so excited about church, beg to go, and ask when he'd get to see Lil' K again. Even more importantly, Ethan is telling me every detail of the stories he's learned throughout the week, asking me to go over his MAP Book every day, and applying the lesson to his own little life. Last night, when he was a little nervous about sleeping in his new room, he sighed and then said confidently, "I can be brave because God is with me! Just like Lil' K!" Thank you for making the Bible come to life for my son. You are an answer to prayer!

Tara Wiley, First Baptist Church
Bossier City, Lousiana

Active Engagement in Action

So what tools are out there? You would have to be living in a cave not to be aware of or inundated with the onslaught of new media-driven tools for children's ministry. However, it can be confusing and scary to know where to begin. Most major ministries have media resources now. The ministries of Willow Creek, Saddleback, Church on the Move, and of course our own company KIDMO are just a few of the entries into this emerging field of effective ministry. Many of the larger curriculum companies also provide offerings in this area. These range from solutions that are designed to be complete programs to supplemental tools that require a little more of your creativity and ingenuity in implementing. Let's look at both scenarios.

Though programs such as ours are designed to be a total experience, many churches are using these resources in varied and unique ways. The complete program is designed to keep your prep time to a minimum, giving a solid, proven format to follow. It contains teaching, worship, interactive learning games, Bible memory, small-group directives, and take-home print resources.

By adding your own elements to those provided, you can customize your presentation. Some alternative approaches include supplementing the programming with your own skits, dramas, videos, and live teaching. You can use a video teaching segment one week and then expound on it the following week with live discussion. Have your own worship leader or kids' worship team lead along with the media-driven worship tools. Have Christian music videos or CDs playing when the kids arrive and during game time. Be imaginative, but remember that relationship takes top priority.

If you are one of the privileged few that has an extensive media department, you can greatly expand your options. Create your own man-on-the-street Bible games like Jay Leno. Rotate kid interviews with your theme and message. Use a popular clip from a family-oriented or animated film to illustrate a lesson. Identify your strongest, most dynamic communicator and create your own video teaching segments. These options are only recommended if you have vast personnel resources and budget. And even then, you need not become the Francis Ford Coppola of church dramas.

Environment

Every bit as important as the media tools you choose is the environment you use them in. Kids can intuitively sense whether the environment they step into is reflective of your culture or theirs. The goal is to create an aesthetic that is inviting, engaging, and screams to Generation M, "Welcome! You matter." The good news is that the media-driven environment is scalable to your ministry size and budget. Instead of investing in large stationary fixtures that serve only one purpose, you can create a flexible, adaptable design that allows you to change with new seasons or themes.

Theming alone is worthy of a treatise. A few key elements are moving lights, media imagery, powerful dynamic sound, lighted gobos (projecting key words or Bible verses on the wall), gaming stations (like Xbox/PlayStation for boys and DDR for girls), and casual seating areas that create conversation stations. One ministry we know assembled a kids council to make recommendations for room layout and design. It was a great success! Nothing communicates that kids matter more than allowing them leadership in their children's ministry. As our own Johnny Rogers says, "If your kids could drive, would they choose your children's ministry?" There are countless stories of kids in the media-driven model waking their parents on Sunday and insisting that they take them to church. Is that scenario not often reversed?

The key objective is to create a place that's safe, fun, and reflective of their DNA. Too often kids are made to feel like foreign visitors in an alien adult land. By embracing their aesthetic values, you gain instant credibility, and you communicate that they matter. This brings about a rapid and sincere openness in their lives and hearts.

A Model of the Media-Driven Active Engagement: KIDMO in Action

To gain a better understanding of how the Media-Driven Active-Engagement Model plays out in practical application, let's walk through our KIDMO program component by component. Delivered on DVD, with lesson plans and print materials on CD-ROM, each KIDMO session contains five distinct yet complementary components, preprogrammed and ready to go.

Front and central in the teaching video is Johnny Rogers. A rising force in children's ministry, Johnny reaches kids with innovative messages and engaging interactivity. The ultimate virtual teacher, Johnny delivers dynamic lessons with fun, fast-paced humor. Each video teaching is divided into three sections: Learn It, Link It, and Live It.

Learn It sets the lesson's theme and presents the big picture. It's highly interactive and dynamic. In keeping with educational psychologist David Ausubel, it creates an advanced organizer that allows students to see where they're going and who's taking them there. It gives assurance of purposeful direction and instructional design. Edward Thorndike's first law of learning, the law of readiness, states that a child must be brought into a state of internal readiness or anticipation for learning to occur. This introductory lesson segment is designed to accomplish this important task.

Link It presents the biblical teaching in a way that is attractive and visually engaging. Its relevant message lets the kids know beyond any doubt that the Scriptures are relevant to the unique settings and contexts where they live today. Whether at home, at school, or on the sports field on the weekend, the Scriptures take on meaningful relevance during this segment of the lesson. This is usually accomplished by an illustration, story, or metaphor.

Live It allows the student to make the connection between relevance and application. After all, what good does it do for children to see how to apply the Scripture if they're never actually challenged to do so? Practical steps are offered during this lesson segment to equip world changers to apply God's Word to their daily lives. One of the distinctives of the Media-Driven Active-Engagement Model is its expectation that children can change the world. They need not wait until adulthood to begin fulfilling the Great Commission. This approach to biblical instruction allows them to join God's army and actively pursue ways in which they can make a difference in the world around them.

Additionally, a memorable Compass Point reminds students of the theme of the lesson. This phrase or mnemonic helps children remember to live out their faith every day.

Following the teaching video, Kwizmo is a lesson review kids eat up like French-fried pistachios! Kwizmo reinforces the lesson, Bible verse, and Compass Point. Competition-based questions, quizzes, and challenges make for a wild and zany time. Leaders emcee, encouraging enthusiastic response and also rewarding teams for correct answers.

The music of KIDMO comes from K'Motion. Delivered in music video form, the music of K'Motion includes on-screen lyrics, with lots of energy to invite participation. K'Motion delivers substantive worship music with the most popular styles kids love. It's worship that's fun and infectious.

Media-driven active-engagement curricula develop visual tools that enhance a child's ability to memorize and recall Scripture. One of the most popular tools used by gifted communicators is adding relevant hand motions to the words of each verse being memorized. In KIDMO's Memory Max, the children are asked to respond with the video and learn the hand motions together. Not only is this approach highly interactive, but it often finds its way into the home or car long after the service time has ended. From an educator's standpoint, this approach addresses the visual, auditory, tactile, and kinesthetic learning styles simultaneously.

Not only does video have the ability to make learning Scripture fun, but it also engages a variety of learning styles in the process, thus heightening the probability that a child will remember the Scripture more readily.

After large-group time, kids are engaged in a more personal and interactive approach—small groups. Print materials for small-group time are available on the included CD-ROM. This time is used to discuss how God's Word can be applied to everyday life. The Compass Point is reinforced through discussion of personal experience. Praying together during this time strengthens the bond between students and their leaders and provides the opportunity for celebration when prayers are answered. Nothing facilitates enthusiastic response more than successfully living the Christian life according to God's purpose. In the Media-Driven Active-Engagement Model, leaders serve more as mentors than instructors, thus ensuring that truth is shared rather than disseminated. This approach allows for learning at the higher levels of the cognitive domain such as analysis, synthesis, and evaluation.

KIDMO print materials further complement the Media-Driven Active-Engagement Model. Leader Q Cards are designed to give leaders a low preparation outline to lead their group time. Each Q Card contains three simple questions that help children apply God's Word to their everyday lives. It is recommended that leaders review the card one minute a day the week prior to the program and prayerfully consider the questions they will process with the children in their groups. The low preparation time and ease of use is one of the strategies KIDMO employs in order to free leaders' minds and hearts to cultivate relationships. This relational investment makes the difference between information and transformation.

KIDMO print materials are used not only during the small-group time but are also sent home with students to encourage parent-child discussion and foster continued immersion in a biblical worldview. MAP Books contain the kids' Mission Action Plans for the week. Full of fun and thoughtful activities, the MAP Books revisit the primary points of the lesson, allowing each child to apply it on a personal level. Designed for home use with a parent, these reviews help drive home the application each week. MAP Books contain practical examples of how to live out the lesson. If parents engage in reviewing the MAP Book with their children, they learn the same lesson points their children learned at church, as well as discover the tangible ways their children are seeking to apply the biblical principle in their own lives. Children can earn points by bringing back the completed MAP Book the following week signed by their parents or guardians.

Finally, prayer request cards are one of the most talked-about and transformational KIDMO accessories. These cards are designed for a small-group setting with leaders handing out cards and asking their group, "How can I pray for you this week?" Leaders then take the cards home and pray for the requests and commitments throughout the week. Amazing transformational stories occur as a result of leaders investing their time and attention during the week.

The media-driven model is meant to be supplemental. Its strength is in its ability to work in tandem with other mediums. Where other models rely on one or two devices to communicate effectively, the media-driven model uses all mediums. In the KIDMO economy, a child processes and reviews the teaching points in the context of relationship in a small group led by a caring mentor. They are equipped with a printed resource in the form of a MAP Book. Children may then reflect and review what they've learned as well as commit to something they will do the following week to live out the biblical principle. Children are often encouraged to engage their parents in the MAP Book learning as well. The advantage the media-driven model has over other models is that it uses a wider variety of tools to expand the potential that deep-seeded spiritual truth might take root. The success of the media-driven model relies on successful integration of print, memorization, interactivity, conversation, thoughtful reflection, and response.

The Media-Driven Active-Engagement Model isn't a parent surrogate. Media alone can create a false intimacy. Instead, this model projects families and communities as the main source out of which faith and virtue are formed.

Through this model it's no longer dependent on the ability of a ministry to provide the best, most creative communicators in each and every classroom at each and every service hour. Through the power of technology, the best communicators, Bible scholars, artists, and educators can translate the Scriptures into a language kids understand and remember. KIDMO boasts an all-star cast of phenomenal talent: directors, producers, actors, screenwriters, graphic designers, animators, songwriters, and musicians. These creative artists share a deep commitment to impact culture through the passionate presentation of intelligent truth. For the same reason that Jesus gave his attention to kids, we commit our greatest resources to kids.

Active-Engagement Methodology in Practice

It's that time again! Search out the nearest moderately attractive member of the opposite sex and ask them, "Are you actively engaged?" Study and note their response. Catalog it in great detail. (That is assuming your target study did not inflict bodily harm on you for the perceived flirtation!)

The Historical Development of KIDMO

In 1988, God planted the seeds of what would later become the KIDMO garden. Living Spring Christian Fellowship, a small church in Garden Grove, California, was home to a number of growing world changers, including the three individuals who would become the founders of KIDMO. The church has remained a small but special place, yet many ministries, some even international, have been birthed there. It's no surprise that something like KIDMO found its beginnings in this humble setting.

Tim Ellis was a worship pastor at Living Spring, Johnny Rogers was an intern in the church's youth ministry, and Bill Baumgart was a pioneer producer in contemporary Christian music and a regular performer in the worship ministry. Over the next three years, Bill and Tim formed a special friendship and shared dreams and visions that would last a lifetime.

By 1991, Bill and his family had moved to Nashville where he flourished as a producer and record company executive. Meanwhile, Johnny was creating his early version of media-driven curriculum at his first full-time children's ministry job at Calvary Church in Newport Mesa, California (now called The Crossing). At this time Tim was growing a fledgling video postproduction company.

Two years later Johnny met with Tim to share his vision for mixing professional video production with children's ministry. Johnny communicated what is now common thought: the Christian message should be taught with the presentation value, story sensibility, and cultural relevance of Nickelodeon and Disney. Tim loved the idea but couldn't imagine any church taking on the risk of embracing it.

Shortly thereafter, Tim and his childhood friend Randy King began developing a children's television show. Tim thought Johnny would be perfect for a key role. It was during this time when the friendship between the three deepened. Randy was in the middle of launching a cable network while serving as vice president of operations for the Fox Broadcast Network. He later became executive vice president of television programming at PBS Affiliate WTTW in Chicago. Meanwhile Johnny was growing his second children's ministry program to more than seven hundred kids at High Desert Church in Hesperia, California. He was stretching the limits of video technology with his experimental media-driven teaching.

In 2000, Tim and Bill were enjoying successes in their respective industries, television and music, when they committed to join forces to synergize their careers and experience to create programs and properties that would make a lasting difference for the kingdom of God. Influenced by people like Bob Buford and Bob Briner, they wanted to live out their "second half" as "roaring lambs." They spent many late nights conspiring together on what that might look like. In 2001, they initiated Orbit Church, with the mission to connect world changers around the globe by providing media-driven content to the emerging church. Their vision was to create thoughtful, heart-inspiring videos that would add life to sermons and meetings. Fine idea, but God had more immediate plans.

In December 2001, Johnny told Tim that he felt like God was doing something special through his latest permutation of media-driven children's curriculum. It so happened that the latest round was for one of the most explosive megachurches in the country: Saddleback Community Church in Lake Forest, California. Johnny had taken the philosophy, scope, and sequence that he had been shaping over the past ten years and captured the teaching on video for several continuous series. He was amazed at how effective the method had become. In fact, Johnny noted that the kids were interacting and responding to his video teaching better than his live teaching! Even more, it solved the problem of trying to provide consistent programming in three different venues spread over seven different service times during the weekend. The production value was down and dirty—shot on a store-bought handycam and edited by one intern the week before—but the results were phenomenal.

Tim visited Saddleback to see Johnny in action and was completely knocked out by what he witnessed: kids shouting back at the screens in response to Johnny's prompts, Scripture recited in unison with enthusiasm, and smiles in crowded rooms everywhere. He immediately called Bill, and together they agreed that Orbit Church needed to redirect its initial efforts into children's ministry with Johnny leading the charge. Thus KIDMO was born.

The new company took the concept Johnny developed at Saddleback, elevated the production value, and expanded the program to include everything necessary for a turnkey soup-to-nuts curriculum. KIDMO includes music videos to run while kids are checking in, worship music videos, teaching, game competitions, Scripture memory, materials for small-group interaction, and a take-home "Mission Action Plan" or MAP Book. Tim provided video production and postproduction support from his team in southern California, bringing network television production value to the content. Bill provided commercial radio production value to the worship music as well as operational oversight in Nashville, Tennessee.

The trio hit the ground running and presented the fledgling curriculum at all three national Children's Pastors' Conferences in 2003. The first series, *FETCH,* was shipped in June 2003 to seventy-five churches. As of January 2006, the company has two facilities in Nashville, employs more than fifty full-time people, and serves more than twenty-three hundred churches. It's the fastest growing children's ministry program in history. By 2008, KIDMO expects to serve more than ten thousand churches reaching over a million kids every week.

Orbit Church recently released Lil' K, its media-driven curriculum for preschool ministries. Similar to KIDMO in function but designed specifically for the developmental needs of three to five year olds, Lil' K is spearheaded by Randy King who recently left his post at PBS.

With the launching of an all-new KIDMO.com, churches have access to KIDMO Kollege, a training forum featuring resources that give children's ministries the creativity and expertise to be transformational and incredibly fun, all at the same time! Interested churches now have the option of viewing clips from each KIDMO and Lil' K series and can now order via the Web site. In addition to the curriculum series, KIDMO currently sells ministry tools to partner churches. Similarly, spiritual formation tools for the family in the form of retail products are currently in development for the 2007 release.

KIDMO's stable of creative talent has been joined by executive talent from some of the largest broadcast and media companies in the world. The company is also praying about using Randy King's expertise to launch the KIDMO Network for the home market. Together KIDMO and Orbit Church are ushering in a new era of innovation and transformation in the Christian community by connecting world changers around the globe. World changers are waiting; KIDMO is ready! How about you?

You have been presented with our story and why God impressed upon us to undertake this journey into active engagement through a media vehicle. Your children's ministry is unique, and your kids are precious. Thanks to Barna, we now know that your role is the most vital in the life and growth of any healthy church.

One of the shining attributes of this ministry model is that you don't have to go it alone! The most consistent comment made from the thousands of children's ministry workers we encounter concerns their struggles with isolation or feeling overwhelmed. Week after week of pushing the boulder of monumental spiritual formation objectives up the mountain has left many a tireless children's worker defeated on the Sabbath battlefield. We are here for you!

The very good news is that you are connected to the body of Christ. And in this age, the world has never been smaller. If community is one of your core ministry values, then partner with us as we share in this global outreach venture together.

Be bold! Step out! Take risks! The rewards are well worth it, and the failures only uncover greater opportunities for success. Will the Media-Driven Active-Engagement Model solve all your problems? No, but harnessed appropriately, it can breathe wind in your sails and carry you to new heights of impact and effectiveness. Christ calls us to be in it not of it. So jump in the media pool and join the transformational fun! The water is just right, and your Generation M kids are already in and waiting!

Responses to Media-Driven Active-Engagement Model

Response by Scottie May

As with the other models, there are points that I can support in the Media-Driven Active-Engagement Model. I acknowledge that technology and media can be effective tools for reaching today's generation of children. I also agree that visuals are a helpful communication medium. Active engagement is a learning approach that I try to bring into educational settings for learners of all ages. I affirm that ministry is culturally conditioned, that

God's revelation of himself is multimedia in the literal sense—
that we have a sensory gospel; "that there is an emerging awareness of the importance of the communal family"; that sharing in
group learning activities can demonstrate Christian faith; and
that relationships are an important way of doing that.

I appreciate the curricular statement that "since each lesson
and series is sharply focused and defined by scope and sequence,
the entire audience is aware of what is being learned, practiced,
and accomplished." (But why, then, do the writers use the word
audience if this model is "active engagement"?) Having affirmed
the above, I have many more concerns about this model than I
have points of agreement.

If you ask children what they would like to do, the response is
often, "Play video games." I wonder if that's really what they want
to do or if that's the way they have become accustomed to oc-
cupying themselves because "everybody is doing it." When given
the choice of watching a video or playing with dad, what would
most children choose? What may be missing that results in the
media-driven model becoming so desirable? I am baffled by their
question, "If your kids could drive, would they choose your children's ministry?" Is this the kind of choice a parent gives a child?
Do parents ask children if they want orange juice or orange soda
pop to drink with breakfast? I hope not. Yet most children would
probably request soda pop. What children enthusiastically want
is not always what is best for them. (I am not suggesting here
that this model is like soda pop, but I am pointing out what I see
as a flawed argument for media.)

Many questions arose for me as I read about this model. Here
are some of them:

- Why is there such an apparent absence of reference to
  the presence and work of the Holy Spirit?

- Does *is* equal *ought*? In other words, does the reality
  of the media age imply that reality is acceptable—even
  desirable?

- If this model has been "formed" to reach Generation M kids, what type of long-term spiritual formation might be happening?

- In what ways are technology and interactive media "discovery-based learning"?

- Do the findings from the Kaiser Family Foundation Study that demonstrate how much time children spend with media justify giving them more?

- If "ministry is culturally conditioned," does this mean we should look and act like the culture?

- What prevents culturally oriented media from distorting the gospel rather than validating it?

- If relationship is the cornerstone of the model, why is it media driven?

I find myself wondering if proponents of this model have explored current literature and research regarding children's spiritual formation—their Christian spirituality. This model appears to lack an awareness of children's ability to encounter God and experience his presence and the inherent attraction that children have to awe, wonder, reverence, and mystery. I have had limited exposure to this model at a training event at a children's ministry conference. The electronic effects were dazzling; the music was full of energy; the volume amped. What does it mean for children that in Scripture Elijah found God not in the wind, in the earthquake, or in the fire but in the gentle whisper (1 Kings 19:11–13)?

The authors seem to be intermingling real-life experiences as in Jesus' teaching with media's imitation of life—that sharing stories around the dinner table is not really different from virtual storytelling. I am concerned with models that employ competition even minimally because it means that in order for me to win, you have to lose. Also, educational psychology demonstrates that although mnemonics have a place in learning information, those devices often yield the information as inert, making it difficult to be internalized. To quote Christian educator Ted Ward,

"It's not that the information is worthless, but the way we teach it makes it worthless."

This model leaves me with the feeling that there is an insidious assumption that children are no longer capable of deep thinking and challenging, reflective engagement. This certainly is not my experience as I work with upper elementary children every Sunday. On occasion I use media to support the aim of a biblical story, so I do not advocate banning media in children's ministry but careful discernment in its use.

Here are a few of the books that help me think about media, culture, and children: Marva Dawn's *Is It a Lost Cause? Having the Heart of God for the Church's Children*; Jane Healy's *Endangered Minds*; John Westerhoff's *Will Our Children Have Faith?* and a couple of Neil Postman's works, *Technopoly: The Surrender of Culture to Technology* as well as *The Disappearance of Childhood.*

I have already identified several concerns that I have with this model, but one more must be discussed. That is principle 3: Whatever Is Helpful Is Biblical. This principle presents pragmatism as the highest value. Are we really free to do whatever is helpful? When pushed to its logical conclusion, pragmatism defends embryonic stem cell research. Pragmatism can gradually replace the sovereignty of our God and our dependence on his Spirit because whatever works becomes acceptable. In this philosophy the end justifies the means. Does practical theology really demand that we be as influential as possible in sharing the gospel with children? Or should the Lord Jesus be our example. He certainly did not try to be as influential as possible, or he would have announced his reign as king and healed all who were sick. Instead he chose to be influential as a humble servant, often leaving throngs of followers to be alone with his Father in prayer. Consequently, I cannot accept that whatever is helpful is biblical, but I can accept that whatever is biblical is helpful—helpful for knowing our God and his story.

Because this model is built in part on active engagement, I am including a taxonomy or way of categorizing levels of involvement that Dr. Linda Cannell, a seminary professor, and I developed. There are many kinds of involvement, but various kinds of involvement are not necessarily equal. Some kinds of engagement seem to facilitate growth and development more than others. Thus, we developed this taxonomy that can assess involvement of children. The levels build on one another, but they don't necessarily have to be present in a linear form. I find the levels useful as I think about models of ministry with children:

Level 1. Passive Experience. The children do a lot of watching something happen.

Level 2. Intentional Interaction. Here children "enter into" the story, engaging in the context of the Bible story, the development of the Bible characters, and God's role in the story.

Level 3. Whole Person Involvement. This level includes worship (meaning more than simply music), celebration, nurture, and mentoring.

Level 4. Cluster of Person Involvement. Here there is intentional involvement of families. The generations of the congregation are necessary for learning at this level.

Level 5. True Community Involvement. Engagement here involves the entire faith community in worship, service, and learning. This becomes the context for much of children's church experiences. Children are welcome in the faith community and active participants. Lifelong learning is the expectation and the norm. The congregation becomes the context where families are learning to be family from one another. Intergenerational experiences are normative and not seen as special events.

Linda and I realize that the structure of many North American churches makes some of these higher levels of engagement difficult to envision, much less to implement, but we feel that these levels have biblical value and can contribute to the spiritual formation of children. Media can play a role in these levels.

A closing thought about the media-driven aspect of this model. Postman concludes his book *The Disappearance of Childhood* by challenging parents to resist much of North American culture for the sake of their children. Recognizing that this will require acts of "rebellion" against norms, he calls for parents to reject the idea of a throwaway marriage in a throwaway culture. He challenges parents to value living near extended family, to teach their children the disciplines of delayed gratification, modesty, manners, and self-restraint. But Postman feels that the greatest challenge to parents "is the attempt to control the media's access to one's own children." The thesis of his book is essentially that media are shaping children in ways that most parents are unaware. He writes, "It is not conceivable that our culture will forget that it needs children. But it is halfway toward forgetting that children need childhood."[11] I wonder if these words have relevance for this model.

Can a media-driven approach be used in children's ministry? Of course it can, in a wide range of ways and settings. But *should* it ever be the primary approach? Time will tell.

Response by Gregory C. Carlson and John K. Crupper

First, it should be noted that many have discounted the methods used in the Media-Driven Active-Engagement Model. We see this somewhat as a personality difference more than a perspective difference. Having commented on the broader streams of Christian spirituality historically in the response to chapter 1, it's also worth noting here that individuals vary in their approaches to spirituality based in some part on their personality or "internal wiring." Gary Thomas, in his book *Sacred Pathways,* notes nine different avenues of spirituality which he calls "sacred pathways." The names he assigns are naturalists, sensates, traditionalists, ascetics, activists, caregivers, enthusiasts, contemplatives, and intellectuals. Each of these pathways

---

11. Neil Postman, *The Disappearance of Childhood* (New York: Vintage, 1994), 153.

relates to God in particular ways. Thomas acknowledges historical movements within the church but also ties these approaches to temperament.[12] If we see that the church ministry to children has become unbalanced, then the present discussion may help fill in some of these necessary "gaps" in teaching. I believe that the sensates, activists, and enthusiasts are reading this chapter with arousing interest. Space will not allow a full discussion of the various forms we gravitate toward in spiritual formation. Many others have noted the multiplicity of valid spiritual pathways based on personality differences.[13]

Second, the Media-Driven Active-Engagement Model is proposing fresh and creative ways to teach the Word of God. While we might not agree with all of their interpretations, one has to admire the creative genius and risk-taking ability that is shown. I can imagine many who fear change will argue with this view, but I find it stimulating, provocative, and helpful, albeit at times overzealous about methods.

Third, the Media-Driven Active-Engagement Model in my view is not a fully developed model at all. It proposes methods but not a methodology. It really seeks to provide creative techniques to accomplish the goals of shaping children in their spiritual formation, but it does not have a comprehensive understanding of the issues of spiritual formation or of a philosophy of Christian education.

The content is not focused. While various popular phrases like "communicating the gospel" are used, there was not sufficient information in this chapter to describe anything more than a cluster of methods. While I am not diminishing these methods, I am concerned that we may not be communicating anything more than popular culture. We must focus squarely on what the gospel is, deal with the content, and not cover it by persuasive man-made methods without spiritual power. "And my message

---

12. Gary Thomas, *Sacred Pathways: Discover Your Soul's Path to God* (Grand Rapids, Mich.: Zondervan, 1996).

13. See for example, Robert Mulholland Jr., *Invitation to a Journey: A Road Map for Spiritual Formation* (Downers Grove, Ill.: InterVarsity Press, 1993); Peter Tufts Richarson, *Four Spiritualities: Expressions of Self, Expressions of Spirit* (Mountain View, Calif.: Davies-Black Publishing, 1996); or Malcolm Goldsmith, *Knowing Me, Knowing God* (Nashville: Abingdon, 1997).

and my preaching were not in persuasive words of wisdom, but in demonstration of the Spirit and of power, so that your faith would not rest on the wisdom of men, but on the power of God" (1 Cor. 2:4–5 NASB). Do we really want to make "the evolution of tools" the validation of the gospel? It's exactly backward! The transcending Word of God makes the method valid! The gospel is the message of Christ dying for our sin according to the Scriptures. He was buried and raised again "on the third day according to the Scriptures" (1 Cor. 15:3–4 NASB). Shouldn't the discussion focus more on message than on method?

There is little that addresses the goal of education. I propose that we would like to see Jesus Christ formed in the lives of children around the world. While the teamwork, retention, and independent learning focal points are applauded, they do not deal with the connection between those methods and spiritual formation. Nothing is uniquely Christian in the proposed Media-Driven Active-Engagement Model. Honestly, I would like to see more integration. A well-entertained, multimedia-savvy young person is not the goal.

Methods perhaps overshadow the message at times in this chapter. In our eagerness to do ministry in practical and exciting ways, we can miss the value of time-tested methods. While we should affirm the innovative and risky things that these developers have done, we should also try to avoid sponsoring the thinking that methods are the only critical factor to distinguish good teaching from poor.

Little is said about the teacher's role, other than it is relational and needing little preparation. Where does the local church have any quality control over the interpretation of the Scriptures that are taught? Can one local congregation influence the emphasis of a particular lesson in order to accommodate a particular theological or doctrinal distinctive they value? Or must every church have the same message? Who gets to choose how often a theme is covered in the scope and sequence of the content? Content "in a can" doesn't allow for much freedom of choice.

The nature of the student in the Media-Driven Active-Engagement Model is too narrow, in our view. To view children as only media participators, where the worst thing that could happen to them is to have a moment of inactivity, is to deny the holistic nature of the child. Children need activity, yes. Children also need to be quieted: "Surely I have composed and quieted my soul; Like a weaned child rests against his mother, My soul is like a weaned child within me" (Ps. 131:2 NASB). We have more of an emphasis upon the actional nature of the child here than we do on the moral nature of the child.

The environment is the strongest element of this model's argument. A sound case for using the environment in creative ways is made.

Our conclusion is this: The authors present some valuable methods and encouragement, but just to say you have a comprehensive philosophy doesn't make it so.

Obviously, there are a few areas where we share agreement. We all agree that media and technology are effective tools for presentation and teaching. The emphasis on participatory learning is much appreciated and necessary for this generation of children in North America. Awareness of how to use media to teach and cause participation is the strength of this group of writers. Cultural relevance may be helped by listening to these creative innovators.

Everyone likes a good story. As such, this chapter was pleasant to read. The stories of life change were encouraging. The exhortation to try new methods is received, and I have no reservations with the innovation described.

Creative instructional methodologies are the highlight of this chapter. Excellent educational endeavors make available to leaders many fresh ways to teach. The principles of review, advanced organizers, and activity would seem to be helpful for children in enhancing learning.

The multimedia approach is said to give more place to the leader to provide relationships. The strategy of multiple groupings: small groups, individual study, and leader helps are sound. Children's ministry should be made a higher priority.

Now let's turn our attention to areas where we are not so quick to agree. First, should we be telling leaders that they don't need to prepare prior to coming to the class (or give them "low preparation" expectations)? Are there not many examples in Scripture of the leader who knows the Scripture (Ezra 7:10; Ps. 1:2; Josh. 1:8; Jer. 15:16; Luke 24:44–45; Rom. 15:41; 2 Tim. 3:16–17; 2 Pet. 1:19–21)? I think we would disagree with the distinctive of little or no preparation needed.

Second, to say that not using multimedia is to disobey the Bible is a fairly strong statement—"whatever is helpful is biblical." If that were true, there are a lot of teachers around the world that are disobeying the Lord! They can't avoid not being "helpful" (i.e. using multimedia). The elevation of multimedia to such an exalted state is not wise. Just because TV *can* be educational doesn't mean it always is. Is this a culturally driven principle that can apply in all times in all places? Obviously, not! While I agree that Paul conducted himself in such a way that "by all means he might win some," he did it for the sake of the gospel. "I do all things for the sake of the gospel, so that I may become a fellow partaker of it" (1 Cor. 9:23 NASB).

Multimedia is a tool but is not the only tool in our ministry capacity. Stories can be told without a screen. The authors' enthusiasm is obvious. At times there seemed to be more evangelistic fervor for presentation software than the power of the gospel. Where does Paul's declaration fit? "And when I came to you, brethren, I did not come with superiority of speech or of wisdom, proclaiming to you the testimony of God. For I determined to know nothing among you except Jesus Christ, and Him crucified" (1 Cor. 2:1–2 NASB).

We should be cautious about saying that because kids want multimedia we should do all our teaching using this methodology. Children want many things, but a mature shepherd must guide and instruct, shape and correct. Do responsible parents give their children everything they want simply because they want it?

"For the time will come when they will not endure sound doctrine; but wanting to have their ears tickled, they will accumulate for themselves teachers in accordance to their own desires, and will turn away their ears from the truth and will turn aside to myths. But you, be sober in all things, endure hardship, do the work of an evangelist, fulfill your ministry" (2 Tim. 4:3–5 NASB).

Are we developing in our children a dependency on media that is almost enslaving instead of helping (reference the quoted verses from 1 Cor. 6:12; 10:23, 33)? It is possible that we are wanting to help our kids, but in reality we are introducing them to the inability to distinguish truth from falsehood. I'm not in the camp of not using media; I'm just saying that it can become addictive and distract from the message.

Tying relevance and media usage is to make the variety of learning methods (even of interactive learning) nonconsequential. Variety needs to include quiet times without electronic prompting. I struggle with the idea of putting Scripture, education, and broadcast truths on the same plane. Is the Bible not the standard by which we measure education? Is the field of broadcasting not an application of means, not an end? To make rules of broadcasting apply to ministry with the same weight as scriptural principle is not legitimate.

Is this approach really being sponsored as a "world changer" invention? I am concerned that a media-driven approach to spirituality is not within reach for *most* of the world's children. Disability alone prohibits nearly 20 percent in some world populations.[14] This does not include those children and churches who do not yet have the capability to provide media. While I hope the world of the media projector and Internet may be available to more Christian education settings, it's a fact that it's not a present reality. In other words, we do not see this collection of methods as being applicable to all cultures.

So, while some of the principles seem culturally narrow, this model overall can help us gain insight into the children and adults we seek to shepherd. It's commendable in relation to creativity but questionable in its foundations.

---

14. The National Organization on Disability, www.nod.com.

Response by Trisha Graves

I enjoyed reading the chapter by Tim Ellis and the KIDMO team on the Media-Driven Active-Engagement Model. The enthusiasm and energy that came across on the written page is indicative of what children experience when they are taught through KIDMO curriculum. Their description of the model is clearly articulated, and the descriptions give thorough explanations that help to address areas that are often criticized by opponents of this model. In reading this chapter, I found myself agreeing with many of the points that Ellis and others write, especially in regard to methodological relevancy, developing a Christian worldview and using multisensory media experiences. While our viewpoints would be more similar than that of the other models, there are some areas where our perspectives differ.

The definitions regarding Generation M kids make a compelling argument as to the enormous role that media holds within this generation. No one can argue that media has no place in the culture of today's child. To me it seems natural and even biblical that technology and media would be used these days to help reach children and enable them to understand better the biblical lessons being taught. This particular model takes a serious look into the "unique distinctives" of our culture and how best the gospel can be presented to this particular group of children.

I agree with Ellis that the Bible presents many examples of Jesus and his followers who used different methods for presenting the gospel to different audiences. While some believe that most media-driven curriculum is for entertainment only, the explanations given in this chapter show that this approach is biblically grounded. Ellis gives some great examples as well as background information to prove that this is a model for spiritual formation, not simply entertainment. While I tend to agree in theory with the statement Ellis makes that "we are free to do whatever builds kids up in their faith in Christ and whatever is helpful is biblical," Ellis and I agree that in order to reach today's children we must be culturally relevant and the Bible must be understood by the children we teach. As Lawrence Richards writes in *A Theology of*

Children's Ministry, "We need to find ways to link the Scriptures with life situations experienced by children, and ways to build their intuitive grasp of truths that will guide their response."[15] Because of children's limited cognitive abilities, children who are given no context for the biblical concepts they are learning will not fully comprehend what is being taught and learn how they might apply in other situations. Many children's ministry professionals believe that biblical teaching must have relevancy in order for transformation to occur.

Where our two philosophies might differ is the extent to which one might go to make a lesson culturally relevant. Advocates of the Media-Driven Active-Engagement Model "might even prefer changing the story to make it a contemporary adaptation so students can discover how to apply the lesson in today's context"[16] or using a different version of God's Word in order for a child to understand better what is being taught. While our models are both based on children's active participation in their faith development, there might be differing opinions as to the extent to which the Bible and its content should be adapted. While we want to transform lives and show children how God's Word is relevant to their lives, those that follow the pragmatic-participatory approach might be more cautious so as not to lose the content and foundation of Scripture. Moses commands us in Deuteronomy 32:46, "Set your hearts on all the words which I testify among you today, which you shall command your children to be careful to observe—all the words of this law" (NKJV). Our hearts are to be captured through relevance, but the Pragmatic-Participatory Model would say careful attention needs to be given to ensure that teaching the Bible remains the foundation. As we see in Hebrews 4:12, "The word of God is living and powerful" (NKJV), and Psalm 119:104, "Through your precepts I get understanding" (NKJV), the power of God's Word cannot be underestimated and does transform thoughts and lives. While relevancy is important, the caution for anyone who values relevancy would be not to remain so focused on making our ministries cultur-

---

15. Lawrence O. Richards, *A Theology of Children's Ministry* (Grand Rapids, Mich.: Zondervan Publishing, 1983), 378.

16. See Michael Anthony's comments on page 41.

ally relevant that the Word of God could become inferior to the relevancy factor.

Another caution is related to placing a high value on relevancy. When relevancy carries a high value, the need for other mediums such as technology, music, drama, and special effects also become greater. While these different mediums can all be successful methods for communicating God's Word, special care must be taken to ensure that the technology or other mediums being used enhance the biblical content rather than detract from Bible learning. For example, a video used during a lesson can be a powerful tool to show a Bible story or real-life application of the biblical principle being taught. Yet when the editing, moving visuals, and special effects overpower a biblical lesson, it can actually diminish the learning that's taking place. There were some interesting findings on the effects of video editing as relates to memory recognition and retention.

> Increasing the frequency of edits—defined here as a change from one camera angle to another in the same visual scene—improved memory recognition, presumably because it focused screen. Attention. Increasing the frequency of cuts—changes to a new visual scene—had a similar effect but only up to a point. If the number of cuts exceeded 10 in two minutes, recognition dropped off sharply. Producers of educational television for children have found that formal features can help learning. But increasing the rate of cuts and edits eventually overloads the brain. Music videos and commercials that use rapid intercutting of unrelated scenes are designed to hold attention more than they are to convey information.[17]

Though it is not evident in every type of curriculum that follows this model, elaborate video production can hinder a child's ability to receive and process information. An overdependence on video cuts and edits when producing video teaching or even worship elements can be counterproductive. As the study shows,

---

17. Robert Kubey and Mihaly Csikszentmihalyi, "Television Addiction Is No Mere Metaphor," *Scientific American* 286, no. 2 (February 23, 2002): 52.

"overloading the brain"[18] with video cuts and editing can distract from the message that one wants to convey. When using this model, it appears that special consideration needs to be taken to ensure that a lesson is effective not merely at holding a child's attention but in communicating the spiritual message that is desired. In some cases that I've observed, the video curriculum was overstimulating for children because it was so frenetic. In one instance, while the Media-Driven Active-Engagement Model held the attention of children during the first few weeks of its showing, the video curriculum was not able to hold many of the children's interest through the latter weeks of the unit. Could it be there was too much of a good thing when it comes to technology and learning in children?

The Media-Driven Active-Engagement Model is committed to reaching children in a culturally relevant way and ensuring that what is taught is understandable given their culture and childlike mind-set. The description given that "God Reveals Himself in Multimedia" aptly addresses why the multisensory experience is important. The paragraph that gives examples of how God communicated in biblical times is powerful and inspiring. There is ample evidence given to the manner in which the message of Jesus Christ should be presented.

While I agree with the need for a multisensory experience and even believe that the media-enhanced method can be an effective example of multisensory learning, there are still many questions that need answers. For example, is depending on a Media-Driven Active-Engagement Model limiting its ability to have long-term effectiveness with children? As energetic and entertaining as it is, does it lose its ability to keep kids engaged week after week? Are children with different learning styles all captured by using media-driven technology? How do children grasp reality if most of what they learn is portrayed on a video screen? Children are able to experience the biblical concepts through characters they might see on the video, yet Ellis describes the value of small groups and discussion times with leaders as vital in providing other real-life experiences that can help children

18. Ibid.

experience that reality for themselves. Do the multisensory methods that are used with a media-driven curriculum become dull or mundane after a while? A wise sage once said, "Your worst method is the one you use the most." Could other senses be engaged, such as smell or taste for example, that might provide children with other varied and memorable experiences and engage in spiritual learning?

Advocates of both models would agree that there needs to be a high value on relationships. We are given many examples throughout Jesus' ministry of the learning that took place in the context of relationships. In the Gospels, Jesus' relationships with the disciples helped to model and teach them how to minister and expand the gospel to the ends of the earth. Examples of conversion and baptism in Acts 8:26–40 and 16:22–34 occurred after God used people to share the gospel message with those who were lost. Spiritual conversations took place in relationship with others. Ellis defines how "high tech can bring about high touch" by saying at each point of contact with the participating children that relationship permeates this model. While Ellis stresses the value of relationships and the role of volunteers in connecting with the children, he also depends on the relationships that the children form with the video characters to meet this need. Yet does a child truly have a "relationship" with a character on a video screen, or is it more role playing that occurs with a fictional character? A child having an affinity for a likable character in a video lesson and answering questions when prompted by a character is different from a relationship with a live person who is teaching or caring for the children and authentically modeling a life being lived with Christ.

Furthermore, Ellis talks about the active engagement that happens through talking back to the characters on the screen. However, a ministry cannot depend on this type of interaction with a video character alone. I think that some children's ministry professionals might turn to this type of curriculum because they see it as a way to get their program implemented. In their mind it's easier to put in a DVD, push play, and have all of their children's ministry needs accomplished. Though a video might be able to hold a child's attention, I appreciate that Ellis gives justification for the teachers and leaders to play an active role in building relationships and modeling their faith through their interactions and discussions. This model also is thorough in its use of other methods such as games, small groups, and other activities to encourage relationship building and Bible learning and understanding.

Ellis states that this model "gives children what they need, what is helpful, and what will build them up, in a way that makes them want it, 'so that they may be saved.'" Some more traditional models in Christian education may not accept that children should be taught in ways that are enjoyable for them to learn. However, I could not agree more that children need to be taught about God in a way that makes them want to learn and come back. Like adults in today's culture, the world offers other things that can compete for a child's attention or even mind and heart. In many homes children have the opportunity to participate in numerous sports, after-school activities, video games, and friendships that don't build up a child's spiritual life and often can be harmful in their spiritual formation. However, when children are attracted to church and learning about the Bible, they are more apt to choose to come back and want to make church activities a priority in their lives. We all know many adults that were turned off by church or "religion" because they were bored or hated going to church as children. Agreeing with Ellis, teaching for spiritual growth can be much more enjoyable and effective if we are able to appeal to children while still teaching God's Word.

The biggest strength I see to this type of model is its ability to enable a church to use published resources within the Media-Driven Active-Engagement Model. It's advantageous for a church to be able to purchase a Bible curriculum that exhibits a high level of excellence, includes various program elements, and captures the attention of the kids with little time and investment made by the ministry. Because of the all-inclusive components of the program and its ability to address the age-old issue of volunteer recruiting, it's no surprise that KIDMO is so popular. While I agree that volunteer recruitment is challenging and that the time spent in preparation is sometimes difficult, I'm still of the bent that live teachers provide an authenticity and legitimacy of faith in action and the Bible as real that is limited in video-driven methods. Yet despite my viewpoint on the benefits of live teachers and that video curriculum can sometimes be overly stimulating and overwhelming for some children, I don't dismiss this model's ability to be effective and powerful in its capacity to influence spiritual life change in children. This particular model, like the Pragmatic-Participatory Model, has the ability to incorporate a broad scope of spiritual components such as small groups, Bible memorization, worship, parent involvement, and prayer. The Media-Driven Active-Engagement Model is meeting the needs of many churches and children. With the advancement of technology and our ever-changing culture, it's exciting to see those advances being applied within the realm of children's spirituality formation.

Index